Gifts of the Gemstone Guardians

Gifts of the Gemstone Guardians

The Mission, Purpose, Effects, and Therapeutic Applications of Gemstones in their Spherical Form

---

Ginny Katz and Michael Katz

Golden Age Publishing
P.O. Box 4487
Boulder, Colorado 80306

Gifts of the Gemstone Guardians

Printed in U.S.A.

ISBN: 0-924700-50-5
Library of Congress Catalog Card Number: 89-080032

Edited by Elizabeth Barile
Cover by Edward Clay Wright, Jr.

Dedicated
to our children
Emily, Eleena, and Eranel,
and to all who live
in the light and sound of God

Contents

THE ASSIGNMENT IS GIVEN

Late one night when the children were sleeping, I sat on our living room sofa, closed my eyes, and turned my attention inward. I began to hear what I thought was the sound of the wind. Then I remembered that the air outside was calm and realized that the sound must be coming from somewhere deep within me.

Suddenly the sound grew louder, and a scene appeared in my inner vision: about thirty individuals sat in a circle around an enormous crystal. A column of light poured into the crystal from above and flowed out of its base, spreading evenly to everyone seated around it.

The individuals before me were as real as the sofa I sat on. Some resembled nothing more than a vortex of energy in human form. Others were distinctly human-looking, and each of these wore a different style and color of clothing. I could see by their gestures that the members of this group were engaged in a lively conversation.

I stood outside the circle. Moments later, my husband Michael appeared at my left side. On my right was a spiritual master with whom I'd had previous encounters: his knee-length maroon robe, weathered skin, and short dark hair and beard were familiar features.

"They are discussing a book," the master said, "a book which will soon be written about them." His deep brown eyes looked sharply into mine.

A man in the circle stood and took a few steps toward the crystal. Then he turned and faced us. He had a long white beard, was dressed in purple robes, and held a staff of white wood. He motioned for us to join the group. The conversation in the circle stopped at once, and all heads turned to us.

With a growing sense of wonder and curiosity, I entered the circle with Michael. As we moved toward the man in purple robes, I had the sudden feeling that something extraordinary was about to happen.

"It is time that the people of Earth learn some truths about gemstones," the man said, "specifically about the effects and properties of gemstone spheres.

"The individuals you see here are Gemstone Guardians. They are the caretakers of the gemstones. It is the time-honored duty of each Guardian to fulfill the purpose of a particular gemstone and to maintain its effects. Recently all the Guardians have been given yet another responsibility: to start working directly with humans to teach them the correct ways to use gemstones.

"The Gemstone Guardians gathered in this circle have been discussing a series of discourses they will give in the form of interviews. These interviews will be an important step in the fulfillment of their new responsibility: they will allow the Guardians to share the knowledge of the gemstones for which they are responsible. These discourses will then be edited and compiled into a book."

My curiosity was growing more intense by the moment. Michael and I glanced at each other. We had been working with gemstones for more than ten years in our business and had become deeply interested in their healing properties. After collecting as many books and articles on the subject as we could find, we had spent long hours studying them.

To our surprise and disappointment, the information available had seemed either vague, incomplete, or too general. Often each of our references had something different to say about the properties of a given gemstone; sometimes it seemed as though they must be describing different gemstones altogether! We had become frustrated but determined not to give up our search for a true authority on the effects of these powerful tools. Now questions began to form in my mind: Had these "Guardians" known of our search? Would they help us find the information we were looking for? And most intriguing: Why were we here now?

As I listened and wondered what was to come next, I studied the rich purple eyes of the man who spoke to us. They reminded me of the finest quality Amethyst. Then he answered my silent questions.

"Through the teachings of your spiritual path, the two of you have learned the art and science of following the light and sound of Spirit and of traveling in consciousness to non-physical places such as this. The tests and trials you have undergone in the past several months have been arranged to teach you discipline, trust in your inner guidance, and how to maintain the focus of your attention."

Indeed, the practice of certain spiritual exercises and contemplations was an important aspect of our daily lives. The sound I had heard when I closed my eyes was part of this daily experience. Nevertheless, I considered it a great blessing when, on occasion, I was able to shift the focus of my awareness away from my physical surroundings and consciously "travel" to an inner world, such as the one I was now experiencing.

"We would like you to perform the interviews with the Gemstone Guardians, for you have earned this privilege," he concluded.

As the magnitude of what we were being asked to do began to dawn on me, it occurred to me that I should feel awe-struck. Yet, on the contrary, it all seemed quite natural. While I fully understood the significance of the task being presented to us, the idea of interviewing the Gemstone Guardians themselves seemed appropriate and even logical. Finally we were being given the opportunity to learn about gemstones, not by reading about someone else's experience, but through our own encounters with the individuals who knew the gemstones best.

"Thank you. We are honored by your trust in us," I replied. Michael nodded his agreement.

My mind raced ahead, and I began to wonder when the interviews would begin. As if he had heard my thoughts, the maroon-robed master said, "Select certain days and times over the next month to conduct these interviews. Nighttime would be best, so that you can be sure your children are in bed and you will not be disturbed. Then sit in a comfortable position and close your eyes.

"Spirit will lead you to the meeting place for each interview. Listen for the word of God. It will manifest as a current of music flowing from the source of life, through your heart, and back again. Follow that sound. Then open your eyes and behold the world that lies before you. The eyes you open will not be physical ones, and often the worlds you perceive will not be physical worlds."

True to his nature, Michael then proceeded to make the most of the opportunity at hand. He began to ask the Guardians for suggestions and advice about the book. He spoke with nearly every one of them—at great length with some and with others only briefly.

As Michael talked with the Guardians, my gaze was drawn to a woman standing outside the circle who radiated a brilliant white light. When this woman saw that the discussions had ended, she joined us in the circle. "This is the Overseer of all Gemstone Guardians," I heard someone say.

"Before you begin your interviews, I would like to give you some advice," said the Overseer. "Don't try to remember everything a Guardian says in the hope that you will be able retain it and write it down afterward. If you do this, much information will be forgotten.

"Instead, Ginny, you should surrender to Spirit and allow it to show you how to enter the aura, or field of energy, surrounding each Guardian. You will not lose consciousness or your identity; nor will you become the Gemstone Guardian. However, your physical voice will be able to speak the words that will flow from the heart of each Guardian. Have a tape recorder ready to capture these words.

"The Guardians will be able to draw upon the words and images stored in your mind. They will use language that is easily understood, so that as many people as possible may come to understand the true nature, purpose, and effects of their gemstones.

"Michael, it will be your role to direct the interviews by asking questions of the Guardians.

"The Guardians will not only speak of their own gemstones, but will share the information needed to understand how all gemstones work. The knowledge each Guardian gives will build on the knowledge given in previous interviews. Therefore, advise your readers to start at the beginning of the book and to read each chapter in order.

"By the way, some Guardians choose to further distinguish their gemstones with the names "earthstone" and "oceanstone": earthstones are the rock of the planet, and oceanstones are treasures of the sea. You will first interview the Guardians of the gemstones, then the Guardians of the earthstones, and finally the Guardians of the oceanstones."

"Do you have any other advice for us?" Michael asked.

"Yes, there is one more thing. As you write the book, imagine yourself within the column of light you now see flowing through the crystal in the center of this circle. It is actually a pillar of love. Write with love and with light—and enjoy your work."

Then the individual I now guessed was the Guardian of Amethyst spoke once more. "I, too, have some words of advice. As you perform your task, you can give or you can take. If you choose to take, your options will vanish. If you choose to give, the number of options available to you will be infinite.

"Let life be the judge of the degree to which you are giving or taking, for the presence of options or the lack of them will be reflected everywhere. The key to successfully completing your task, regardless of the number of options presented to you, is focus. Although I am referring to the completion of the book, this advice can be applied to any project."

Then the maroon-robed master indicated that it was time for us to leave the circle. We did so, and the Guardians returned to their discussion.

"The first interview will be with the Guardian of Quartz," said the master. "Choose a time for the discourse, and remember to follow Spirit to the meeting place."

Then the scene vanished. Once again, my living room became the focus of my awareness. I sat without moving or opening my eyes for several minutes. I wanted to absorb the experience I had just had and to steady the rising excitement in my heart. But before I could compose myself or contain my excitement, I jumped up and hurried to the bedroom where Michael sat in contemplation.

He opened his eyes as I entered the room. His expression suggested a profound knowingness. "Tomorrow night we meet the Guardian of Quartz," he said. I smiled. We had already begun what promised to be one of the greatest adventures of our lives.

1
QUARTZ

We met the Guardian of Quartz among billowy clouds. The scene resembled the classic image of heaven. White mist surrounded us as far as the eye could see. Yet my heart knew that we were standing somewhere on the Earth. The ground felt firm, unlike anything I would expect if I were standing on a cloud.

The Guardian stood with his arms folded. He was wrapped in a white cape that radiated a soft light. Unfolding his arms, he opened his cape to reveal his body, which was made of clear Quartz crystal. Astonished, I blinked my eyes, whereupon the crystal changed into a human body dressed in soft white pants and a shirt. I studied the Guardian's features carefully. He appeared to be about thirty years old. His hair was light blonde, shoulder length in back, and short on the sides and in the front.

Then I noticed that the Guardian held a large, single Quartz crystal. As I watched, the crystal grew into a city of crystals. In the next moment, this cluster was transformed into a Quartz sphere large enough to fill both his hands. Then he placed the sphere beside him and, pressing the palms of his hands together, bowed to us.

Michael and I returned this silent gesture of greeting. Then trusting my inner guidance as my spiritual teachings had taught me, I moved closer to the Guardian of Quartz. I looked into his dark brown eyes; and as he gazed into mine, I thought for a moment I would be lost in the light that surrounded him. Then, without a word, I moved into his aura.

From that moment I was able to see what the Guardian saw, feel what was in his heart, and speak with my physical voice the words he would speak.

Energy flowed through his body continually. Like a waterfall, it entered his head from the universe above and flowed into the ground through his feet. I wondered how this energy would return to its source and thereby complete the cycle. As he began to speak, I knew. It returned to the universe through his voice.

Quartz exists almost everywhere, *the Guardian began,* either as a constituent of another rock or by itself. It is found both within the Earth and on its surface.

I am most effective for humans when I am shaped into a sphere. In this form I allow the life force to flow through the mind, memory, and emotional levels to the physical body. This flow of life force then balances all aspects of the human.

I bring balance to all that I touch. If I am worn around the neck, I balance the whole being. If worn over specific areas, I balance those areas.

When I am in crystalline form, my effect is different. The crystalline form does not have the balancing effect of the spherical form, nor does it have the power of the spherical form for aligning the inner aspects.

Those who wear Quartz in crystalline form feel the energy of the Earth. Specifically, they feel the life force that the crystal receives through one end, transforms in its crystalline matrix, and then gives to the Earth's atmosphere through the other end.

The Quartz crystal's energy is a grounding energy, because it is energy of and for the Earth. It is only in this sense that crystalline Quartz has a balancing effect. When one is more grounded, one tends to feel more balanced.

Most Quartz crystals have a pointed end and a non-pointed end. Because of the nature of the crystal's matrix, energy is compelled to flow only in one direction through the crystal: into the non-pointed end and out of the pointed end. It is neither correct nor incorrect to wear the crystal pointed "up" or "down." A crystal's energy flows are universal. It is how one relates to these flows that will determine the direction in which one chooses to wear the crystal. Individuals will tend to wear it in the direction that lets them feel the most energy.

Regardless of the form in which I am used, my mission is

simply to keep the planet alive. Now, the question may arise, Why would I want to assist human beings, so many of whom seem to be destructive to the Earth? The reason is this: humans are not just destructive; in fact, humans and the Earth give and take from each other.

Many feel that humans only take the good from the Earth and give back the bad. This is not so. A human's greatest gift to the Earth is the human's connection with the life force, sometimes called Spirit or the healing force.

Quartz can only collect and use the life force already contained within the Earth's atmosphere. Humans, on the other hand, have the capacity to connect with Soul, the source of the life force. By wearing the spherical form of Quartz, humans become more balanced on all levels. This, in turn, gives them a greater ability to bring even more life force into the Earth's atmosphere. The more in balance an individual is, the more life force can flow through the individual into the atmosphere.

So, from one point of view, my mission to help humans is somewhat selfish, since my primary mission concerns the life of the Earth planet. By helping humans attain balance, I allow a greater flow of life to enter them and therefore a greater flow of life to enter the Earth.

One of the greatest gifts that people can give to the Earth is to wear Quartz in spherical form. The more that people wear Quartz in spherical form, the more life force will be available to the planet.

The Early Years of Quartz

Quartz was born when the Earth was born. The early Earth can be compared to a human fetus. When a fetus is in its mother's uterus, it grows and changes, but it does not yet have its own life. It shares its mother's life. So it was with the Earth. There were thousands of years when the Earth was forming that it did not yet have a life of its own. During those years, the Earth shared the life of the universe.

As soon as a critical point is reached, the baby's Soul enters its body and the baby is born. When this critical point was reached for the Earth, the life force entered into the Earth planet. It was within Quartz that this life force was encased.

Of course, there were other crystals present which were also enlivened by life force. Each of these crystals performs a specific function for the Earth planet. In this way the Earth is similar to humans, who have many organs, all of which are necessary for their survival. Like humans need their organs, the Earth needs all of its crystals and minerals to survive.

As time passed, the clear Quartz crystals grew, as they are always growing before they are harvested from the planet. As they grew, some were implanted with vibratory rates, or essences, that gave them color. These vibratory rates also gave the crystals their missions, or purposes. Some of this implantation was done by people from other planets. Some of it was done by the Earth herself, via divine guidance. In other words, the Earth knew what she needed. As the Quartz crystals grew, other elements were added to fill those needs, and so other Quartz derivatives were born.

During a child's early years, it grows rapidly and seems to have no end to its energy. Similarly, during the early years of the planet, the Earth had so much energy that its crystals grew very quickly. They even pierced the soil and grew out of the ground like plants. Now Earth is in her middle years, and just as humans in their middle years do things more slowly than a child does, Earth's crystals grow much more slowly.

The Age of Lemuria was an ancient era when a highly civilized race of people inhabited a continent which was eventually destroyed by earthquakes. The Lemurian continent now lies beneath the Pacific ocean.

During this age, Quartz grew out of the ground in beautiful crystals like flowers exist today. My crystals were not worn as jewelry in the way that people now wear crystals. Although some people who have memories of the Age of Lemuria seem to remember wearing crystals as jewelry, these people do not remember correctly. Quartz crystals were worn around the neck or head and on other areas of the body. However, this was done for the purpose of transferring information into the crystal.

Now, this concept of information transfer may be difficult for people today to understand. The Lemurians, on the other hand, knew that many things—including feelings, information, and even sicknesses—could be transferred into a Quartz crystal. They transferred their experiences and technology into crystals for the potential use of future generations.

You see, they knew that it is much more effective to record information in a crystal than it is to record on paper, which deteriorates and is easily burned or destroyed. Recording on paper was also avoided out of respect for the trees.

Information transfer is most effective when a crystal with a well-defined, six-sided nature is used. Crystals can contain more information more efficiently than the best computers humans have ever created. However, they do not process information like a computer; they only contain it.

Since you lack knowledge of certain technology, explaining the transfer mechanism would be pointless. Those who have the technology may one day impart this information. To do so now would be like explaining how to bake a cake when you don't have a bowl to contain the batter or an oven to cook it in. Besides, if I did explain the transfer mechanism, and you decided to transfer information into a crystal, how would you know that you weren't writing over other valuable information already contained in the crystal?

At the destruction of Lemuria, the Quartz crystals growing on the surface were destroyed Earth-wide. Only those crystals hidden in rock were not broken. They were protected from the violent upheavals that occurred between the Ages of Lemuria and Atlantis.

The Age of Atlantis occurred after the destruction of Lemuria. Like Lemuria, the Atlantean continent and its civilization were destroyed by earthquakes. Atlantis now lies beneath the Atlantic ocean.

During this age, people began to wear Quartz crystals because they sensed the crystals' power. People found that when they wore the crystals, their super-natural abilities increased as some of the crystals' power was imparted to them. The crystals they wore were typically no less than three inches long, and often as long as nine or ten inches. They wore them over the heart, over the stomach, or in headbands.

The headbands consisted of metal crowns. When the crystal was placed in the center of the crown, at the top of the head, and with the point upwards, the crystal helped individuals to have out-of-body experiences. Although these experiences were often wonderful, afterwards those who had them would feel depleted.

When the crystal at the top of the head was pointed downward, its wearer often gained super-physical powers. However, these experiences had time limits, and if practiced for more than only short periods of time, the body would become completely exhausted.

Others wore crowns in which a crystal was placed in front of the forehead. This was done primarily for the purpose of communicating with beings from other planets. Extraterrestrials visited Atlantis frequently. They often lived among the people of Atlantis and taught them how to use these crowns for interplanetary communication.

Quartz Today

"Will you speak about your effects today?" asked Michael.

Yes, *replied the Guardian of Quartz.* This is where our attention should be. And it is time that some truths be known.

To understand Quartz, one must understand some basic principles of crystals. These principles apply to every crystal on the planet. Of course, crystals are found in clumps and clusters, with double terminations, and in all kinds of unique manifestations. However, the basic crystal has two ends: a non- pointed end which receives energy; and a pointed end, out of which energy flows.

Energy flows in one end of the crystal and out the other. Therefore, when placed on physical bodies, crystals can suck energy out or pour energy in. Their effect is indiscriminate. That is why it can be extremely dangerous to place crystals on the body. If you place the non-pointed, energy-receiving end of a crystal over a disharmonious area, energy will be sucked out of the body, flow through the crystal, and leave through the pointed end. Yet, there is absolutely no way of telling whether the crystal is pulling disharmonious energy or positive life force out of the body.

Now that you have this information, I, as the Guardian of Quartz, take no responsibility for the misuse of my crystalline form.

However, in the spherical form, there is no giving or receiving end. Quartz's energy swirls around the sphere, continually giving its energy to the entire aura of the wearer. This effect is enhanced when the spheres encircle the neck.

When you place spheres over a disharmonious area, you can know without a doubt that the effect will only be beneficial, because the Quartz will attract life force to that area. It will also call life force to the corresponding areas on the individual's inner levels. This is useful, because disharmony may not only be physical; it can manifest on the emotional and mental levels as well.

To understand Quartz and other crystals, you must also know that all crystals are alive. As the planet was forming, the life force of the universe was directed and focused toward Quartz, which was to become the bearer of the planet's life energy. The life force is a combination of light and sound. As Quartz crystals manifested and became more physical, the highly focused power of this light and sound was trapped inside the crystalline matrix.

This light and sound that once had all the force of the universe behind it is now contained in the form of the crystal. This is the life force of a crystal. This is also why, although crystals are small, they can be so powerful. When a crystal is fashioned into a sphere, the life force that is compressed in the crystalline form—and that once possessed all the power and love of the universe—is still present. Once the crystal is cut into a sphere, its energy becomes more available to humans and more in harmony with them.

* * *

Now that you have this information, I shall explain in greater detail my purpose for the planet: I collect, distribute, reflect, and absorb the energies that flow in and around the atmosphere, so that the Earth can use them for its sustenance.

Crystals can only work for the planet if they are unharvested—that is, still touching the Earth. If you return a harvested crystal to the soil, it will work for the Earth again. It doesn't matter how you plant it; you can bury it in the soil or simply lay it on the ground.

Crystals have concentrated, compressed life energy within them. They give life, good feeling, and harmony to any environment or atmosphere. However, they cannot assist the Earth directly if they are placed in the home or worn around the neck. They must be touching the soil.

* * *

Those who wear spherical Quartz will receive the life force from two areas: first, from the energy that is contained within the Quartz and that is thrown into the aura; and second, from the life force within the individual's own inner aspects, which is then drawn to the physical body. When increased life force enters the individual, the inner aspects become more balanced. Then even more life force is allowed to flow to the individual's physical level.

What does this mean for the individual? The more life force that is present, the less room there is for disease or anti-life; for isn't disease anti-life?

Just as I brighten the Earth's aura, I brighten my wearers' aura. I decide which vibratory rates are best for their physical body in the same way that I do this for the Earth. And just as I help the Earth to maintain balance, I help the human to maintain balance. The life force consists of a current of light and sound. My ability to attract this current is what allows me to create balance in the individual. The increase in life force which results from this balance manifests as a brightening of the individual's aura.

The light and sound I attract not only nourishes the physical body, but nourishes the inner aspects as well—namely, the emotions, memory, and mind. The inner aspects are touched by the life force as it flows through them into the physical body. It is also through this process that I help to align the inner aspects.

I may appear to protect the individual who wears me, because I help bring into balance everything that comes into the physical body. But I do not provide protection; with my help, the individual simply becomes more able to place all experiences in perspective or balance. Once an individual is in balance, all situations are handled in a more self-controlled, dignified way.

Because of this, I seem to have the effect of protecting individuals from the negative emotions of others. Again, the receiver of negative emotions will just become more able to place them in perspective and put them in balance. Positive emotions will appear to be enhanced, but only because the individual having the emotion will want to hold onto it longer and enjoy it more.

To achieve greater mental balance, Quartz spheres will sharpen either analytical or creative thinking, depending on the needs of the individual. For example, to balance a particular individual's mind, the creative aspect may have to be stimulated and the analytical aspect quieted. This is the sacrifice one will make if one wishes to move toward a more perfect mental balance. Then, a greater amount of life force will be able to flow through the mind to the physical body. Once greater mental balance is achieved, both aspects of the mind will naturally be strengthened.

As soon as the spherical form of Quartz is worn, its energy begins to saturate the aura, and I become awakened. During this process, I get to know how much life force the individual needs in order to achieve greater balance. Then I can initiate the changes needed for this balance to take place.

When I am in crystalline form, I will have no affinity for the aura of the one who wears me. It doesn't matter whether the crystal worn is large or small. I have no way of learning the aura or the needs of the individual. This is because the energy flowing out of the crystal and into the aura is not reflected back to the crystal. The crystal's energy is compelled to flow with great focus and force only in the directions dictated by the facets of the crystal. Nothing comes back.

In contrast, when Quartz spheres are worn, their energy radiates like the sun and fills the individual's entire aura. As the aura becomes saturated, the Quartz's energy bounces back and forth between the spheres and the aura. In this way, I get to know the individual.

Often, in the process of whatever must take place for the Earth to achieve greater balance, the Earth experiences earthquakes and volcanoes. Similarly, during your own movement toward greater balance, you might experience eruptions and foundation shakings. This is the cost of balance. The more out of balance you are on any level, the more upheavals will have to occur before balance is established. However, because my nature is one of balance, I will bring your entire being into balance in a balanced way, slowly and steadily. However, upheavals may still occur.

Before an earthquake occurs, a tremendous tension builds. The Earth wants to change and become more balanced and in harmony. But there is tension. There is resistance. Once the earthquake occurs, of course, the tension is released.

This may be compared to what you might undergo when working toward greater balance. The tension will build somewhere in your life, and then there will be an "earthquake." During this time you may say, "Look what the Quartz is doing. It's certainly not making my life more balanced!"

Once the earthquake is over, and greater balance and harmony than ever before is attained, you will understand what has actually occurred. You will realize the true nature of your changes, especially if you understand the way in which Quartz works.

The movement toward balance will occur in proportion to the mass and quantity of Quartz you wear. If only one or two strands of Quartz spheres are worn, the earthquakes may simply be little tremors. The length of the strand you wear does not matter. It is the mass and quantity of Quartz that will determine the effect. The greater the mass, the stronger will be the effect.

Quartz Therapies

"In what ways can the spherical form of Quartz help people through their changes?" Michael asked.

So, you want to know how change can be promoted—how the life force can be focused by placing Quartz on disharmonious areas of the physical body? In other words, you want to know about healing?

"Yes."

Some may wish to call me a healing stone. However, in reference to Quartz, the word "healing" is misleading and vague. Healing often refers to an instant, overnight change. I assist individuals in their changes by allowing them to find a balance in all aspects of their lives. If I am worn on a continual basis, I will even work to reflect those forces in people's lives that may upset the balance; and I will attract what is needed to maintain balance.

In my quest for balance, I support and encourage the natural energy flows in the physical body. If these energy flows are already in balance, they become stronger.

The physical body contains seven energy centers. (See Chapter 2, "Lavender," for a detailed discussion of energy centers.) Individuals who have imbalances in their energy centers and in the energy that flows in and out of them can place Quartz spheres over each energy center. This will gently encourage a readjustment of the inflow or outflow of energy.

Specifically, take seven strands of Quartz spheres, each at least sixteen inches long, and place one strand in a pile over each energy center. Start at the lowest energy center on the body. You can make the piles neat by placing each strand in a swirl. Quartz spheres that are six millimeters in diameter will have a very gentle effect. Eight-millimeter Quartz is probably ideal. Ten-millimeter Quartz may be a little too strong for most people. The treatment should last at least a half hour and perhaps up to an hour. It may be done once or twice a day, as needed.

When you are finished, remove the strands, beginning with those at the top energy center and working down. Before you have completely removed the Quartz from all the energy centers, place one strand around your neck and wear it until the next treatment.

When a gemstone therapist gives this treatment, the therapist may hold a handful of Quartz over each energy center before starting the treatment. This procedure will provide a progress report by allowing the therapist to sense the quality of the energy flows. It will help the therapist determine whether the flows are moving correctly, what the direction of the flows are, and how strong the movement is.

Placing one long strand of Quartz spheres up the center of the body across these energy centers will not be effective, because such a procedure lacks focus. Each energy center may need to open, close, or readjust its energy flows in a different order. When separate piles of Quartz spheres are placed on the energy centers, each center can work with the inner aspects of the individual independently. Then the doors of the energy centers will open, close, and readjust in the order that is most beneficial for the entire individual.

You can perform this treatment with the assurance that you will not be hurting yourself. As a result of these treatments, you will notice that you have more energy. You will be able to give and take on many levels in a more balanced way.

If your energy centers are already working well, this treatment will only strengthen you.

Anyone with any kind of illness probably has an imbalance somewhere in the flow of energy through the energy centers. Therefore, this treatment will assist anyone who isn't feeling well or who is seriously ill, either mentally, emotionally, or physically.

I will have a similar effect when used in crystalline form. However, I must strongly caution you. Users of the crystalline form must be very knowledgeable if they are to achieve the same beneficial results that come automatically from the use of the spherical form.

If my spherical form is placed over the energy centers, I will know how best to balance the physical body's energy centers. However, in my crystalline form there is a directed flow from one end of the crystal to the other. If you point my crystalline form at or away from an energy center, you will playing a dangerous game unless you know *exactly* what the body needs.

Some may think that they have this knowledge, but Quartz spheres know without a doubt exactly what the body needs. As the spheres' energy saturates the aura and bounces back and forth from the aura to the spheres, the Quartz learns everything about the individual. Because of this, the spheres can act in the best interest of the individual.

* * *

Now let's discuss another therapy. As Quartz balances an individual's inner levels, they align themselves like vertebrae or joints do in the physical body. Quartz spheres can be placed over the spine or around any joints to attract life force into the area.

For example, you may place a long strand or several strands of Quartz along the entire spine, starting at the top of the head, touching the curve at the neck, and reaching to the tail end of the spine. This will bring more life and light into the spinal column. It will also assist in the alignment of the spine. This is because, just as life flows through the inner bodies and aligns them, so will it align the joints that the Quartz touches. This treatment can be done for as long and as often as you like.

For those who have relatively healthy spines, this will be enough to "adjust" them. For those who have serious spinal problems or injuries of any kind, this will greatly assist in the body's own healing. I say the body's own healing, because I do not directly cause a healing.

This treatment might also help the physician or chiropractor to work more effectively on the area. It would be ideal to have someone place the Quartz along your back while you were waiting on the adjustment table for the physician.

Placement of Quartz along the spine will provide assistance before and after back surgery. Before surgery, it will bring greater life to the area and prepare it to withstand the trauma of the surgery. Afterwards, this treatment will help to heal the trauma. It will not heal the actual condition that created the need for surgery; that condition is seated on a fundamental level. The trauma of surgery occurs on a more superficial level and is easily assisted by the balancing effects of Quartz.

You can also wrap a generous amount of Quartz around other joints in the body, such as fingers, knees, and feet. This will not take away the pain of arthritis; there are other gemstones that will work more effectively for this. However, it may help bring more life into the area and help changes take place.

The placement of Quartz spheres around the area of broken or sprained joints will be an excellent therapy for these joints. In other words, conditions that are more acute than chronic will respond more favorably to this type of Quartz therapy.

Do not expect Quartz to perform specific healing for the body. Such healing would be one step beyond my mission. I simply bring the life force, which is also known as the healing force, into the body. But, to be honest, there may be a healing effect when I am used.

* * *

Quartz attracts all seven colors of the rainbow in a very gentle way. Quartz's presence on the physical body will call these color rays to the body, correcting any imbalances in light or color rays that an individual may have. Often a disharmonious area is so tight that it does not allow a certain color ray to come in, even if that color ray is needed for optimum balance and health. Quartz calls the color rays so gently, that the body is less likely to resist the healing influence of the color rays. It will recognize these colors as acceptable, desirable, and soothing. Therefore, you can place spherical Quartz over any area of the body that needs color therapy.

For this treatment, have the Quartz touch the skin and be open to the air, not hidden under the clothing. It must be open to the sun, even if it is just to the sunlight coming in through the window. Again, this can be done as often as you wish.

Quartz is also beneficial for bringing light into those areas that are particularly sensitive, such as the eyes. The eyes are made of delicate tissue. The best way to bring color rays to the eyes for the purpose of color healing is with Quartz spheres.

Now, there are many reasons that people get headaches, and many gemstones can help this condition. People who suffer from headaches have numerous choices if they wish to use gemstones for assistance or to actually heal the cause of the headache. This is because gemstones tend to heal causes and rearrange patterns, so that the same condition does not recur again and again.

To use spherical Quartz for the eyes or for headaches, place the Quartz in front of your open eyes. The light that Quartz calls to the body cannot penetrate the bone. However, it can enter the brain through the eyes.

Look through the Quartz into an area where the sun is shining and, of course, not directly into the sun. If you cannot look outside because you are lying in bed, just look through the Quartz into the room where the sunlight is coming through the window. It is not good to look into artificial light; in fact, it can be destructive.

The Quartz should be layered as thickly as possible, so that you see nothing but the Quartz and the sunlight through it. This will bring all seven colors into the eyes and brain, will soothe strained eyes, and may ease headache pain.

If this procedure aggravates your headache, but your intuition still tells you that your headache will be helped by Quartz, follow the same procedure using moonlight instead. You should look directly at the moon through the Quartz spheres.

The use of Quartz with sunlight or moonlight is related to the concept of yin and yang headaches. It is not my function to discuss yin and yang. If you suffer from headaches and wish to know more about yin and yang energies and how they relate to headaches, the moon, and the sun, seek out someone who is familiar with Oriental medicine and who has this information.

This therapy may be practiced for as long as you feel comfortable. When you are tired of looking through the Quartz, you may close your eyes and let the Quartz rest upon your face.

* * *

Quartz does not absorb disharmony. However, when Quartz is used for therapy, disharmonious energy may become attached to the surface of Quartz. To burn away this energy after the therapy is completed, place the Quartz in the sun for several hours.

Quartz Tomorrow

As people begin to wear the spherical form of Quartz, and as their inner bodies become aligned and more able to accept the flow of life force, their consciousness will awaken and their inner worlds will become more real to them. As their consciousness awakens, they will also become more aware of the greater functions of Quartz. They will discover new therapeutic and scientific applications as well as new ways to use Quartz in everyday living.

You see, as the consciousness of the people expands, awakens, and is raised, so will the consciousness of the Earth be expanded, awakened, and raised. Why? Because humans will give more life force and spiritual energy to the planet. Since the Earth is comprised of such a large percentage of Quartz, I too will become uplifted. As I am uplifted and raised in consciousness, I will become more able to help humans rise even further in consciousness. This cycle will escalate in an upward spiral.

Although the people of Atlantis and Lemuria may have had greater technology, their consciousness was not as evolved as the consciousness of people today. That may be hard to understand. Consciousness has been evolving since life began on the planet. Yes, there have been ups and downs and hills and valleys; but, overall, consciousness has been expanding.

The people of Atlantis did not have the consciousness, the awareness, or the spiritual readiness to carve Quartz into spheres. They just weren't ready for it. They were not ready for the great upliftment that the balancing effects of Quartz would bring. They were not ready for the increased flow of life force that spherical Quartz would bring into the physical body.

It has only been in the last few generations that the consciousness has been ready for the effects of the spherical form of Quartz. Quartz will remain a tool. It is my dream that it will become a tool as common as the hammer in every household.

Remember, the crystalline form of Quartz is for the Earth. The crystal takes universal life force and converts it into the kind of life force that can be used as fuel by the planet. The process is similar to the way that you eat food and convert it into fuel for your body.

There is nothing wrong with wearing Quartz crystals. They will make people feel good because of the energy the Quartz crystal gives. Yet, it is like food that cannot be digested; it cannot make the body grow. It is like smelling the aroma of fresh bread baking in the oven. It smells wonderful, but your body can't live on the aroma.

In spherical form, Quartz can take the energy that is in your aura, metabolize it, and return it to you in a more usable form. It can call to itself the life force that exists all around you and in all your inner levels. It can bring this energy into the physical body in a form that the body can "digest" and use for its growth in consciousness.

As the spherical form increases the flow of your life force, it will expand your awareness and might even increase your ability to communicate telepathically. This communication may occur among other wearers of Quartz who, along with you, may form a group of light-receivers for the planet. Communication can also be developed with other wearers of Quartz who live on other planets.

* * *

Tomorrow night you will meet the Guardian of Lavender. Lavender will explain in more depth what I mean when I speak of inner levels and energy centers. Lavender and I work similarly, yet differently. Remember, my principal focus is for the planet. You will find that Lavender's focus is for the human.

Until we meet again, may the blessings be.

"May the blessings be," replied Michael.

I slipped out of the Guardian's aura. He lifted the large Quartz sphere lying beside him, nodded his head, and smiled. Then the white mist that surrounded us gradually diminished until nothing was left in my mind's eye but the memory of this unusual experience.

This was only the first of our interviews with the Gemstone Guardians. We felt a mixture of inspiration, awe and now eagerness—to meet the Guardian of Lavender.

2
LAVENDER

I closed my eyes and found myself, my husband, and four others sitting in a circle among the same soft clouds that had set the scene for our interview with the Guardian of Quartz. At the head of our circle stood the Guardian of Lavender. He had perched one foot on a cloud which seemed as solid as a rock, and rested an elbow on his knee. He had been waiting for the listeners to arrive.

Lavender's hair was white and curly and fell to his shoulders. Viewed from the back he would appear to be an old man, but the rest of his features suggested a man in his early twenties.

He wore a dark lavender cape over simple, highly textured cotton clothing. His skin was fair, but most compelling were his eyes, in which deep lavender irises surrounded royal purple pupils. He did not focus his attention on any one individual, since his gaze would have been too powerful and penetrating.

I stood and moved next to him. He looked at me and nodded his head. Instantly I was pulled into his aura like a magnet.

Looking through his eyes, I saw him scan his audience. Then he focused his gaze a foot or two above his listeners' heads, studying the light that entered each of them from above. Soon he began to speak.

We are here for a purpose. You wish to learn of the gemstone Lavender. Indeed, I, as the Guardian of Lavender am not Lavender. Lavender is simply the gemstone of which I am in charge. The Lavender gemstone encases the vibratory rate that it is my duty to protect. It is also my responsibility to make Lavender's energy available to the planet.

We will limit this discussion to the effects of Lavender on Earth humans.

"Do you mean there are humans on other planets?" asked a listener.

Yes. Would it surprise you if I said that I am one? Would it also surprise you to know that the Guardians of some gemstones may even have physical bodies on your Earth planet? A Gemstone Guardian need not be from another plane of existence.

Those of you who have attended from the planet Sarshauné may wish to wait for the next lecture to learn about the effects of Lavender on their own planet.

"Sarshauné?" asked Michael.

Yes, the people of that planet have been working closely with gemstones for ages. As far as gemstones are concerned, Earth and Sarshauné have a strong connection. Both planets are Quartz-based, and it was the Sarshauné's ancestors who introduced the Lavender essence to the Earth's Quartz.

The Sarshauné's lifestyle is very different from yours, as is their climate. Their technology has made life simple for them. Technology has also provided them with what is perhaps their greatest challenge—how to prevent their minds from becoming as simple as their lifestyle.

"Why did they bring Lavender to Earth?" Michael inquired.

The ancestors of the Sarshauné mastered the Quartz crystal. It was they who taught the Atlanteans about crystals. Of course, the Sarshauné were not the only ones. There were people from other planets who also influenced that Earth civilization.

The ancient Sarshauné could use their crystals to see into the future and into the past. They could see that the destiny of the two planets would one day cross, but only if the Earth also had Lavender.

Through close work with their own Lavender, they had developed a keen state of consciousness. The alignment of their inner bodies was so well managed that they could, at will, become clear channels for Spirit. This also made their inner guidance much clearer.

There were some who followed their inner guidance more closely than others. These people knew that Lavender should be planted on Earth. Yet, others on Sarshauné resisted this idea. These others were responsible for governing their planet and for upholding the law that prohibits people from indiscriminately planting gemstones on other planets.

Still, those who followed their inner guidance knew what must be done. They began by trading the mature form of Lavender crystals with the Atlanteans. After much trading, the governing group of Sarshauné saw that Lavender was indeed harmonious with the Earth and gave permission for the Lavender seeds to be planted there.

Now, you probably want to know how a gemstone is planted. To understand the process, you must realize that crystals are living things. They are like plants that grow from seeds. If you plant berry seeds indigenous to China in Iowa—and the seeds grow—there will soon be Chinese berries in Iowa, where they never existed before.

If you plant seed crystals in a healthy environment on another planet, they will also grow. And, after a few thousand years or so, they will evolve into mature crystals.

Gemstones can also be planted within crystals that are already indigenous to the planet. In the case of Lavender, the vibratory rate characteristic of Lavender was planted in the Quartz crystal. Your scientists will say that the difference between clear Quartz and Lavender is a mineral contaminant. But that is not the whole story.

Before the vibratory rate of a gemstone can be planted in another gemstone, the minerals characteristic of the gemstone to be planted must be transformed into super-physical energy. In simple terms, super-physical energy is a sheath of energy that surrounds the physical body of an object or being. Super-physical energy is only slightly more subtle than physical energy.

Whenever you wish to make any kind of physical change, it is always more effective to begin by making the change on a more subtle or fundamental level first. This is because subtler levels, such as the super-physical, are more flexible and changeable than the physical.

Minerals are one of the basic building blocks of the physical universe. Even more basic than minerals are the molecules and atoms which make them up. Therefore, if you wish to change a mineral into super-physical energy, it is most effective to first transform its molecules and atoms into super-physical energy.

When a mineral's molecules and atoms are converted into super-physical energy, its vibratory rate is raised. This makes it more charged, excited, and alive. It also gives the mineral greater power and energy.

It was not difficult to find the veins and arteries of the clear Quartz growing in the planet. The Lavender, in its super-physical form, was simply placed into this circulatory system. Since it was not the intention to make all the Quartz on the planet Lavender, it was planted only in certain veins. Quartz accepted the Lavender as a gift. It allowed Lavender's vibratory rate to travel along Quartz's network of veins and arteries to areas where it then concentrated the new Lavender energy.

Once the Lavender vibratory rate reached these areas of Quartz and was securely planted, the Lavender vibratory rate reverted to its physical form. From then on, Lavender grew in these areas, rather than clear Quartz.

Now, why would clear Quartz accept Lavender as a gift? The reason was perhaps selfish, but it was one that would benefit all. Quartz knew that when Lavender matured and was worn by people, it would open the flow of life force to a much greater degree than could the clear Quartz. As the Guardian of Quartz has already explained, the more life force that a human can bring to the planet, the more life the planet itself will have.

So the Earth accepted the gift of the Sarshauné readily, happily, and gratefully.

The Early Years of Lavender

I did not exist on the planet during the Age of Lemuria.

During the Age of Atlantis, Lavender was shipped to the Earth and traded, as I have mentioned. The general populace never knew exactly where the Lavender came from. Only certain miners conducted business with the interplanetary traders. Since the people knew that these well-known miners worked in faraway lands, they assumed that the Lavender came from the Earth.

During the Age of Atlantis I worked, as I do now, to align all the inner bodies of man and woman. This allows a greater life force to flow through to the physical body directly from the source of the life force itself.

People wore me because I gave them feelings of joy, happiness, and upliftment. These feelings often came from the higher awareness attained when Lavender is worn. This awareness, in turn, led to an ability to see from a greater viewpoint. I also brought comfort during hard times, since I gave people a knowingness that a greater reality lay beyond.

Lavender was shunned by the royalty and nobility of Atlantis, because they felt it did not have enough power. They also felt that it was not worthy of royal adornment, because it was distributed so widely among the populace. It was only worn by those few nobles who took counsel with true spiritual leaders and sought upliftment rather than power.

At the destruction of Atlantis, the interplanetary trade ceased. The Earth then began a new cycle. It was a darker cycle, characterized by ignorance and greatly influenced by power.

However, the Sarshauné knew that when the Lavender they planted became plentiful enough to be noticed and mined, the next cycle would begin. This new cycle would bring with it an era of greater consciousness, science, and technology.

Lavender Today

Who I am today is who I always was, and who I always will be. I, as Lavender, am ageless. My effects will continue into eternity. What will change is the ways in which people use me. These changes will occur as people's consciousness grows and opens to a greater awareness of my properties.

I do not directly benefit the planet; that is the mission of clear Quartz. My mission is to benefit humans. I can also work with animals, but not as effectively.

To understand my purpose, you need to understand the concept of inner bodies. The Guardian of Quartz referred to these inner bodies as inner aspects or levels. He also mentioned energy centers. Energy centers must be explained, since they are key to an understanding of how I, as well as other gemstones, work.

People are not just comprised of physical bodies. Everyone knows that they also have emotions, memories, thoughts, and a subconscious. Some are also aware that they have an intuition that offers guidance, especially during times of danger and at other crucial points in their lives.

If you could see beyond your physical body and into your inner aspects, you would see that your emotions actually take the form of a body. This emotional body, sometimes referred to as the astral body, completely surrounds your physical body like a sheath. As with all the inner bodies, the depth of the emotional body varies, depending upon the individual. The emotional body may extend anywhere from a few to many inches away from the physical body.

If you looked a little further you would see another sheath, or body, surrounding your emotional body. This is the part of you that stores memories and where many of the patterns of the past are kept. I call this the memory body, though it is sometimes referred to as the causal body.

If you looked even further, you would see yet another sheath, which is known as the mental body. This body surrounds the memory body. It is the source of a river of thoughts that continually flows through the memory and emotional bodies and into your physical brain.

Your subconscious is yet another body. It is a relatively thin sheath that surrounds the mental body.

Just beyond your subconscious is the aspect of yourself that is by far the most beautiful. It is not quite right to call this area a body, because in essence it is pure Spirit. This area is Soul itself. It appears as beautiful white, yet slightly golden, bright light.

Beyond Soul lies what I shall call the Worlds of God. Here is the infinite and divine source of all life. The life force—the current of light and sound which is also known as the healing force—originates in the Worlds of God.

As I have described, your inner bodies extend away from your physical body and form your aura. Paradoxically, these inner bodies—your emotions, memories, mind, subconscious, and Soul—also lie within you.

Now, this concept of inner bodies may be somewhat difficult to accept or even to grasp. However, it must be considered if one is to have any understanding of the way gemstones work with an individual's inner aspects.

Also, just as your physical body exists in the physical world or plane of existence, your emotional body exists in the emotional plane, and your memory body exists in the memory plane. Your mental, subconscious, and Soul bodies also each exist in their respective planes.

Since you have a physical body, your primary focus is on the physical plane. But there are many beings, including several Gemstone Guardians, who do not have physical bodies. They live and work on one of the inner planes. Still, the Guardians' spiritual duties often require that their attention be on the physical and other planes on which their gemstones exist. Similarly, just because your primary focus is on a particular plane does not mean that you are limited to that plane. Weren't you able to move your attention to this inner plane to meet me and obtain this information?

In each inner body there are seven doors through which the life force flows from its infinite source into the physical body. Some call these doors "energy centers"; others call them "chakras."

Ideally, the corresponding doors in each of your inner bodies line up with each other. When the doors are not aligned, the flow of life force through the inner bodies to the physical body is impeded, and problems arise. For example, if the emotional body is shifted to the right or left, resulting in a misalignment of the doors, emotional difficulties may result. Those with mental problems may discover that the mental body has shifted one way or another. People who are caught up in the past may find that some of the doors in the memory body are blocked. Since these misalignments and blockages also inhibit the flow of life force to the physical body, there may be physical problems as well.

The seven doors, or chakras, in the physical body are located down the middle of the front of the body. The first is the base chakra, and it is situated over the base of the spine. The second is sometimes called the sex chakra, or sacral chakra, and is seated halfway between the pubic bone and the navel. The third, called the stomach chakra, lies in the vicinity of the stomach. The fourth is the heart chakra, which sits in the center of the chest over the heart. The fifth is the throat chakra, and it lies at the throat. The sixth, known as the brow chakra, is situated between and slightly above the eyebrows. This chakra is also called the spiritual or inner eye. The seventh is the crown chakra, and it lies at the top of the head.

When worn, I align all the chakras in all the bodies. When this occurs, the life force can flow unimpeded through each of the inner bodies and nourish them. As all the bodies become nourished, the individual becomes stronger, more creative, and more loving. In other words, the individual becomes a greater human being on all levels.

I will help individuals to master themselves on all levels. Mastery of the inner bodies is the whole purpose of Lavender. I will open the brow chakra and thereby give greater awareness of the inner bodies. This awareness is essential for the mastery of these bodies.

I also help people become aware of Soul and its connection with God and the infinite. This awareness brings upliftment; and when enough people are uplifted, civilization is transformed. This is because the people's needs and desires change. Then lifestyles, health, and technology naturally evolve to fulfill these new needs and desires.

At this time in the Earth's history, a greater alignment of the inner bodies is needed, so that the flow of life force can increase. When the inner bodies are aligned, greater balance can occur on all levels. For example, individuals who have spent much time at universities "stuffing" their mental bodies may have neglected the equal development of their emotional bodies. By wearing Lavender, these individuals will learn to become more balanced; and life will provide them with the experiences needed to help them achieve that balance.

* * *

As part of their desire for spiritual unfoldment and advancement, many people are striving to become perfected. This striving is being expressed to some extent in the currently popular practice of cleansing toxins from the physical body. However, those who only put their attention on their physical bodies and think that by cleaning the body they can become spiritual, have it backwards.

If you wish to perfect the physical body, you must first work to align your inner bodies. Then the life force can flow more easily through the chakras to every part of your physical body. In this way you can become cleansed, balanced, and healed.

"How long does it take for one's bodies to become perfectly aligned?" asked Michael.

It depends on how out-of-alignment your chakras are, as

well as the size, quantity, and quality of Lavender worn. Perfect alignment may never be achieved. However, the closer you come to alignment, the better; because the more aligned you are, the more life and healing force will flow through you.

* * *

The highest quality Lavender has a distinct lavender color with small areas of purple. The purple supports my mission; for what is the purple ray? It is the ray of wisdom, spirituality, and divinity. It goes hand in hand with my purpose. The Lavender must be cloudy in parts, because the cloudiness gives it strength. Yet it must also be clear in places; this clarity is important, for it symbolizes a clear openness of all the chakras.

Lavender Therapy

When Lavender is worn by individuals who have illnesses that are difficult to diagnose or that don't fit textbook descriptions, their unclear and confusing symptoms will often disappear or be resolved. Those symptoms that are lodged very deeply, or that exist because the individual requires certain lessons or experiences, will become clearer and more easily diagnosed. This will occur because of the alignment of the individual's inner bodies and the resulting increase in the flow of life force. It would be wise for these individuals to wear Lavender for at least one or two weeks before seeing a physician.

Now, regarding specific therapies, I will start with the top of the head, where one can wear a "tisrati." This is a strand of Lavender which encircles the head, like a headband. It lies over the brow chakra and above the ears.

A Lavender tisrati will open the connection between the brow chakra and the crown chakra, increasing communication between them. This is significant, because this connection is closed or inhibited in most people today. The tisrati also strongly directs life force to all the energy centers of the physical body.

When it encircles the head, the tisrati causes one's skull to expand slightly. This may take pressure off headaches. If you have a headache caused by physical pressure or too much emotional or mental activity, this will help to open the area and let the life force, or healing force, flow through and bring balance.

First, hold the Lavender in a pile over the crown chakra just to prepare it for what is going to happen. You will only need to keep it there for a few minutes. However, if it feels good and eases your headache, you can keep it there for as long as you wish. Then place the tisrati around the head. It should fit loosely, but it should also stay in place. The tisrati can be worn as long as it feels comfortable.

Wearing a strand of Lavender around the neck will strengthen the effects of the Lavender encircling the head. Indeed, wearing Lavender around the neck while it is also being placed anywhere else on the body will increase its effects. For Lavender to be most effective, it is best that the Lavender worn around the neck be a strand of spheres without knots between them.

Although my balancing force is not as strong as Quartz's, my ability to open the physical body to the life force is much greater. An individual may also wear a strand of Quartz during any therapy where Lavender is being placed in a specific spot. This will help the physical body to accept in a more balanced way the changes that will occur when greater life force is called to the area.

The effects that the Earth human will experience when wearing the Lavender tisrati have yet to be fully researched. However, it is known that the tisrati has great effects on the inner bodies and on the way in which the physical body relates to them.

* * *

I can assist any area of the body that needs alignment. I can also help open up any area that is tight.

Place Lavender over any tightness in the body, and let it stay there for as long as you wish. At the same time, wear an Aventurine necklace to bring the healing energy of Aventurine to focus on the area from the inside. If worn by itself, Aventurine will find the organ with the greatest disharmony (See Chapter 3, "Aventurine"). But if Lavender is placed over a specific area, for example, a tight calf muscle, the Lavender will act like a magnet and draw Aventurine's healing energy to that area.

These gemstones can be worn for as long as the individual feels the tightness. Often if the tightness is acute, the relief will come within minutes. For a longer-lasting effect, the Lavender should not be removed as soon as the area feels better. Leave it on for a while, and continue wearing the Aventurine.

I am being purposely vague regarding time, because each situation will be unique. Judge for yourself how long to practice any therapy that involves Lavender. Wearing Lavender will open up the inner bodies, making your intuition about this and other matters clearer. The more you use your intuition, the clearer it will become.

Lavender can also be placed along the spine to relieve tightness and to encourage alignment. However, for significant results you will need many strands of Lavender. One strand placed from one end of the spine to the other will not be very effective. The muscles that extend two or three inches from either side of the spine affect the bones of the spine. Therefore, the Lavender should ideally cover the entire area, including those muscles. If that cannot be achieved, cover as much of the area as possible.

* * *

Anyone who has a disease in the physical body that is threatening or inhibiting life can benefit by wearing the strongest combination of physically healing gemstones yet known: Dark Green Aventurine in one necklace and Emerald in another necklace.

Diseases are not just manifestations of the physical body. They exist as disease or disharmony in the inner bodies at the same time. Wearing Lavender with this combination will direct the attention of the healing rays of Emerald and Aventurine to the inner bodies as well. However, the Lavender should not be worn until you have been wearing the Emerald and Aventurine for two or three weeks. This will give the Emerald and Aventurine a chance to work with focused attention on the physical body first.

* * *

The inner bodies are like spiritual joints. Lavender moves them into alignment and thereby allows more healing force to flow through them. This process is also reflected in the joints of the physical body, especially in the fingers, toes, and spine. The improved alignment and increased healing force that the Lavender brings to these areas will manifest as a decrease in pain.

For this therapy, wrap as much Lavender as is comfortable around the painful area—for example, the fingers and hands. If there is enough Lavender, layer it. It will feel wonderful. A strand of eight-millimeter Lavender spheres 60 to 100 inches long would be ideal. Ten-millimeter spheres may be too large for some people, and six-millimeter spheres will not be strong enough.

The gemstones will feel so good that individuals may want to sleep with them as well. The more that they keep them on, the better.

* * *

Whenever you place a strand of Lavender on the body for a specific therapeutic purpose, its effects will be enhanced if another strand of Lavender is worn around the neck. Neither strand should contain knots between the spheres.

Knots cause a separation between the spheres. In unknotted Lavender, one bead draws energy and gives energy to the next. Therefore, the effects of unknotted Lavender strands are stronger than those of knotted ones: the whole is greater than the sum of its parts. I do not know of any other gemstone that has this quality; therefore, you can assume that it is fine to place knots between other gemstone spheres.

Lavender strands can be knotted if your intention is only to align the inner bodies and open the flow of life force to the physical body.

Perhaps in the next one or two hundred years your grandchildren will enjoy necklaces not bound by knots and containing gemstone spheres which need not be pierced by drills. Today the need for string and knots to connect gemstone spheres is simply a technological limitation of the Earth planet.

"There do not have to be knots," explained Michael. "They are just safer. If an unknotted strand broke, the spheres would fall and roll in all directions."

I understand, Lavender replied.

"How long does it take for Lavender to begin working on an individual?" Michael asked.

I begin my work as soon as I am worn.

* * *

To cleanse Lavender, place it under hot or cold running water for five minutes. This will wash away any of the wearer's energy that may have been picked up by the gemstone.

I also recommend that you remove the information I pick up from a wearer's aura, so that I will be fresh for the next wearer. If I am working with an individual on a specific therapy, and that person has been using the same Lavender repeatedly, the Lavender will get to know the patterns of that individual's aura. It will get to know exactly how to adjust the inner bodies so that all the chakras line up more perfectly. This information will be different for everyone. It is this memory that is good to wash away before another person wears the Lavender. To do this, place the Lavender in bright sunlight for at least one hour.

Lavender Tommorow

My mission will remain the same throughout eternity. All that will change will be people's realization of the greater ways they can use all gemstones, particularly Lavender. This change in understanding will result from the expansion of individuals' consciousness.

Let me also say that the Sarshauné use Lavender for assistance with practically every condition. Everyone on the planet uses Lavender at some time in their lives.

The best gift you could give someone with whom you are having disharmony is a Lavender necklace . . . and hope that the person will wear it.

If you are a president or a diplomat planning to negotiate with another president or diplomat, one of the greatest gifts you could give yourself and the one with whom you are meeting would be Lavender. You should wear the Lavender while you negotiate. Then your attention would be lifted above the arena of the physical. You would be able to look down at your situation from a greater viewpoint. When looking down you might also be able to see each other's nations in a different way, including the intertwining connections between them.

If you wear Lavender while you sleep the night before the negotiations, you might have dreams of the karma between the two nations; and your understanding of the entire situation may be expanded.

The more people that are effected by the positive changes Lavender initiates, the more that others will want similar experiences and results. This is how I see the people of the Earth learning Lavender's benefits and the ways in which it can be used in their lives.

* * *

The people of the Earth must start thinking and seeing beyond their own planet. The time will come, as destiny has already ordained, that the Earth people will become aware of civilizations from other planets. When this time arrives, the people of the Earth may wish that they had better prepared themselves to accept this awareness. Wearing Lavender is an ideal way to uplift oneself and prepare for the events of destiny.

It doesn't matter what religion you practice, what spiritual master you follow, or what name you call God. Lavender transcends the divisions that Earth people have made between religions, because it connects you with Soul, your very own spark of God.

I have spoken of how I, as Lavender, bring the life force into the physical body. There is another who brings healing force to an area from inside the physical body. This gemstone is named Aventurine.

Come, I will take you to meet the Guardian of Aventurine.

3
AVENTURINE

We left the clouds behind and entered an immense field of short grass. "In this field you will have the opportunity to gain greater wellness on all levels. Here you may ask for whatever you need to gain this wellness, and the answer will be immediately and clearly given," explained the Guardian of Lavender.

We walked across the field, covering what seemed to be a great distance. Yet I knew we had hardly gone anywhere at all, for I sensed that time and space were illusions here.

We entered an area of waist-deep green mist which moved in the rhythm of waves. It seemed as though we were standing in an ocean. Yet the waves did not move our bodies, but instead seemed to flow through them. Soon the energy propelling the waves became more powerful, for we had arrived at their source.

In front of us was a man sitting cross-legged on a platform, as if in meditation. The waves of energy through which we had walked emanated from him.

Lavender spoke again: "May I introduce you to the Guardian of Aventurine."

The Guardian's eyes were closed, and his hands rested comfortably in his lap. His round form reminded me of a Buddha. His skin was the color of Dark Green Aventurine, and his clothing was the color of the gemstone's light green variety.

When he opened his eyes, the waves of energy coming from his being reversed direction and receded into him. He appeared to be gathering his energy as the waves compressed more tightly into his aura.

The white of his eyes created a sharp contrast to his light green irises and dark green pupils. He looked at us, as though he was looking through us, seeming to know exactly what we needed and exactly what he could give.

He motioned for us to sit in a circle in front of him. Then he left his platform and joined us on the grass, completing the circle. Once seated, he used his hands to open a hole in the ground in the center of our circle.

Now you can see into the physical universe. There is your planet Earth. The continent you call Africa is bathing in the sunlight.

If you look at this planet with the eyes of knowingness, you will see that all over the planet people are ready for an awakening. It is the awakening of their true Selves. Some will call this a greater spirituality, enlightenment, or Self-awareness. Some will call it a heightened sensitivity. And some will call it God's love shining upon them. Regardless of its name, it will be characterized by a renewed sense of Spirit and a greater understanding of all life, including one's relationship with one's Self and God.

I am here to help prepare individuals for this great awakening. My purpose is to heal the physical body, especially the most vital organs; for when the body is no longer ailing, the attention can be shifted away from it to focus more clearly on this awakening.

This is my function for the people of Earth. On some other planets, the people have already experienced this quantum leap. There I am used abundantly for other purposes and in ways similar to those in which the people of Earth will one day use me.

The Early Years of Aventurine

Aventurine has been a part of the planet for a long time. I, as Aventurine, did not form when the planet formed. I evolved as the planet evolved. As the Earth prepared itself for humans, I was also prepared.

Only those very few who had the awareness to obtain the knowledge of gemstones used me for my true purpose.

Information about the true purpose of gemstones is available to all. It is kept in libraries within the inner worlds or is periodically given by the Gemstone Guardians in lectures such as this one. It is best that individuals wishing to learn more about gemstones study in these libraries or attend these lectures. It is inconsiderate to be repeatedly interrupted in my contemplation by individuals who wish to communicate directly with me. During the contemplation in which you first saw me, I was maintaining the flow of vibratory rate to all the Aventurine in existence; at the same time, I was enlivening and empowering this flow.

To assist in my mission, the information I will give you must be shared. If given by a Guardian itself, one can be sure that the information is as current and correct as possible for the conditions of a particular time and place.

Throughout history I was given to the patients, friends, or family of those few who were aware of my effects. They soon found that, although the rough form of Aventurine had an effect, it wasn't until the Aventurine was smoothed and rounded that its greatest effect on the physical body could occur.

Aventurine Today

To understand my purpose, you must know how I work. You must also grasp the concept of vibratory rates. The phrase "vibratory rate" has essentially the same meaning as the words "energy" and "frequency." Your body is comprised of a multitude of frequencies, energies, or vibratory rates. I will use the phrase "vibratory rate."

Each organ in your body has its own vibratory rate; and within an organ are many vibratory rates, especially if the organ or part of the organ is diseased.

The Earth planet has two basic varieties of Aventurine: light green and dark green. We will limit our discussion to these two varieties, for what good would it do to learn what exists in other places? The finest, gem-quality Aventurine does not exist on the Earth planet.

The light green variety has little or no dark green flecks. The dark green variety is actually Light Green Aventurine so infused with flecks or particles of flecks, that it appears dark green to your eyes. Therefore, the light green variety that contains no flecks is composed of one vibratory rate, and the dark green variety is composed of two: the light green vibratory rate and the vibratory rate of the flecks.

The vibratory rate of Light Green Aventurine is the power behind Aventurine in both the light and dark green varieties. It is this power that throws the vibratory rate of the flecks into the wearer's aura. The more transparent the Aventurine, the finer the quality and the greater is its effectiveness. This is because the more light that is able to enter the gemstone, the more power it will have to throw the energy of its flecks into the aura.

The flecks contain the type of Aventurine energy that can move past the physical barrier of the crystal and enter the aura. This is why, of the two types of Aventurine, Dark Green Aventurine can assist an individual most profoundly.

When Dark Green Aventurine is worn around the neck, the vibratory rate of the Aventurine flecks fills the aura and enters the physical body through the breath. As it is with almost anything that is inhaled, the Aventurine vibratory rate first enters the lungs, then the blood stream, and then every cell in the body. This is how the whole body becomes introduced to Aventurine vibratory rate.

Although the Aventurine "molecules" are distributed throughout every cell in the body, they maintain communication with each other. When enough Aventurine vibratory rate has entered the body, it detects the organ that possesses the greatest disharmony. Then all the Aventurine vibratory rate already in the body, plus any additional vibratory rate that is breathed in, surrounds that particular organ.

When the organ is surrounded by Aventurine vibratory rate, it recognizes that a change is about to occur and that it will no longer be able to hold on to its disease. Physical matter resists change; and anything that is diseased especially resists the healing energy of the Aventurine.

An individual can help the Aventurine vibratory rate enter the organ by breathing deeply. Deep breaths bring more oxygen to the organ. The Aventurine vibratory rate latches onto the oxygen molecules and rides on them into the organ. Of course, deep breathing will also increase the amount of Aventurine vibratory rate entering the body, because there will be more breath entering the lungs. Deep breathing will be most effective if one waits until the aura is saturated with the Aventurine energy before one begins.

If a necklace of ten-millimeter Dark Green Aventurine spheres is worn, the aura will become saturated within fifteen minutes. It may take up to 45 minutes for saturation to occur if eight-millimeter Dark Green Aventurine spheres are worn.

Once any amount of Aventurine vibratory rate—no matter how small—enters the target organ, it opens the door for more Aventurine vibratory rate to enter. Then it gradually distributes itself as evenly as possible throughout the organ.

To assist in this process, the wearer should periodically breathe deeply for just a minute or two. Of course, one should be careful not to hyperventilate.

As more and more Aventurine vibratory rate enters the organ, the disease or disharmony has no choice but to exit. Then it is up to the body to metabolize most of this disharmony—that is, unless a strand of Emerald is also worn around the neck.

Emerald carries the green ray, which is the healing ray. The green ray is that part of the life force which specifically focuses on raising the vibratory rate of the physical body. When the physical body's vibratory rate is raised, healing occurs.

When Aventurine is worn with Emerald, it will focus Emerald's green ray on the target organ. Then the body won't have to bear the burden of metabolizing all the toxicity that the Aventurine vibratory rate expels from the organ. The green ray, supported by the Emerald vibratory rate, will disintegrate the disharmony and actually metabolize it for the body.

In other words, the Aventurine vibratory rate targets the organ and expels the disharmony; the Emerald vibratory rate helps to metabolize the disharmony.

When the target organ is no longer the most disharmonious organ in the body, the Aventurine vibratory rate slowly leaves the organ. If the individual is still wearing Aventurine, the Aventurine vibratory rate will find the next organ with the greatest amount of disharmony. Then it will begin working on that organ. The Aventurine will continue this process as long as it is worn.

Aventurine will focus on the most vital organs, particularly those contained within the torso. Now, you may recall that the Guardian of Lavender mentioned an exception to this rule—that is, if Lavender is placed on an extremity or anywhere else on the body, the Aventurine will focus on the area dictated by the Lavender.

Aventurine Therapy

The Dark Green Aventurine works from the inside of the physical body and is most effective when worn around the neck. Light Green Aventurine works best when it is placed over a specific area of the body. In this way, the two varieties can be used together for maximum effectiveness.

To illustrate this, let's say that the target organ is the spleen. Once the spleen has been saturated from the inside with Dark Green Aventurine vibratory rate, the Light Green Aventurine should be placed on the skin over the area of the spleen. This will support the spleen and help it to regain its strength as the Aventurine vibratory rate completes its work and moves on to the next target organ.

Even a diseased organ contains some vibrant, healthy cells. When Light Green Aventurine is placed directly over an organ, its vibratory rate focuses on these healthy cells. It allows their vitality to spread to every other cell in the organ. The action is similar to that of the "domino effect."

To understand how Light Green Aventurine works, recall that it has the power to throw its life force at any green flecks contained in it, compelling them to enter the aura. When placed on the skin over an organ, it throws its life force toward the healthiest cells in the organ. This compels them to spread their healthy vibratory rate to the cells next to them. These cells then spread this vitality to the cells next to them. This continues until the whole organ has gained greater vitality.

I have other effects when my light green and dark green varieties are used together. For example, if one's liver is healing from a disease, one can wear Dark Green Aventurine around the neck and Light Green Aventurine over the liver. The Light Green Aventurine will support the action of the Dark Green Aventurine. It will do this by stirring the disharmonious vibrations in the liver, loosening them, and encouraging them to be sloughed off.

Light Green Aventurine also has a soothing effect. This is because it spreads the highest vibratory rate in an organ throughout the organ. This, in turn, helps to expel the disharmonious vibratory rate released by the Aventurine's stirring action.

In addition to entering the body's organs, the vibratory rate of Light Green Aventurine gets reflected into the aura.

The body's energy flows, or meridians, are particularly sensitive to the vibratory rate of the Aventurine's light green color. When this vibratory rate is reflected in the aura, the meridians become stimulated and slightly charged. This slight charge raises the vibratory rate of the entire body by one or two degrees, which is just enough to strengthen the entire body. When the body's vibratory rate is raised, whatever is the weakest organ also becomes more apparent.

When the Light Green Aventurine vibratory rate is reflected into the aura, it is also breathed in by the wearer. As soon as it enters the body, it focuses on the weakest organ. When it has finished distributing the organ's highest vibratory rate around the organ, it moves to the next weakest organ.

Like the vibratory rate of the dark green variety, the Light Green Aventurine vibratory rate will move from one organ to the next, starting with the weakest. If I am worn long enough, it is possible that every organ will be treated. It is also possible that the very first organ I worked on will again receive my attention. The longer I am worn, the stronger the organs become. Naturally, this leads to a strengthening of the entire body.

If you wish to make a particular organ as impenetrable as possible, wear Light Green Aventurine around the neck and place a second strand over the organ. The vibratory rate of all the Aventurine worn will be focused on the organ over which the second Aventurine strand is placed.

Once the organ's own highest vibratory rate is spread throughout the organ, the Aventurine will continue to uplift the vibratory rate of the entire organ. In this way, the organ will become stronger and stronger. This strengthening process will progress as quickly as the rest of the body will allow.

Using Light Green Aventurine in this way can make an organ so strong that it will be practically immune to disease. Therefore, this treatment can be used periodically if, for example, you would like to increase your liver's resistance to disease because your family has a history of liver cancer.

Again, to accomplish this, one should wear Light Green Aventurine around the neck and periodically place another Aventurine strand over the liver. The first time you apply the Aventurine over the liver, keep it there for fifteen minutes. Next time, keep it there for half an hour. Gradually increase the time increments until you can bandage the Aventurine to the liver for several days. It is important to increase the treatment times gradually. Otherwise, the liver may become overactive, and other imbalances may be created.

If practiced by a relatively healthy individual on an organ that is relatively free from disease, this procedure will act as a preventive therapy. The strengthening effects will increase over time. It may take one, two, or perhaps three months before changes become obvious, depending on the constitution of the individual and how easily he or she accepts change.

* * *

Dark Green Aventurine can be placed over any area of the body, including the head, to soothe and ease pain. You may wonder why this is so, since this effect seems to contradict what I have said about the action of Dark Green Aventurine.

Aventurine naturally identifies areas of disharmony, no matter where it is placed or worn on the body. Therefore, if the Aventurine is held several inches away from a disharmonious area, it will start to send its vibratory rate toward that area. However, since the Aventurine vibratory rate cannot enter through the skin, it will bounce back to the Aventurine. Aventurine will continue to send vibratory rate toward the disharmonious area, and the skin will continue to reflect the vibratory rate back to the Aventurine. This process will create a feeling of heat in the Aventurine.

Now, if one were to actually touch the skin with the Aventurine, there would be no space for the Aventurine vibratory rate to bounce back and forth. Yet this will not stop the Aventurine from attempting to send its vibratory rate toward the disharmony.

To help you understand what happens when Dark Green Aventurine is placed on the skin, recall how you first perceived my energy when you entered my aura. It was as though you were walking through waves of green energy, which passed through your body in a rhythmic motion. It is the primal nature of Aventurine to move rhythmically, like the breath.

When Dark Green Aventurine is placed on the skin with a hand holding it there, it acts like it has been put in a corner. Its vibratory rate cannot infiltrate the aura, because the hand is blocking it. Its energy cannot bounce back and forth between itself and the skin, because there is no space to do so. It is cornered. As a result, its consciousness shifts to its primal nature.

When an animal is cornered, its primal nature (represented by its will to survive) will surface. This will happen with any living being. One must not forget that gemstones are living beings; the expression of a gemstone's life is simply confined to the limitations of its crystalline form.

When cornered between the hand and the skin, the Aventurine will revert to its primal nature. It will begin to emanate its energy in a wave-like motion, just as I did when you approached me. These wave emanations are not restricted by anything physical. They will flow through your body in a wave-like motion and in the rhythm of the breath. It is this energy that is immensely soothing and will take away the pain.

"Why would someone want to work with Light Green Aventurine to help an organ, when the darker variety is so much stronger?" Michael asked.

The light green variety has its place—especially on this planet, where so much of your medicine is chemical.

The body knows how to rid itself of toxic foreign substances. Most of these substances will cause diarrhea or vomiting as part of the body's effort to force them out. However, when the foreign substance is not overtly toxic (as in the case of most drugs and some chemicals), the body does not know how to deal with it. It does not know how to pass these foreign substances through the system in order to excrete them. Because many of these foreign substances, such as drugs, are actually designed to be in harmony with the body and have a specific effect on it, the body becomes confused about how to handle them.

After the drug has done its work, the body wonders, "What do I need this drug for now? What do I do with it? How do I get rid of it?" Although the drug may have provided a benefit, the body will not know what to do with it once the drug's work is completed. So the body will encapsulate the drug and isolate it from the rest of the body. More specifically, if a drug is targeted at a specific organ and enters it, the body's protective mechanism will encapsulate the drug in that organ to protect the rest of the body from the drug's toxicity.

I find it interesting that the pharmacists and physicians of Earth who design drugs have perfected a healing system only halfway. They are ignorant—or choose to be ignorant—of the fact that even though the drug may appear to be metabolized, its vibratory rate remains in the body.

If the organ which has encapsulated a drug is the same organ that is being targeted by the Dark Green Aventurine necklace, the Aventurine vibratory rate will infiltrate the organ. It may then recognize pockets or encapsulations of drug as clumps of disharmony. It will work to loosen these up and dispel them from the organ.

Now, if the organ has been accumulating the vibratory rate of drugs for years, a potentially serious situation may arise when the Aventurine starts moving these drugs out into the body. The drugs will suddenly start circulating in the body, and the body will not know what to do with them or how to remove them.

The Light Green Aventurine can assist in these cases—especially if it contains some flecks—since it will work more gently on the organ. However, it will not be as effective at healing unless it is worn with a strand of Emerald. The Emerald will assist in actually disintegrating the disharmony.

The Emerald will enhance the healing effect even though, to my knowledge, it only works on natural toxicity. By natural toxicity, I mean the toxicity produced by a living organism. It does not know how to disintegrate toxicity born in a laboratory.

Wearing the Light Green Aventurine and Emerald together will allow the organ and the area surrounding it to become less disharmonious. This will help the organ, the area, and the whole body to become stronger and more able to deal with the encapsulations of the drug toxicity.

Either variety of Aventurine allows the green ray, or healing ray, to enter the body. Often those in pain become so tight that they can focus on nothing but the pain. I allow the body to relax and open itself to the green ray. Emerald is the gemstone that carries the green ray. When I am worn with Emerald and my vibratory rate targets, for example, a diseased liver, the green ray will be drawn to the liver.

I was not going to mention Aventurine from other planets, but I will say that a fine, gem-quality Aventurine does exist on planets other than the Earth. By gem quality, I mean Aventurine so transparent and beautiful that it begs to be cut into a faceted stone to reflect the light for all to see and enjoy. This quality carries enough healing energy within itself to render an Emerald necklace unnecessary.

This quality of Aventurine does not exist on the Earth for a reason. It seems that on Earth, physical healing must occur more slowly. Perhaps this is only because physical illnesses exist on this planet for a purpose.

* * *

I will enter the aura, infiltrate the body, and identify the organ of greatest disharmony at the same rate for a healthy individual as I will for an individual who has any major illness, such as cancer. However, the individual with cancer, for example, should breathe deeply as much as possible to help my vibratory rate enter the diseased organ. Remember, my greatest effect is on organs.

The deep breaths are necessary, because a disease such as cancer wishes to repel with all its force the Aventurine vibratory rate. Cancer is like a living entity. It knows that my vibratory rate is the beginning of its demise, so naturally it wishes to push my energy away.

Individuals with diseased organs who wish to use gemstones and other non-chemical methods to aid their healing should wear a necklace of high-quality Dark Green Aventurine spheres and a necklace containing Emerald in rounded form. If they are fortunate enough to be under the care of a gemstone therapist, they may be able to wear a single strand of much larger, rounded Emerald whenever they visit the therapist's office. If worn for at least 30 minutes, this would give the body a high dose of green-ray vibratory rate.

The individual should support the gemstones' action with other therapies that increase the strength and vitality of the entire body. Therapies that focus on supporting the eliminative organs should also be used, so that the cancer or other disharmony can leave more easily.

If a cancer is removed by surgery, or if a cancer patient appears to be healing because of the action of the gemstones, the Dark Green Aventurine and Emerald should still be worn. This is because, once a cancer vibratory rate is in a body, it often lingers after the manifestation of cancer has been cleared.

* * *

Where gemstone therapy clinics exist, a patient's time is respected. Patients are given attention as soon as they walk in the door and identify themselves to an assistant. The assistant then refers to the patient's file and gives the patient preliminary gemstones to wear. These preliminary gemstones are ordered by the therapist to prepare the patient for the therapist's treatment. This practice also shows respect for time of the therapist, who will be in great demand. This demand will be created because gemstone therapy works.

Gemstones will work better than any of your other medicines, because their vibratory rate remains constant. In contrast, if you take an aspirin or an herb, its vibratory rate changes as soon as it touches the tongue. Its effects on a monkey or in a test tube will not be the same as its effects on a human. This is because the vibratory rates of monkeys, humans, and test tubes are all different. Also, the way an aspirin will work on one human is not the same way it will work on another.

The vibratory rates of gemstones are consistent. They work from one human to the next in a similar way.

* * *

The time it takes for Aventurine worn around the neck to work will depend on the size and quality of the Aventurine. It will also depend on the degree of toxicity in the organ and the degree of overall toxicity in the body. Also, the work of Aventurine may take three times as long without Emerald.

To be more specific about time, let's first place disease or degree of toxicity on a scale of zero to five. "Zero" indicates perfect health, and "five" indicates a level of toxicity so great that there would be virtually no life left in the organ being measured. We will also assume that ten-millimeter Dark Green Aventurine spheres are being worn.

Those people with conditions that register "one" on this scale should wear Dark Green Aventurine alone for perhaps one month. After that, they could begin the procedure of holding the Light Green Aventurine over the targeted area. If Emerald were also worn, the time required would be considerably reduced. Individuals in this category include those who are relatively healthy, but who have aches and pains or organs that are not as strong as they would like them to be.

Those with conditions that register "two" may need six months of wearing Dark Green Aventurine alone. If worn with Emerald, that time could be cut in half.

Those with conditions registering "three" may need to wear the Aventurine for nine months to a year.

Those whose conditions register "four" and "five" must have very toxic bodies for their organs to possess such a low degree of life force. These individuals will need to wear Aventurine for at least three to five years. Again, the use of Emerald would greatly reduce this time requirement. Unfortunately, a body this toxic may not live that long, unless it is supported by other therapies. These could include other gemstone therapies.

* * *

I will give and give infinitely. I do not absorb, although certain disharmonious energies tend to stick to Aventurine. Because I give so much, the same strand of Aventurine can be worn by many individuals. Still, it will be considerate to cleanse the strand before it is given to the next wearer.

To prepare Aventurine for another wearer, place it under hot and then cold running water (or vice versa) for about thirty seconds. Then place it in the sun for at least an hour.

Aventurine Tomorrow

I was purposely vague in describing therapies, because my uses are so diverse. With the relatively short time we have had together, I could only give you an overview of my nature, so you can begin to use me correctly.

Indeed, I will assist all life, including animals. A collar of Aventurine would be a wonderful gift for a dog or cat who isn't feeling well.

In the future I will be assisting humans on greater levels than they have ever imagined. However, I will not give you this information until you are ready for it.

Look not to the gifts of the future. Enjoy and appreciate

the value of the gifts you have today. Indeed, they are more valuable to you than any future gift, which you cannot yet use or fully appreciate.

The people of Earth are in the process of taking one of the greatest steps in their history. Use the tools that are already available to you to aid in this process. These tools are gifts. They have already been given. It is only up to each individual to unwrap and accept the gift.

* * *

It seems most appropriate that the next Guardian you meet will be the one in charge of Emerald, for we work so closely together.

For those who are aware of such things, I wish to say that I too am aware of the fact that I am the third Guardian interviewed who manifests in a male form. I have chosen for your fourth interview a Guardian who also manifests in a male form.

You will find that the majority of Guardians manifest in this form. Know that this is for a purpose. You should also know that, in the hierarchy of Guardians, the one who oversees us all manifests in the female form. And this also is for a purpose.

May the blessings be!

The Guardian of Aventurine rose and returned to his platform. He sat down and closed his eyes, and once again the waves of green energy began to flow from his being.

I glanced down at my planet through the hole Aventurine had made in the ground. His wave emanations poured through the hole and surrounded the Earth, touching and enlivening every Aventurine crystal on the planet.

As my attention followed these waves, I realized that I too was moving closer to the planet. In the next moment, I regained the awareness of my physical body. I opened my eyes just as Michael was opening his. We smiled at each other, and our hearts filled with gratitude for the knowledge unfolding before us.

4

EMERALD

As I closed my eyes I wondered what the Guardian of Emerald would look like. The sound inside my head grew particularly loud, making it especially easy to follow. It led me to a small dark amphitheater where three others, including Michael, were already awaiting the arrival of Emerald.

We stood in the center of this amphitheater, bathing in the glow of what appeared to be seven floodlights. Each of these lights showered one of the colors of the rainbow on us. The colors continually moved, as if dancing to the rhythm of music. My heart danced with them as I watched, awe-struck by their beauty.

Suddenly the green ray grew larger, and the other six rays receded, until they just flickered quietly in the background. Within the green light an Emerald crystal began to materialize. When it was fully formed, the crystal stood about six feet high and three feet wide. Like a magnet, the Emerald began to draw into itself all the green ray that showered from above. The green ray moved with increasing speed, so that soon it was pouring into the crystal with considerable force.

After several minutes, the crystal began to take the shape of a tall figure shrouded in an emerald-green cape. As the figure straightened, the hood of the cape fell off and revealed the head of a man. He appeared to be in his thirties and had short black hair and a closely cropped black beard. He opened his eyes, and green rays of light shot from them, piercing the darkness that surrounded us. A moment later his eyes became a more familiar dark brown.

Then the ceiling of the amphitheater disappeared, revealing a starry midnight sky. At the same time, the seats in the amphitheater vanished, and we found ourselves standing in the middle of a vast grassy field.

I approached the Guardian of Emerald. We looked deeply into each other's eyes, and again his eyes became green. The color overwhelmed me. Feeling somewhat intoxicated, I turned and stepped backward into his aura. . .

I am glad all of you were able to travel the sound and meet me halfway between your world and mine. Let us begin.

Emerald is found throughout the physical universe on every planet where life is evolving. Only those planets that are just rocks in space, which support no life or only primitive forms of it, have no Emerald.

My purpose for the Earth human who wears Emerald is the same purpose I fulfill for every other being throughout the universe who wears Emerald. I provide the green ray, which is essential for the life of all plants, animals, and humans.

I have been the bearer of the green ray since the beginning of time. Since I am not bound by time as Earth humans understand it, I am still in my prime. I will continue to be the bearer of the green ray for as long as your imagination can stretch into the future.

I work specifically on raising the vibratory rate of the physical body. The vibratory rate of Emerald, in combination with the green ray, uplifts the state of consciousness of the physical body. When this upliftment occurs, the wearer's attention can more easily focus on the greater states of consciousness that lie beyond the physical.

In order to uplift an individual, I resolve the weakest link in the chain. The weakest link is always the lowest vibratory rate in the body; it is often the source of disease.

The Early Years of Emerald

Emerald was not present when the Earth was born.

When a planet becomes ready to support life, it is the duty of the Guardians of the Physical Universe to direct the implantation of the seven gemstones that bear the color rays. Emerald is one of those gemstones.

As the Earth evolved and developed a capacity for life, it

reached a stage where it began to prepare matrices to encase that life. When the Guardians of the Physical Universe noticed this and saw that Spirit wanted life on the planet, they fulfilled their duty to direct the implantation of these gemstones.

You will soon learn of the other six color-ray-bearing gemstones. Not all of these gemstones were present when I was planted on Earth. This is because, at that time, some of the color rays were carried by different gemstones than they are now.

I was not planted in the same way Lavender was, since I have no relationship with Quartz.

"I understand that you belong to the beryl family on this planet," said Michael.

Classify my crystalline nature as you wish.

Before I explain how I was planted, let me say this. Some wheat seeds are planted to produce flour for eating. Other wheat seeds are grown specifically to bear higher quality seeds for replanting. Emerald crystals have similar classifications.

There are a few coveted and highly protected Emerald crystals with a life energy so intense, that only one race of people in the universe can handle the responsibility for them. These Emerald crystals are like the wheat seeds that are grown to produce more seeds.

The Earth is a living planet. It contains super-physical channels act in a way similar to your blood vessels. Some people call the places where these channels reach the surface the "power points" of the Earth. When the Earth was ready, representatives from the race of people I mentioned planted a cluster of these special Emerald crystals in a channel beneath a power point. This special cluster became the "mother crystal" of all the Earth's future Emeralds. The mother crystal gave the Earth a blueprint, or pattern, for making crystalline matrices to contain the Emerald's energy.

The Guardians of the Earth decided where on the planet the mother crystal's vibratory rate should be planted. There it would begin to manifest Emerald crystals and then distribute them around the planet.

The base of the crystal cluster was somewhat circular. The cluster itself was about one-and-a-half to two feet wide and one foot high. You should know that these dimensions are only approximate and that, ultimately, the actual shape and size of the mother crystal does not matter. However, it is good for you understand that it was not a mile wide.

The race of people to which I referred has the responsibility of planting mother crystals throughout the universe. These include more than just Emerald crystals. They have a technology and spiritual awareness far beyond anything even your science fiction writers have yet conceived. Although they use space ships, they are not bound by the limitations of the physical universe. They move from one end of the universe to the next in little time. This race works directly with the hierarchy of Guardians in this physical universe and in non-physical universes, as well.

When Spirit directs the attention of a Physical Universe Guardian to a planet that is ready to support life, the Guardian then notifies this race of people. When presented with a planet ready to support life, and ready to be implanted with at least the seven color-ray-bearing gemstones, this race begins to research the planet.

They are like scientists. They scan the planet for its energy channels and power points; then they chart them. Because the planet is preparing to support life, all types of data about the planet must be gathered and stored.

Of the millions of planets in the physical universe, there are always many preparing for life. Therefore, this race of people keeps very busy.

After the mother gemstone crystals are planted, certain members of this race continue to record data. One space ship of these people, whose lifetimes span much greater lengths of time than yours, stay with this planet for hundreds of your Earth's years.

Some of the things they monitor include: how the planet receives the gemstones; whether the planet forms crystalline matrices as well as it can; whether the proper connections are being made between the mother crystal and its offspring; and how the planet responds to the new light rays that, because of the gemstones, are now available to the evolving life.

Those of you who are students of the sound as well as the light know that when I refer to a light ray, I also mean the sound that accompanies the light. Gemstones carry light and sound. It is just tedious to say "light and sound" repeatedly. The word "light" is more easily understood by most people, since it is a more obvious quality of gemstones.

Mother crystals still exist on the planet. When your people

have attained a certain level of technology and earned the responsibility, you may be able to locate mother crystals and dig them up. However, you will not be given this technology until you are responsible enough to take care of these crystals and know what to do with them. No mother crystals have yet been uncovered on the Earth planet.

"Do all gemstones that exist have mother crystals?" asked Michael.

No. Lavender, for example, does not have a mother crystal; its vibratory rate was planted in Quartz.

As a planet constructs crystalline matrices to house the vibratory rate of a mother crystal's offspring, mutations can form. This is one reason that this race of beings monitors the planet for several hundred years or sometimes thousands of years. Of course, they also regularly monitor every planet they have implanted with gemstones. Yes, some of these beings do visit the Earth every once in a while. They do not walk the planet, because they are very different from the Earth's inhabitants and would be too noticeable. They scan the planet to monitor, for example, changes in life forms and power points; and they always record data.

If a planet begins to develop mutations in a desired matrix, these people have ways to make sure that the intended matrix does not continue to change, but grows according to its original form. However, if the mutation has already formed, it will continue to grow. These mutant crystals are not necessarily bad or undesirable. Usually the planet creates the mutation in order to help it balance the energies of newly planted gemstones.

In ancient Lemuria, my crystals often grew up through the soil. They were clear, bright green, and had few inclusions. Although I was not used for specific healing purposes, the people recognized and respected Emerald. During this era the life force was fresh, clean, and new. It was easy to carry the green ray into the Earth's aura and into people's auras, as well. It was as effortless as the sunshine.

Between the Ages of Lemuria and Atlantis, there was much shaking within the Earth. In fact, many of the crystals that were once so clear in Lemuria's age cracked internally and formed inclusions. These inclusions made me less powerful, since they inhibited the flow of the green ray. On the other hand, my power was also increasing during the Age of Atlantis as I entered my prime.

In Atlantis my powers were researched, and certain qualities of the vibratory rate of my crystal were discovered. You have heard of chemical warfare. There is also such a thing as gemstone warfare. I hesitate to speak of this. However, there are some things you must know, even though they are not pleasant.

Most of the black inclusions you see in an Emerald are the result of foul play. When this foul play occurred, the black inclusions were not visible. Otherwise, it would have been obvious to the gemstone's recipient that the Emerald had been tampered with. This Emerald brought disease of both the mind and body.

The Atlanteans responsible for this foul play were assisted by individuals from beyond this planet. Not all extraterrestrials have the best intentions.

This is one reason that it is so important for each individual to expand into awareness of the Self, or Soul. Then one can directly touch the truth and Spirit that lies within oneself without the help of anyone else. Then, when confronted with the unknown, one need only look within one's own heart to determine whether the intentions of the unknown entity are honorable or dishonorable. Then one can act accordingly.

Lavender, with whom you have already spoken, is one of the best gemstones available to help one establish this communication with one's true Self.

At the destruction of Atlantis, the Emerald on your planet needed serious attention, and many were called upon to assist. We devised a way to transform the destructive vibratory rate that had been placed within all the Emerald crystals on the planet. We transformed it into what appears to be black flecks.

Today these black inclusions are no longer harmful and there is nothing that one could do to transform them back into harmful energy. But they will always serve as a reminder that gemstones are powerful tools—more powerful than you may realize. When misused, powerful tools are highly destructive. When used with good intentions, an open and loving heart, and a clear and understanding mind, the benefits of such tools can be astounding.

Can you explain why the Emeralds that have recently been mined also contain black flecks?" Michael asked.

Many Emerald crystals that have grown since the Atlantean era contain black flecks. Unlike most other inclusions, these flecks are a living part of the Emerald. They are like mutant genes: although the flecks are now benign, their vibratory rate continues to reproduce and grow within the Emerald crystals.

Emerald Today

To gain a better understanding of my purpose, it will be helpful if you understand what color rays are, where they come from, and why they are important to life.

In a far part of the area you call the mental world, at the top of a mountain too high even to imagine, lies an important crystal. Before the white light of pure Spirit can touch the worlds below, it must first flow through this crystal. As it does, the white light is separated into seven color rays: red, orange, yellow, green, blue, indigo, and violet. This occurs in the same way that sunlight shining through a crystal hanging in a window is separated into the colors of the rainbow. This white light of Spirit is also known as the life force and the healing force.

The seven color rays are all essential for life and for health. A deficiency in any one of these colors moves one away from optimal life and health.

Every planet has a unique ratio of color rays. This ratio is essential for the life and state of consciousness that the inhabitants of the planet are destined to achieve. The Earth, for example, has less yellow and indigo than the other rays.

As the people's consciousness grows and expands, their need for greater amounts of color rays increases. At the same time, they become ready and able to receive more of these color rays. They can use the rays as tools to improve their lives. It is hard to work with color rays in their pure form, because they are not physical. However, the gemstones that bear these color rays are physical and therefore can be used like any other tools.

Why are people today unable to directly accept the color rays that surround them? It is simply because of the vibratory rate of the physical plane, where there is more negativity than positivity. This vibratory rate manifests as a general weakness in the physical body's ability to receive the seven color rays.

In the past seventy years the consciousness of the people has been rising to greater heights. With this rise in consciousness, people require a greater velocity and volume of green ray. Now that I am in my prime I cannot get any stronger. However, individuals can fulfill their need for the green ray by wearing me.

* * *

In addition to the life force that has differentiated into the seven color rays, there is undifferentiated life force. It is this unmanifested, latent life force that enters the base of the Emerald crystal. Inside the crystal it becomes energized in such a way that when it shoots out of the crystal's point, it takes the form of pure green-ray energy.

Wherever an Emerald crystal is placed, life force will be drawn into the base end. Therefore, if the base of an Emerald crystal were placed on the body, the life force of the individual would drain into the crystal. This is dangerous and could even cause death if placed on certain points of the body. Only the pointed end of an Emerald crystal should be directed at toxic areas—or any other areas—of the body.

Fortunately, Emerald crystals on this planet are relatively harmless. This is because the crystals readily available to you are usually small. An Emerald of the size that would be capable of doing severe damage would be beyond the budget of most people.

A person who wishes to wear an Emerald crystal around the neck will not experience a negative effect as long as the crystal is only pointing either up or down, and not at the body. If the crystal is pointing up, its green-ray energy will focus on the head; and this can only be beneficial. Actually, I personally would not wear an Emerald crystal pointing away from the head.

A crystal is compelled to draw life force into itself. It cannot do otherwise because of the way the crystal's molecules are arranged to form the crystal. It is a law of the universe.

When I am faceted, energy can only flow into the point or base of the faceted stone. Then it radiates in all the directions dictated by the facets. Therefore, if one wears a faceted Emerald as a pendant over the heart, as a ring, or as earrings, the wearer should not be concerned that the Emerald is drawing energy out of the body. There will be some slight pull of the body's energy in through the molecules that make up the point of the stone, but this effect will be negligible. Besides, the green healing ray contained within the faceted stone, and which shines into the aura, provides a benefit which will greatly outweigh this effect.

A faceted Emerald can only radiate the energy it already contains within itself. Therefore, its power is governed by its size. A quarter-carat faceted Emerald can only fill with green ray a small dome in the aura over the place the Emerald is worn. A nine- or ten-carat faceted Emerald worn as a pendant over the heart would throw off enough green-ray energy to fill the aura over the entire head and torso.

Now I will discuss Emerald in rounded form. The rounded shapes I will speak of are the sphere and the rondelle. The rondelle is a sphere that is somewhat flattened on two opposite sides. Like a faceted Emerald, a rounded Emerald can only radiate the energy, life force, or vibratory rate already contained within that Emerald.

To illustrate the difference between faceted and rounded Emerald, let's look at a hypothetical situation. Let's see what would happen to a one-carat faceted Emerald and a one-carat rounded Emerald if we sped up time by thousands of years. Also assume that I, as the Guardian of Emerald, do not feed these two gemstones any additional life force during this period of time.

Which of these Emeralds would run out of energy first? Based on what I have already said, you might guess that the rounded Emerald would run out first. However, a faceted Emerald radiates green-ray energy indiscriminately and always at maximum velocity. In contrast, a rounded Emerald does not begin to radiate maximum Emerald energy until it is enlivened by a wearer's aura. Then, as soon as the aura is saturated, the Emerald slows down and gives to the aura only what is needed to maintain saturation. Therefore, the life span of the faceted Emerald is perhaps one-fifth or one-tenth the life span of the rounded Emerald.

The faceted Emerald will radiate green ray into the atmosphere regardless of whether it is being worn or not. It is compelled to do so because of the way its crystalline matrix has been shaped by the stone cutter. When a rounded Emerald is not being worn, it emits only a very low amount of energy. However, as soon as it touches an aura, it becomes enlivened and begins to radiate at maximum velocity until the aura is saturated.

Every Emerald will give some degree of green-ray energy. The closer in color the Emerald is to the green color of the rainbow, the more powerful is the gemstone. Also, the clearer the Emerald is, the greater is its power. This is because cloudiness inhibits the velocity at which Emerald can radiate its green ray.

White inclusions will inhibit less than black inclusions, which actually block the green ray from flowing past them. Fractures, small lines, or tiny crystals that might be observed in an Emerald do not inhibit the power of the Emerald to radiate the green ray, especially if it has a good color.

If you wore only one half-carat, round Emerald around your neck, that one Emerald would radiate its energy into the aura at full velocity until the aura became saturated. However, an Emerald that size would probably not be large enough to saturate the aura. Therefore, it would work at full velocity 24 hours a day. If you wore five or six carats of Emerald, the Emerald would probably not need to radiate at full velocity all the time. This amount of Emerald would be enough to saturate the aura of the average individual within six to twelve hours.

If you are wearing Emerald for therapy, your aura should maintain saturation for 24 hours a day. The Emerald will know if the aura drops below 100-percent saturation. It will increase its velocity until the aura once again reaches full saturation.

Between the emotional body and the physical body lies a layer of super-physical energy. For the sake of simplicity, I will call this layer of energy the "physical aura." The physical aura surrounds the physical body. The physical aura is surrounded by the emotional aura, which is surrounded by the mental aura. If enough Emerald is worn, it will begin to saturate the emotional aura after it has saturated the physical aura. It takes longer to saturate the emotional aura than the physical aura; and it takes even more time and perhaps more Emerald to saturate the mental aura. This is why individuals who wear Emerald and Aventurine necklaces, and whose physical disease or disharmony is resolved, must continue to wear at least the Emerald necklace. That way, the inner auras can also be saturated with green ray, and the corresponding disharmonies in these areas can be resolved.

Disharmonies in the physical body manifest as aches, pains,

tumors, hardness, stiffness, tightness, etc. Disharmony in the emotional body can manifest as unbalanced emotions. In the mental body, disharmonies can express themselves as mental aberrations, such as greed or anger. These mental and emotional disharmonies almost always lead to physical disharmonies.

Therefore, once you take care of the physical disharmonies, you must take care of the inner disharmonies. Otherwise, they will manifest once again in the physical body. Perhaps they will manifest in a different place or as a different condition, but they will return.

This is why someone whose physical body is overburdened with disharmony may wish to wear Emerald for the rest of his or her life.

Remember, the Emerald energy can start to work on the inner bodies only after the physical body's aura can maintain Emerald saturation and there is enough Emerald mass to supply the extra velocity needed.

My effects on the emotions and mind are secondary to my effects on the physical body. If individuals who wear me understand how I work on the physical body, their minds and emotions can be at rest. They will know that they have a very powerful tool helping them to heal their physical conditions.

It is important to know that there are actually two forces working within Emerald. One is the Emerald energy that carries the green ray, and the other is the vibratory rate of Emerald itself. It is Emerald's vibratory rate that prepares the emotions and the mind for the new state of consciousness that will arise once the Emerald's green healing ray resolves the physical disharmony. This is Emerald's way of assisting in the actual resolution of a condition.

It is not the green ray alone that disintegrates disharmony; it is the green ray in combination with the vibratory rate of Emerald. If this were not the case, green-ray color therapy alone would be sufficient, which it is not.

One can "consume" the green ray much more effectively by wearing Emerald than, for example, by constantly eating spinach and collard greens. This is because spinach and collards do not stay green very long. Even the deep green juice of wheatgrass changes in vibratory rate when it enters the body. Although it carries much life force, the matter which supports the green energy of the wheatgrass juice—or of any other green vegetable—changes considerably when it is digested. On the other hand, when one wears Emerald, one receives the green ray and the Emerald vibratory rate constantly.

There is something else you should know. You might wonder why, when an aura becomes saturated with green ray, it does not stay saturated. Disharmony and Emerald vibratory rate are opposites. Emerald vibratory rate has the power to cancel out and disintegrate disharmony. However, if the Emerald is removed from an aura that is saturated with Emerald vibratory rate, then any disharmony still present in the aura will fight with the remaining Emerald vibratory rate. If the disharmony is strong, the Emerald vibratory rate will be used up and dissipate rather quickly.

It is not possible to wear too many Emerald spheres or rondelles. A necklace of 75 to 100 carats of Emerald would be very effective therapeutically, because it would easily keep the physical body saturated. It would also put enough velocity behind the Emerald vibratory rate to infiltrate the inner bodies after physical saturation has been achieved.

By velocity, I mean the speed at which the Emerald energy can enter the aura. The velocity of a large or small rounded Emerald is the same. The size of an Emerald simply determines the power behind the velocity. In other words, the speed is a universal constant for all Emeralds; the power behind the speed is determined by the Emerald's size.

Another factor to consider when trying to achieve maximum Emerald effectiveness is the distribution of Emerald throughout the aura. For example, five one-carat Emeralds would be less effective than 25 Emeralds with a total weight of five carats if these 25 Emeralds were spaced around the neck. This spacing enables the Emeralds to touch a greater portion of the aura.

Emerald Therapy

The effect of Emerald vibratory rate on cancer is one of shock. Cancer is like a living entity. It works to maintain its own life which, of course, exists at the expense of its host.

When introduced to the pure green ray and the vibratory rate of Emerald, the cancer entity becomes so shocked that it cringes and becomes a little more compact. Then, if Dark Green Aventurine is also worn, the Aventurine will be able to enter the diseased area more easily. This will occur for two reasons: first, the cancer has become more isolated; and second, as the cancer entity is shocked, it will let down its guard.

Once the Aventurine enters a cancerous organ, it works remarkably well with Emerald. Aventurine works from the inside of the organ to dispel disharmony and spread healthy, harmonious vibratory rate throughout the organ's cells. The Emerald stands at the gateway of each cell with a "hose" which shoots green ray at the exiting disharmony and disintegrates it. It essentially sucks the life out of the disharmony. This is the power of the green ray; it is the perfect opposite of cancer.

* * *

Emerald spheres or rondelles can also be placed over specific areas on the body. Let us use the liver as an example. If Emeralds are placed on the skin over the liver, and sunlight is allowed to shine on them, the rounded Emeralds will begin to act like crystals. The side that is accepting the sun's energy will become the base of the crystal, and the side that is touching the skin will direct the green ray like a laser into the liver.

If the Emerald is worn over the liver but under clothing, only the energy that is already inside the Emeralds will be able to infiltrate the organ. Also, the penetrating effect will not be as deep. Sunlight provides a great push, allowing the entire organ to be flooded with the green ray within minutes.

The individual will be greatly assisted in this effort to heal the liver if that person has been wearing ten-millimeter Dark Green Aventurine spheres for a minimum of several hours beforehand. Of course, this assumes that the Aventurine will also target the liver as the organ of greatest disharmony.

If an individual with liver disharmony wants to work with this therapy, he or she should place a strand of rounded Emeralds on the skin over the liver and lay in the sun for a half hour each day. In fact, this therapy can be used on any area of disharmony—such as broken bones or areas that are healing from other injuries or surgery.

Alcohol is a drug which is metabolized by the body but leaves its mark on the liver. A liver damaged by alcohol will be assisted by placing Emerald, plus a strand of Quartz, on the skin over the liver and then lying in the sun. It would be ideal to form the two necklaces into a neat spiral; this will enable them to intermix and be distributed evenly over the area. The Quartz will act like a window through which the Emerald vibratory rate can work on healing the areas in the inner bodies that are affecting the liver.

A liver which has been damaged by too much alcohol comprises a different situation. The alcohol is also an entity, but it does not latch onto the physical body like the cancer entity does. Instead, it clings to the aura of the individual. Alcoholism is actually an inner-body disharmony; that is why, when treating it, Quartz should be included with the Emerald. The Quartz will align the inner bodies with the physical body. It will open a door through which the Emerald vibratory rate can easily begin to saturate the inner bodies, even before the physical body is completely saturated.

If you want to focus primarily on the physical body, use Emerald by itself or wear it with Aventurine. If, in addition to your physical body, your inner bodies require Emerald's vibratory rate to resolve your physical situation, wear Quartz along with the Emerald.

By the way, the addition of Quartz would not be indicated in a condition such as liver cancer. The cancer is a malicious entity which has grabbed onto the liver. In order to eradicate it, the individual will need to place maximum focus on the physical level. Only when the physical body has become stabilized, should the focus be shifted to the inner bodies.

* * *

Emerald will probably not be effective when placed over stomachs that are hurting because their owners have eaten the wrong food. I would only help to soothe and heal the stomach if it were actually damaged or hurt by eating that food.

* * *

When an Emerald necklace is worn around the neck along

with a necklace of Aventurine, the Emerald vibratory rate enters the body through the breath. The Emerald vibratory rate effectively rides in on the Aventurine vibratory rate.

If an Emerald necklace is worn by itself, the Emerald vibratory rate first floods the aura and locates areas of disharmony. Then, like the eagle which has spotted its prey, it swoops down on these areas. The Emerald vibratory rate focuses on the disharmonious areas and enters them by diffusing through the skin.

Emerald vibratory rate can enter the body through skin, muscle, or bone. Those with head pain could wrap the Emerald strand around the head like a headband or place it over the specific point of pain. If your Emerald necklace contains 75 to 100 carats of Emerald, I suggest that you place it on your head for only one minute at a time every fifteen minutes. Necklaces containing five to fifteen carats of Emerald can be placed on the head for longer periods of time or perhaps indefinitely, if it feels good. It should be removed as soon as it feels uncomfortable.

Individuals with diseases that affect the entire physical body can benefit most by wearing an Emerald necklace containing as much Emerald as they can afford. The Emeralds should be spaced around the neck so that they can touch as much of the aura as possible. Because the disharmony of such diseases is so great, it will take much Emerald energy to maintain physical body saturation. The war between the Emerald vibratory rate and the disease vibratory rate will be a massive one. The individual will need as much healing energy as possible.

Those individuals whose energy flows are so severely imbalanced that their illness is noticed by society—and who might even be housed in a special institution—should precede Emerald therapy with a gemstone therapy or other therapy that corrects the energy-flow imbalances. Those who have minor energy-flow imbalances will have no difficulty using Emerald from the start.

Emerald Tomorrow

I will assist people who use Emerald as a tool for resolving their greatest disharmonies. Once the disharmonies are resolved, the attention can be placed on greater aspects of growth. This will allow people to move more swiftly in their personal and spiritual evolution.

When I say "I" or "me" in reference to Emerald, I do not mean I, the Guardian of Emerald. I am referring to that part of me which is Emerald itself.

Yes, I am rare and precious and therefore expensive. As a general rule, the more precious a gemstone is, the more power it has and the stronger are its effects. Because it is so powerful, less of the gemstone is needed on the planet. Therefore, it is naturally more rare.

Do not underestimate the healing power of the gemstones that carry the color rays. Emerald's specific purpose is to assist individuals in their physical changes and upliftment.

If all you had were Emerald and Aventurine, your gemstone "tool box" for physical-body assistance and healing would be almost complete. I do not wish to negate the importance of other gemstones and their significance for speeding up the resolution of certain isolated conditions. However, if you cannot see a gemstone therapist, and you are working on healing a condition by yourself, then Emerald and Aventurine are indispensable.

There is still much to learn about Emerald, as the stories of my past only suggest. My nature is to assist in the upliftment of human beings. I, as the Guardian of Emerald, am ready. Emerald itself is also ready. Now it is up to you.

Recognizing that the discourse had ended, Michael and the others thanked the Guardian of Emerald, who responded by nodding his head. As I turned to thank him, I found that I was no longer in his aura, but was facing him. Again he looked into my eyes and then held my hands, which now clutched a strand of Emeralds.

Then his body vanished, and the green-ray floodlight appeared in its place. The sky also disappeared, and we found ourselves standing once again inside the amphitheater. Soon the other six colored floodlights reappeared in their former positions.

We looked at one another, silently assimilating the experience we had just shared. Then, one by one, each of us walked away in separate directions.

5
ROSELLE

(Rose Quartz)

Four individuals stood waiting for my husband and me beside a thick, pale pink fog. We joined them, and acknowledged one another with silent looks. Then we all joined hands and walked into the mist.

The fog quickly turned into a light pink rain. This gentle rain did not make us wet, but seemed to cleanse and soothe our emotions. Through the rain we saw a figure shrouded by a misty pink light approach us. I knew she was female by the quality of her energy, although the light radiating from her face made her features hard to see. When she arrived, she folded her hands and bowed her head in greeting.

I walked up to her and asked permission to enter her aura. She shook her head and stepped back. The rain seemed to stop in mid-air, and the pink mist that surrounded her body became absolutely still. Then out from behind the mist stepped a woman.

She had long, dark blond hair. Her eyes were brown. The shirt and pants she wore appeared loose-fitting and comfortable. Her shirt revealed muscular arms. She seemed as ordinary as anyone; yet the light in her eyes and radiance of her body made her seem like no one from the Earth planet.

The pink shell of misty light that she had once occupied came alive again, and its energy began to swirl like a whirlpool. Again the rain began to fall.

The Guardian looked at us and smiled. I am Roselle, *she*

said. Then she invited me to stand next to her and connect my consciousness with hers. In this way I could relay her words.

In many ways I am just like you. I have a family, and I have children. But I also have a spiritual responsibility: I am the Guardian for Rose Quartz.

My name is Roselle. I would be grateful if you also called the spherical form of Rose Quartz "Roselle." This will help distinguish the properties of the spherical form from those of the crystalline form, which is commonly known as Rose Quartz.

I do not live on the Earth planet. I live on a plane which has a vibratory rate higher than that of the physical plane. My world is unseen by physical eyes; yet it is as real to me and its inhabitants as your world is to you. Many people who see me every day have no inkling of my spiritual responsibility as Guardian of Rose Quartz; and I do not advertise it. I say this to help you understand the possibilities of who and what a Gemstone Guardian might be. Before I give you an overview of my purpose for the Earth planet and for the humans who live there, why don't we all sit down? The rain has stopped, and the sunshine is warm.

When I am in spherical form, my purpose is to help individuals move beyond their emotions. Emotional disruptions often act as great stumbling blocks or locked doors for an individual. These disruptions inhibit one's changes and growth. They stand between oneself and one's greater understanding and experience of Spirit, Soul, and God.

Emotional disruptions are caused by feelings which would rather not be expressed or which cannot be expressed because a physical pain is too great. These emotions might even be positive ones, like love, joy, or happiness.

I help bring the attention of those who wear me to their emotions. I also bring the attention to those particular aspects of the emotions that are blocked and therefore act as closed doors in the emotional body. I help the individual to open these doors.

Then I help to resolve emotional disruptions. I do this by stirring unexpressed emotions and gently stimulating the heart to open. This allows these emotions to be expressed at last.

One's heart will only open if the body is ready to accept the feelings I have stirred. I will not force the heart to open. In other words, I allow the individual's true nature to be stirred and felt; then if the body allows, the door will open and this true nature will be expressed.

I do not heal emotions; the word "heal" is misleading. I simply help an individual to resolve suppressed or misunderstood emotions. These emotions include long-forgotten feelings that have been pushed deep within as a result of one's upbringing, social pressures, culture, or other factors.

When I am in crystalline form, my focus is for the planet. I act like a magnet, drawing the Earth's vibratory rate upward toward the emotional plane. My magnetic influence pulls the Earth's energy to a higher state of consciousness.

This movement toward a greater awareness is part of the Earth's evolution. For this purpose, I need not be planted in the Earth. I can be anywhere in the atmosphere, so long as I am in crystalline form.

The Early Years of Rose Quartz

I was not present at the birth of the planet. I evolved as life evolved on Earth.

Any thinking or feeling that fish, reptiles, or mammals do is directly related to the physical functioning of their brains. These thoughts and feelings are mostly a product of habit and instinct. As humans evolved, they could not grow beyond this purely instinctual, physical state of consciousness until there was enough emotional energy on the Earth to allow this growth to occur.

So, when the Earth became ready for human beings to start evolving, the light ray that gives life to the emotional plane was directed toward the Earth in a great beacon. It enveloped the planet and began filling its aura. This light ray from the emotional plane was the pink color ray.

Once the Earth's aura contained enough of the pink ray, the pink ray vibratory rate collected at the Earth's power points. Then Quartz directed this vibratory rate along the Earth's veins and arteries to the many places in the Earth where Quartz was already forming and growing. When this pink energy was accepted by certain Quartz crystals, it took hold and began to spread through them.

As this occurred, Rose Quartz was born, allowing both the Earth and the humans living there to become connected with the emotional level of life. This gave the evolving humans a conscious awareness and recognition of their emotions, which the animals did not possess.

By the way, today most animals still react, feel, and think only on an instinctual level. However, those animals who have been touched and loved by humans, and who are growing along with them, are given a special gift most of their owners are not aware of. Because their owners are in touch with their own emotions, these pets become more in touch with theirs. Pets actually encourage a greater emotional connection with their owners. They encourage their owners to open their hearts and love them, and thereby direct a stream of love and emotion toward them. This love raises the pet's consciousness and provides it with the gift of being more in tune with its own emotions.

During the Age of Lemuria, I was not considered very important. At that time, my pink color had not totally infiltrated the Quartz crystals destined to become Rose Quartz. In other words, these crystals were not yet entirely pink. Even though the pink ray had been accepted by the clear Quartz, it took thousands of years for entire pink crystals to grow on their own.

In the Age of Atlantis, my crystals had become fully pink and were clear and new. When something is new, extra energy and excitement is often associated with it. This is true of anything, whether it is a new book, a new movie, or a new baby.

In the early and middle part of that era, the people did not know that Rose Quartz was a relatively new gemstone. When people held the crystal, they felt excitement and enthusiasm for life. Why? Because they could feel the upliftment that Rose Quartz was giving to the planet and to the atmosphere around them. Upliftment is exciting, since it brings a greater amount of energy. Therefore, single Rose Quartz crystals that could be easily grasped in the palm of the hand were valued highly. At that time I was not fashioned into spheres; nor was I cut in any way, except to isolate single crystals.

Toward the end of the Atlantean era, I was most treasured by those who relied on my help in order to maintain a positive attitude, despite the negativity that was building on Atlantis. I helped these individuals to gain a greater connection with their true emotions; and this helped them to remain balanced. I also protected them from some of the negativity. Rose Quartz crystals today do not have the protective value that they had during the era of Atlantis.

The Rose Quartz crystals available throughout the Age of Atlantis were clear, pure, very beautiful, and basically free of inclusions. Of course, when the Earth shook at the downfall of Atlantis, almost every crystalline structure on the planet was cracked or broken.

Rose Quartz Today

To understand my purpose, you need to know a little more about Rose Quartz. Today, few well-defined Rose Quartz crystals are found; it mostly occurs in a cloudy, rock-like form.

Rose Quartz is still spreading on the planet. A tremendous amount has been born since the time of Atlantis. This growth is preparing the planet for greater consciousness. As more Rose Quartz becomes available, the magnetic pull toward the emotional level and the momentum of the upward spiral of energy on the planet will increase. The spread of Rose Quartz also serves to balance the downward spiral that this planet is currently experiencing. We see this spiral expressed as increased crime, corruption, and negativity.

Since the Age of Atlantis, the positive and negative forces—the upward and downward spirals—have been struggling with each other.

This opposition is also the reason that Rose Quartz has become so cloudy. The constant struggle between these two forces creates a conflict within the crystalline matrix and causes this cloudiness.

Today, Rose Quartz in crystalline form can do little for humans other than to remind them of their emotions. Of course, if someone has an affinity for a Rose Quartz crystal, if they like the way it feels, and it has become a friend for them, I encourage them to enjoy it.

When Rose Quartz is shaped into spheres, it can greatly assist humans. In this form it can help open the doors in the emotional level that have blocked an individual from greater spirituality, self-awareness, or self-understanding. These closed doors often manifest as suppressed, hidden, or unacknowledged emotions. People often don't express certain emotions, because these feelings don't fit the concept of the spiritual or moral beings they want to be, or they are not in harmony with the religious, social, or political values these people were taught as children.

Emotions that are not expressed prevent or inhibit one from receiving the flow of spirit force, life force, creative force, or healing force (call it what you will) to enter the physical body.

When physical pathologies are the result of suppressed emotions, I can assist in healing the cause of the pathology. Of course, other treatments should be used to heal any physical symptoms. I can also assist when physical healing is being inhibited by certain suppressed emotions.

My mission is to awaken suppressed emotions, and this occurs in two phases: In Phase One, I stir suppressed emotions, allowing the individual to acknowledge, understand, and then feel these emotions; in Phase Two, the individual is encouraged to express these emotion, let go of them, resolve them, and move on.

Did you notice the significance of numbers in this formula? There are two phases and four steps to each phase. The number two represents the emotions, and the number four represents the physical. That these two numbers intertwine in this formula means that the emotions are provided with a greater tie to the physical. This gives them an easier path for expression.

In general, you will find that I can assist women through these two phases more effectively than I can assist men. This is only because men have a more difficult time letting go of suppressed emotions than women do. Of course, most men easily express and let go of emotions that are felt spontaneously and that they do not wish to suppress. If a man wishes to be assisted by Roselle, he must be totally willing to acknowledge and re-experience his suppressed emotions. This is often difficult for a man.

My action is not violent. It is subtle, yet effective. I only give what the individual can handle. Since women have stronger emotional constitutions than men do, they can wear greater amounts of Roselle without feeling imbalanced. One might think that women are emotionally weak, since stereotypically they cry often; but it takes great emotional strength to let go and cry.

Even after I am worn for just a few hours, I begin to work on the individual's emotions. If I am taken off, my effects will continue to be felt until the momentum wears off or until I am worn again. If I am worn continually for a few days—long enough to saturate the aura—I will still influence the individual even when I am not worn. However, I can do this only if I am in the same room as the individual.

Some say that I remind people of positive emotional qualities, and that I promote feelings of goodwill, friendship, and love. This is the effect of my color. However, judging a gemstone by the properties of its color alone can be misleading. A gemstone is not simply its color. It also has energies apart from those of its color. I have a focused, clear, and specific purpose which is not defined by the vibratory rate of my color. It just so happens that the pink color ray is the most effective vehicle for my mission.

Often people need to use their minds to rationalize certain emotions before they can resolve them, let them go, and move on. Those who wish to understand why they are feeling a certain way, when there is no logical reason for it, can benefit from wearing Roselle. Just as I act like a magnet to draw the energy of the physical plane upward, I also act as a magnet to pull mental plane energy downward. As mental energy is drawn to the emotional level, a greater understanding of the emotions occurs.

So, Roselle does affect the mind, but only in direct connection with my purpose.

Roselle Therapy

To assist human beings, I must be in spherical form and, ideally, be worn around the neck. This is the easiest way for the aura to be filled with my energy. When the aura is filled, the whole body can be uplifted in a way similar to that in which the Rose Quartz crystal uplifts the Earth's physical consciousness.

Lavender is an ideal gemstone for people to wear before seeing a physician. When wearing Lavender, any peripheral symptoms that may be clouding a patient's true problem will diminish or resolve. Then the physician will be able to diagnose the true condition more easily. However, if a doctor determines that the cause of an individual's condition is an emotional suppression, then Roselle would be the ideal pre-treatment gemstone to wear.

Generally healthy individuals who are looking for tools to

help them get through certain emotional blockages can benefit from wearing Roselle. They can choose to wear six-millimeter, eight-millimeter, or ten-millimeter Roselle spheres. People will be attracted to the size that is most comfortable for them. If you are first attracted to the six-millimeter size, you should encourage yourself to graduate to an eight-millimeter strand after several months. Then, after several more months you should move on to a ten-millimeter strand, because the larger the spheres are, the stronger are their effects.

It is important to follow your intuition. If the six-millimeter spheres feel comfortable for you, wear them. Move on to eight-millimeter spheres when you feel that the smaller size has given you a greater emotional understanding and clarity, but you still have blocks and feel that it's time to wear something stronger. When you are ready for even deeper work on your emotions, wear the ten-millimeter spheres.

A size larger than ten millimeters would only be appropriate for individuals who have worn a ten-millimeter strand for several months, and are still having difficulty with unusually stubborn emotions that don't want to be expressed.

If individuals are having trouble expressing and/or letting go of their emotions, they would be helped by wearing Ruby along with Roselle. Ruby's powerful love will give them the confidence they need. They'll know that they will still be loved and have love if they express the feelings they have been suppressing.

* * *

I can assist individuals who know they have emotional problems or whose emotions are so disharmonious that they are considered emotionally ill by society's standards. I will help them regain some emotional strength. I will also prepare them for a gemstone such as Rhodocrosite, which has a strong ability to break up emotional patterns and to cleanse and rebuild the emotional body.

The treatment is this: Place a small amount of Roselle in a neat spiral over each of the seven chakras for at least one hour every day. You might even fall asleep with the gemstones in place. Because Roselle has the crystalline matrix of Quartz, it will work on balancing the chakras. However, it will focus primarily on creating that magnetic effect of uplifting the vibratory rate of the physical body so it will be in greater harmony with the emotions. This action will also harmonize the connection between the physical and emotional bodies. Often the most apparent, and therefore the most critical, emotional disharmonies occur when this connection is faulty.

On the mental level, this therapy will help individuals to better understand their emotions. On the emotional level, it will allow suppressed or hidden emotions that are creating disharmony to become more apparent. And on the physical level, it will help individuals to express these emotions and to resolve the disharmony that has been caused by their suppression.

Eight- or ten-millimeter Roselle spheres would work best for this therapy, since six-millimeter spheres might be too weak. You will only need a twelve-inch strand of Roselle over each chakra. It does not matter whether or not there are knots between the spheres.

If you only have one or two strands of Roselle, do not place them in a line up the body over the chakras. Each chakra should have its own individual strand of Roselle. If you only have a few strands, you could place a spiraled strand of Roselle over each chakra—starting at the base chakra—for ten minutes. This will work, but it will not be as effective as placing strands on all chakras simultaneously for an hour. This is because the Roselle will only be working on each chakra for ten minutes.

To achieve the strongest effect, between these treatments wear ten-millimeter Roselle spheres around the neck. The strand should be long but comfortable. Also wear a shorter length of eight- millimeter Quartz spheres. The ten-millimeter Roselle is suggested because of its greater focus and force. However, by itself it might be rather strong; the Quartz will allow the effects of the treatment to occur in greater balance. As it balances the individual, it will bring healing energy through all levels and thereby help to resolve the situation.

If suppressed emotions have caused a physical disharmony, then a Roselle necklace can be worn along with Emerald and Aventurine.

If the physical disharmony is most critical to your wellbeing, make the Aventurine the longest necklace, the Roselle somewhat shorter, and the Emerald the shortest necklace. If the physical condition is apparent, but the emotional disharmony is most critical (because its energy is greatly feeding the physical disharmony), then ten-millimeter Roselle should be the longest necklace, and the Aventurine should be the middle-length necklace.

* * *

Sometimes when individuals are emotionally upset, they feel tightness in the stomach. Holding Roselle over the stomach will soothe this upset feeling. This procedure will often be more effective for easing heartaches than holding the Roselle over the heart itself.

The next time you are releasing emotions—whether or not as a result of Roselle's influence—it will be comforting to take off your Roselle necklace, hold it in your hands, and cry. Go ahead and release those emotions as you clench the Roselle in your hands. When people cry and hold Roselle in their hands, they will tend to hold their hands over one of four chakras: the stomach; the chest; by the chin over the throat; or near the eyes over the brow. They will subconsciously hold the Roselle wherever it feels most comforting. This is because the body will know which of these chakras most needs the Roselle vibratory rate to help the individual get through the release.

* * *

Now something you must clearly understand about gemstones is this: When the Guardians say, "Gemstones assist people in their changes," they mean that the gemstones will initiate changes. However, they will also support the individual through the changes and help the changes occur in balance. Gemstones can also force changes. If individuals who are reluctant to change wear certain gemstones, they are in effect saying, "I give the gemstones permission to force the change, because I want the change. I just can't do it myself. I'm stuck and need help."

Even if gemstone wearers are totally ignorant of their effects, the gemstones will still do their work.

* * *

"Over 95 percent of the spherical Roselle currently available

on Earth has been dyed. How does that affect your work?" asked Michael.

Dye makes the color of Roselle appear more pink, but it does not make the vibratory rate of Roselle any stronger. In fact, the dye will inhibit my action. If you used dyed Roselle for any of the therapies I have mentioned, you would get no results. It is not dangerous. It just doesn't work, and it does not fulfill my mission. However, dyed Roselle can assist in soothing emotions.

Let the Rose Quartz that people would want to dye remain in the Earth, for that is where it will do its greatest work. Rose Quartz that you consider low in quality because it lacks striking pink color is still beneficial for the Earth. So let it remain there. Only harvest those crystals that do not need to be dyed and that can be truly beneficial to people. Harvest Rose Quartz as you would harvest medicinal herbs: choose only the best.

I know that Earth humans will have many economic and business objections to that suggestion. But my advice is for the ears of those who have pure ethics in mind. Unfortunately, they may be the select few. Although it does not take economic considerations into account, the scenario I described would be the ideal way to harvest Roselle.

Those who want to wear Roselle as a therapeutic tool should only use the finest quality, natural, undyed Roselle that has good color and some transparency.

* * *

Roselle should never be worn touching gold.

The combination of Roselle and gold will bring destruction to the wearer. Do you know why? It is important to know why. If you have discovered any property of any gemstone, it will mean little, unless you know why that property occurs.

Gold tends to lock an individual into his or her current state of consciousness; and it tends to close the heart. These effects are in direct conflict with the mission of Roselle.

When gold is worn with Roselle, the emotions will be stimulated and grow out of proportion. For example, if the amount of your suppressed anger could be compared to the size of a sparrow—and you wear gold and Roselle together—your suppressed anger will grow to the size of an elephant.

Yes, the effect is that strong, because my vibratory rate enlivens and strengthens gold. I also make its effects more erratic and unstable. When emotions grow out of proportion from the influence of Roselle and gold, these emotions surround the individual like a bubble. The individual becomes lost within that bubble.

Of course, gold has its positive qualities; but when it is worn with Roselle, I turn it into a monster.

* * *

Before an individual's Roselle is worn by someone else, it should be cleansed. This is because an individual's vibratory rate will cling to it. The most effective way to cleanse Roselle is to place it under cool running water for about thirty seconds, and then to place it in the sun for about one hour.

Roselle Tomorrow

Roselle is not a particularly strong gemstone, especially when you compare its strength to that of the color ray bearers. However, Roselle is a tool that should not be overlooked, especially if one has any emotional disharmony at all.

Roselle may even be used simply to know oneself better. It could be quite enlightening to discover what emotions you may be suppressing. It could be an interesting experience in self-awareness and self-understanding to wear Roselle and observe the emotions that start coming up and the ones you try to suppress. You may not realize you have been suppressing anything at all. The experience will also allow you to recognize which of your attitudes are causing you to suppress certain emotions. Therefore, Roselle could be included in every self-help seminar, if only because it can tell people so much about themselves.

My mission will continue into the future. Rose Quartz will continue to grow and spread, because the planet needs it. The planet needs a force to balance and counteract the downward spiral that seems to have such a strong pull on it. Roselle is also needed to strengthen the upward spiral being experienced by the planet. Roselle in spherical form will continue to be available to those individuals who wish to open the closed doors in their emotional bodies. This opening will allow more life force to flow into their physical bodies.

I see no changes in the appearance of my crystal, in the availability of high-quality crystals, or in the way I affect humans. The only changes I foresee in the ways that people use me will result from the opening of the intuition. It will guide people to other ways this tool called Roselle can be used.

You will find that some gemstones are more powerful than others. That is why some Gemstone Guardians must be Guardians full-time and totally committed to their work. Perhaps this is why I, as Roselle, am able to take the responsibility of being a Guardian and yet still have a family and lead a somewhat normal life.

You may never know whether your next-door neighbor is a master of the life force or adept in the teachings of light and sound. But as you wonder about this possibility, your attitude of wonderment and curiosity will bring with it a certain humility. Next to some gemstones, we can all be humble—no matter how small their size may be, compared to ours.

* * *

Tomorrow I will introduce you to a special friend. I do not get to see her often myself. She is the Guardian of Ruby. The gemstones she and I care for can do wonderful things for the human when we are worn together.

Do not hesitate to wear Ruby with Roselle, for she will give light and life to my effects. She will help uplift the individual to greater heights than I ever could alone.

Roselle smiled briefly. Then she stood up and re-entered the shell of pink, swirling energy. We watched, amazed at her ability to do this. Then she placed the palms of her hands together, bowed her head to the group, and walked away.

6
RUBY

We sat in our living room and prepared to meet Ruby. Already her presence was strong. The room began to fill with feelings of love and joy. It seemed as though all the molecules in the air were turning themselves inside out, changing into particles of greater and greater energy; and this energy was love.

I closed my eyes in order to become more attuned to these feelings of love that I knew must be related to Ruby. Indeed they were, for a woman appeared on the screen of my inner vision who clearly was the Guardian of Ruby. She was standing in the pink mist in which we had met Roselle.

Red energy swirled and flowed around the Guardian's body, forming what appeared to be a floor-length gown. Her hair was dark, almost purple-red. A red ray either shone from her eyes or was reflected by them—I could not be sure which. Gloves covered her arms. The only skin I could see was that of her face and neck; it was unusually white.

She extended one hand to Michael and one to me, and together we walked through the mist and pink rain to the Guardian of Roselle.

When the two Guardians met, they held the palms of their hands together and bowed slightly to each other. Then Roselle turned to us and said, "I see you have already met the Guardian of Ruby. Follow her. Perhaps you and I will meet again somewhere in time. For now, farewell!"

Ruby led us to the edge of a cliff where about fifteen listeners were already gathered and awaiting her discourse. The wind was strong, yet it did not ruffle our hair or clothing. Peering over the edge of the cliff, I saw clouds below and, thousands of feet beneath them, the ocean. Despite the distance of the water, the roar of waves crashing against rocks could be distinctly heard. Still, we were not distracted. Our attention was focused on Ruby.

She seated herself close to the cliff's edge, and the listeners gathered in a semi-circle around her. She started to speak and I remembered my duty. Feeling conspicuous, I stood and approached her. She seemed to understand my intent and drew me toward her. Then I fell into her consciousness. . .

When each of you first felt my presence, you experienced what Ruby does naturally. It changes the molecules in the atmosphere. It turns them inside out, in a sense, to reveal the love that created them. And what is this love? It is the divine love that created all molecules and atoms. You can call it the love of God.

Those who wear the faceted form of Ruby find that the red ray I project into the aura teaches them to become more aware of their emotions and more comfortable with the vibratory rate of the red ray.

In spherical form, I provide a direct link between the emotions and the physical body. I allow my wearers to more fully experience the reality of the emotional body.

The Early Years of Ruby

The chemical matrix of my crystals, known as corundum, was formed when the Earth was formed. It collected in pockets in many places around the planet. These pockets had a certain geographical relationship with the Earth's power points as they existed at the birth of the planet. The corundum pockets were located at specific distances from the power points.

If you study the major deposits of corundum and the power points of the Earth, you will discover this relationship. This is because corundum, of any color, strongly desires to be positioned at a certain distance from the power points—not too near and not too far. It will even cause shifts in the planet in order to achieve this distance.

Power points have shifted several times since the birth of the planet. Each time the power points shift, the minerals and crystals that need to be a certain distance from the power points are drawn to these distances like magnets. This force compels the plates of the Earth's crust to move, so that the crystals can realign and relocate themselves at the ideal distances from the power points.

I am saying that corundum has the power to force the Earth's patterns to change. Do you think that a human's patterns are hard to change? My friends, there is nothing harder to change than the physical matter of a planet; and if corundum can do this, it can easily change a human's patterns. It is just a matter of applying the proper tools correctly.

Corundum was colorless at the birth of the planet. Red Corundum, or Ruby, came into being when the vibratory rate of the red ray entered the Earth planet and combined with the crystalline matrix of corundum. Remember, when a planet forms, it is not given the color rays until it is ready to support life. So although corundum had formed, it was not infused with the life of the color rays until the planet was ready for it.

Ruby is not just the red ray or just the vibratory rate of corundum. It is the combination of the two. It is the way in which the vibratory rate of Ruby uses the red ray and throws it into one's aura that makes its effects different from those of any another source of red ray, red color, or red light.

It was not until the Age of Atlantis that the people of Earth needed the strong vibratory rate of corundum behind the red ray. Prior to that, there was another carrier of the red ray. The reign of this previous carrier had declined rapidly. This carrier had gladly taken the responsibility of bearing the red ray, but it faltered when it could not handle the long-term responsibility. Its crystalline matrix was too weak to handle the vibratory rate of the pure red ray over a long period of time, and this weakness caused an imbalance. This imbalance corrupted the gemstone and its Guardian, and the two became a negative influence on the people of Atlantis.

Because of this corruption, a new carrier of the red ray had to be quickly acquired. So, the Guardian of the planet, the Guardian of the universe, and whoever else was required to make such decisions focused the red ray like a laser toward specific deposits of clear corundum.

The transfer from the old carrier to the new occurred almost instantaneously (by Earth standards, in about 100 to 200 years). This was all the time needed for the corundum to change from clear to pink to a true red. So, if your next question is whether pink Ruby is an immature form of red Ruby, the answer is yes.

On most other planets, the red ray is planted in corundum at the same time that the other six color-ray carriers are planted. I do not know why the Earth was different in this respect.

When I was given the responsibility of bearing the red color ray, the previous carrier resisted. It would not let go of the responsibility it had grown out of. Therefore, to protect and maintain my mission, I had to create a mask of power. This was necessary to keep my predecessor from influencing my work.

Unfortunately, people soon noticed this mask of power. They labeled Ruby a stone of power and then misused this power for themselves. I was meant to be a gemstone that taught the force of love. It was never my intention to carry the force of power.

The greatest misuses of Ruby occurred near the end of the Age of Atlantis. Fortunately, most of the knowledge concerning the misuse of my power sank beneath the waves along with the continent of Atlantis.

After the destruction of Atlantis, I was treasured by royalty and nobility, because my high-quality specimens were rare and precious, and because remnants of my power remained.

You see, as long as I was wearing this mask of power, I was unable to fulfill my mission as the force for love, which is the positive aspect of the red ray. Today there are other gemstones and earthstones that carry the element of power. These are available to satisfy the need for power possessed by individuals in a certain state of consciousness.

My predecessor's energy has greatly waned and does not fit the expanding consciousness of most people today. Because my predecessor's energy has weakened, my power mask is no longer necessary. It seems as though a cycle has ended, and I can begin my reign all over again. This time I can do it right, because now I have no need for a mask to protect myself or my mission. Now, the consciousness of human beings is ready for Ruby.

Because I have experienced the conflict between power and love, and have resolved it within myself, I can assist others who are also experiencing this struggle. I can give them the strength to move beyond this conflict.

The color red may always be a symbol for power; yet it is also a symbol for love. My predecessor allowed the red ray to enter the body principally through the base chakra. You can imagine what state of consciousness would allow this to occur and the results it would have.

I bring the red ray in through the heart. Often the heart is so thankful for my presence and the love I bring with me, that it freely opens its door to my vibratory rate as well as to the red ray.

I could continue discussing my past in greater detail, but my importance for the present is what you really need to know.

Ruby Today

If one's body tenses at the discussion of emotions, this is a sure sign of red ray deficiency. One may say, "I'm willing to learn about emotions," but the eyes will say, "I'm afraid. I'm not ready. I don't want to know."

If you feel tension, try to be aware of any imbalances that you may also be feeling. Then try to recognize the nature of these imbalances in light of what I have just said.

On one level, emotional mastery means control of the emotions. Emotional control implies emotional balance, understanding, and the ability to regulate how much emotion you want to exhibit in a certain situation. But this is not the mastery that Ruby teaches; this is only the effect of the mastery.

The emotional mastery Ruby teaches means total awareness of the emotional body. The emotional body exists in an emotional world, just like your physical body exists in a physical world. The emotional world is very different from the physical world; yet it is also similar in some ways. There are trees, mountains, oceans, deserts, jungles, birds, flowers, cities, and houses. There are also good people, bad people, and problems, just like there are in the physical world.

The emotional world is a more beautiful place than the physical world. The light is greater; colors are more vibrant; the sound current of the life force can be more easily heard; and energy or vibratory rates are more easily seen. Understandably, the founders of some religions who have glimpsed this world have called it Heaven.

The greater awareness and knowledge one has of this inner world, the more that its tools, laws, and principles can be used in the physical world. If you are using Ruby, you will not need to consciously "travel" or project yourself in any way into this world in order to master it.

Let me draw an analogy to help you understand the potential of emotional mastery, for I see that this concept may be difficult for many people to understand.

Let us say that the physical world is like high school, and that the emotional world is like college. Let's also assume that you are a high school student who enjoys chemistry. One day you start to wear Ruby in its spherical form. Soon thereafter, whenever you walk home from school, an inner urge guides you to the nearby university. There you begin to sit in on a first-year college chemistry class. As a result, you start to realize that your high school chemistry is much more basic than you had previously thought.

Every day you still have to attend your high school chemistry class. But the more college chemistry you learn, and the more your knowledge and awareness expands, the easier your high school chemistry assignments become. Your high school chemistry becomes easier, because you have seen a greater point of view. You also begin to realize the reason you are in high school: to prepare for college.

In this analogy, the power of Ruby opened your awareness and understanding to enable you to accept college-level information. Without Ruby, you would not have been ready for such information until you had completed high school. Ruby speeds up the process. It allows "college-level" information to be understood by "high school" students.

If you are still in high school, college-level information will make your high school work easier. This is the point of the analogy: If you are still in the physical world, knowledge of the emotional world will make your life much easier. It will place your life in perspective.

To understand Ruby, you need to understand the kind of love that Ruby teaches its wearers. It is not human love, for human love implies needs and expectations. My love implies freedom. My love is a noble and powerful love. It turns one's attention toward that which is greater than oneself.

Humans need love. They need human love; yet human love alone does not sustain them, because it does not provide their emotional bodies or their interpersonal relationships with enough nourishment. Humans also need divine love.

Human love says, "I need your warmth. I need you to hold me and kiss me. I need you to tell me where you're going, so I'll know where you are and won't worry about you." Divine love says, "I will love you regardless of what you do. I love you regardless of who you are. I love you even if you go someplace and forget to tell me where you're going. And I'll love you when you return. I love the Soul that is inside your physical body. I love that which gives you life. I love that part of you which is God."

Divine love gives individuals the freedom to be who they really want to be. This freedom nourishes them and their relationships. It gives them space to grow. Ideally, the individuals in a relationship should be able to share both human and divine love.

Unfortunately, most people today do not understand the difference between human love and divine love. Even those who understand the concept often have no real idea of how to open their hearts and give divine love. The necessity of divine love may make sense mentally; but when it's time to express divine love emotionally, few people know where to start.

Ruby teaches this. Ruby will open your heart and give you a taste of what divine love is. Then it will show you how to be a vehicle through which divine love can enter your life. This love will then touch others around you, even if they're not wearing Ruby themselves. They will learn from your living example.

Ruby's love is powerful. Divine love is powerful. An example may help explain what I mean. A husband may tell his wife from a human-love point of view, "Please stop smoking, because it's bad for your health, my health, and the kids' health." To return the human love, the wife will want to stop smoking and try to do so. However, because it's hard to let go of a habit, she may encounter one obstacle after another. Even though she wants to stop and realizes mentally that it's not good for her children's health, the struggle to quit may be too great.

If the husband has divine love flowing from his heart, and asks his wife to stop smoking from the point of view of divine love, his words may be exactly the same. However, behind the words he will be saying, "Please stop smoking; but I will love you even if you continue to smoke, and I will love you if you stop." If the husband is truly a vehicle for divine love, and the wife sincerely wants to quit, the divine love flowing through her husband will give her the power to do so. Love is power. Of course, power is not necessarily love.

* * *

My direct effect on the physical body is to support all the chakras. I also specifically strengthen the heart chakra and those below it.

I have my greatest effect on the emotional level. The red ray exists on the subconscious, mental, memory, emotional, and physical levels. However, it seems to collect in the emotional level, where it forms a bridge to the physical level. Therefore, Ruby will lead individuals from the physical to the emotional level. It is up to the individual to choose whether to stay at this level or to continue toward even greater states of consciousness.

Some of the red ray gets diluted on the emotional level, giving the area an overall appearance of pink. The color pink causes a stirring of the emotions. This is important for maintaining emotional health, just as your blood circulation is important for maintaining your physical health. Indeed, the emotional aura, which surrounds the physical body, contains little needle-like lines about two inches long, which can be compared to your blood vessels. It is along these lines that emotional energy flows.

When Ruby is worn, I gently encourage these lines to point in the direction of the heart. This mechanism allows the red ray, the feeling of love, and an awareness of the emotional level to flow through the heart chakra and filter into the physical body.

Contrary to some people's concepts about the meaning and symbolism of different colors, every color ray is a spiritual ray. This is because each color ray is a vibratory rate which comes from God. When color rays enter the body, they bring spiritual upliftment. They provide a bridge from the inner, spiritual worlds to the physical world.

Each individual is in greater harmony with one particular color ray than with any of the other color rays. This color may be called the individual's "main color ray." Individuals who wear the gemstone that bears their main color ray will have an easier time expanding their consciousness, being uplifted, and moving closer to God. In other words, wearing your main-ray gemstone will be a significant step on the road to greater spirituality.

There is an Earth-wide deficiency in the availability of the red ray. This means that those whose main color ray is red are not being provided with a sufficient amount of red ray to meet their needs. Once this deficiency is alleviated, many of them will be able to find their personal avenues for spiritual unfoldment.

* * *

Ruby gives the mind the power to orchestrate a greater relationship between the physical and emotional bodies. It empowers the mind to create the opportunities in your life that will allow you to become more in tune with your emotions. This is because the mind is primarily responsible for bringing things into your life or for removing them. In other words, it is mostly your mental processes which lead you to decide to change jobs, move to a different location, or perhaps to take college level classes when you are still in high school.

When you begin to wear Ruby, your mind will see that your heart is opening. It will see that you are preparing to accept the knowledge of your emotional world. When you are ready, the Ruby might, for example, encourage your mind to decide to attend a certain lecture. Perhaps this lecture will present techniques for becoming aware of your emotions; or it may present a healing method that the mind thinks is necessary to clarify the connection between your emotional and physical aspects.

It is interesting to note that, just as Ruby brings the emotional level to physical awareness, blue corundum (also known as Sapphire) brings the mental level to physical awareness.

* * *

The faceted form of Ruby behaves differently than the

spherical form. A faceted Ruby reflects the red ray, making this form of Ruby appear much more beautiful than a Ruby sphere. However, the red ray reflected by the faceted Ruby cannot directly enter the heart. It must first enter the consciousness through the eyes.

Fortunately, only a few people can afford faceted Rubies, especially since they are nothing but toys. The spherical form of Ruby is not a toy; it is life-giving. I feel sorry for those of my children who are faceted and worn as knick-knacks. However, they do serve the simple purpose of allowing the eyes to become comfortable with the red ray. In effect, they open the consciousness to the red ray from the "back door." Then, when the individual is ready, Ruby spheres can be worn, which will allow me to enter the consciousness through the heart.

The crystalline form of Ruby has the same ability that crystalline Emerald has to force its energy into the body. It can do this if the crystal is pointing at the body in such a way that energy will flow into the body. Therefore, crystalline Rubies should only be used as elements of more involved therapies.

I would not recommend pointing Ruby crystals at any area of the physical body unless you are a physician who is well-versed in gemstone and color-ray therapy, and you know exactly what you are doing. This is because, compared to the other color rays, the red ray is very strong in the physical world. Too much red ray directed at an organ can easily imbalance it, because the red ray could be infused into the organ at the expense of the other color rays. And it is the balance of all colors that promotes health.

Ruby crystals can be quite effective in restoring balance to organs or places in the body that are deficient in the red ray. However, you must know exactly when the deficiency has been corrected and, therefore, exactly when to remove the Ruby.

At your present level of technology, you are unable to measure the exact effects crystals have when placed on the physical body. These measurements are especially important when placing color-ray-bearing crystals on the physical body. You still need to develop instruments which will measure precisely how much color ray an organ has and what the ideal amount for that organ is. Once you have developed such instruments, then anyone who knows how to use the instruments can be trusted to safely apply color-ray-bearing crystals to the physical body.

Ruby Therapy

When I am worn in spherical form, the first thing I do is open the heart. This will occur no matter where the spheres are worn on the body. As the Ruby spheres spread their energy throughout the aura, the heart chakra is located. This information is reflected back to the Ruby. Then the flow of red ray is directed toward the heart center, and it opens.

When the heart chakra opens, the red ray will identify and collect in any disharmonious area in the emotional body that is causing a physical-body disharmony. The red ray will also be directed toward the corresponding area of disharmony on the physical body.

When this occurs, the mind will be able to see the connection between the emotional cause and the physical symptoms. This will allow the mind to start to understand the relationship between the cause and the symptoms. When this understanding dawns, you will have taken the first step toward resolving the disharmony. This is because, once you know the reason for a certain condition, you will know better where to focus your attention to resolve it. Attention brings with it life force, and life force consists of a perfect balance of all color rays. When your attention is focused on a situation, you are in effect directing the seven colors rays to that situation. The natural result will be a restoration of balance.

* * *

Often emotional disharmony is caused by congestion in the emotional body. When the heart is opened—and feelings start to flow, be felt, and expressed—this congestion will loosen. This will allow more life force, and thereby greater harmony and balance, to flow into and through the emotional body. In other words, Ruby will heal disharmonies in the emotional body.

Once the emotional congestion is dissolved, any conditions that it has caused in the physical body will no longer be fed by it. For example, you may have a congestion in the emotional body which manifests in the physical body as chronic stomach distress. The emotional congestion feeds the physical condition with disharmonious energy. This process will continue until the emotional-body congestion is resolved. When it is resolved, the disharmonious energy will no longer be there to feed the stomach distress.

Now, the congestion in the emotional body will not be the only factor contributing to the physical condition. There are two other aspects which must be resolved if the physical condition is to be healed. Surrounding the emotional body congestion will be emotional patterns; and surrounding the physical condition will be physical patterns. Both these sets of patterns have been formed by some influence—actions, reactions, or feelings—that was repeated over a long period of time. Like emotional congestion, the emotional patterns will continue to feed energy to the physical patterns until the entire condition is resolved.

Ruby will first work on relieving the congestion. Then it will work on changing the patterns in the emotional body that surrounded this congestion. At the same time, the individual should work on changing the physical patterns.

One of the most effective ways to change physical patterns is to change one's diet and exercise routine. You have conscious control over your diet and exercise patterns. By changing them, you can easily influence your other physical patterns. The more radically you change your diet and exercise routine, the more swiftly your other physical body patterns will change.

However, if you only rely on changes in your diet and exercise routine to change physical patterns, you will either get nowhere from the start, or you will get very far very quickly, and then reach a plateau and get nowhere. You can completely resolve the stomach distress situation—or any other physical condition caused by emotional factors—only if you change your emotional patterns as well as your lifestyle.

"Are you saying that people who focus only on diet, lifestyle, and exercise, and do not wear Ruby, will not resolve the cause of their physical conditions, no matter how radically they change?" Michael asked.

In most cases, yes. They will not resolve the cause of their conditions even though a new diet, lifestyle, and exercise program may result in physical changes. However attitude is also an important factor. If you are one of the rare individuals whose desire to change originates in your heart, from Soul within, then you will have the power of divine love behind your change. As long as that flow of divine love exists, it can melt your patterns and assist you in your changes on all levels. In this case, you would not need to wear Ruby.

If you truly want to change and are willing to make the effort, Ruby can be a great tool. As I have said, Ruby will open your heart, linking you to the source of divine love. Ruby is so strong that it will force an individual to open up. Even if the individual is not willing, or has no awareness of Ruby's effects, Ruby will still give powerful love. Love is the force and power behind an individual's strength, willingness, and ability to make changes.

* * *

There is another aspect of Ruby, which I will just touch upon. The warmth of Ruby's color tends to relax one's hold on one's patterns. The fire of the color red brightens disharmony. It burns out whatever stands in the way of making the change. After a fire, the land is destroyed; but new life will grow in place of the ashes. Now, Ruby does not leave ashes and charred emotions; it does not work like that, although the fire analogy was appropriate in other ways.

The only circumstance in which Ruby cannot easily open the heart is when the body is so ill and out of balance, that the imbalance is easily recognized by society. This individual's heart would repel Ruby. Another therapy would first be needed to allow balance to occur. Then I will be able to heal and comfort the heart, just as I do for any heart that accepts me.

* * *

The size and amount of Ruby used will determine the amount of force Ruby will put behind the changes it initiates.

Five or six carats of .25- to .33-carat Ruby spheres will open the heart immediately. Within seconds it will reflect the red ray onto emotional body congestions. This amount is good for gentle, yet effective work.

Ten or twelve carats of such Ruby spheres would be very strong, and effective for therapeutic purposes. Within minutes this amount of Ruby will fill the individual with powerful love energy. It will begin to change the individual's disharmonious emotional patterns very quickly. At the same time, the red ray will start to saturate the aura, causing these emotional patterns to relax, break up, and release their hold on the individual's physical patterns. This action is important, because it is physical patterns which prevent physical diseases from resolving.

Beware of wearing fifty carats or more of Ruby. This may create an imbalance. The force of the red ray behind this much Ruby might be too powerful for most people of the Earth, unless they have been wearing Ruby for a long time and just need some extra Ruby to make additional changes.

There will be some individuals who resist Ruby even though they are deficient in the red ray. Part of their resistance may come from a past-life memory of the negative ways Ruby was once used. Again, this misuse was the direct result of the conflict between Ruby and the old carrier of the red ray. Now that this is finally resolved, I can get on with my mission unimpeded.

These individuals would benefit from wearing either a small amount of Ruby (such as one carat) or the gemstone that carries their main color ray. This would help to prepare these individuals to wear a larger amount of Ruby, such as would be used for therapy.

* * *

Ruby initiates changes within minutes. As more love enters the individual (and the individual becomes accustomed to the love and accepts it), the more love will be given and the more the heart will open.

Ruby can also benefit those who consider themselves healthy but who want to become healthier and less restricted by their emotional patterns. This includes those who know they have congestions and disharmonies in their emotional body. It also includes those who have not yet achieved the emotional mastery they desire.

Remember, the red ray alone, or the red of any other gemstone, will not have the effects that the red ray of Ruby has. This is because Ruby is the carrier of the pure red ray of the life force, and this red ray is supported by the vibratory rate of Ruby.

Ruby Tomorrow

Once people are accustomed to using Ruby as a tool and are comfortable with the vibratory rate of Ruby, they will be able to use much larger amounts of it. These larger amounts can be used for short periods of time for specific, more radical, and much swifter pattern changes, which will result in the resolution of physical and emotional disease.

Unfortunately, this may not be possible for at least two or three generations. At that time, your people will be more accustomed to the vibratory rate of gemstones; and large quantities will profoundly affect them within minutes or hours.

* * *

The next Gemstone Guardian you meet will be the Guardian of Rhodocrosite. Rhodocrosite also works on patterns by breaking them up, cleaning them out, and making new, more harmonious ones. Ruby affects patterns by bringing more fluidity into the emotional body, which loosens patterns and diminishes their influence.

Ruby gives individuals love and strength, and opens them up to the infinite source of love, which is Spirit. This allows people to make the changes they wish to make. It will allow them to grow into the individuals they wish to be, for my love also implies freedom.

"Thank you for sharing. May the blessings be," said Michael.

As I turned away from Ruby, I suddenly felt as though I didn't know her anymore, whereas only a moment earlier I had understood everything about her.

Ruby paid no further attention either to me or to the listeners. She seemed preoccupied as she turned her head away from us and gazed beyond the cliff out over the sea. Something over the water had caught her attention.

7
RHODOCROSITE

Ruby's gaze was focused in the distance, where a tornado was forming. The other listeners and I had not yet seen it. Our attention was still on Ruby as we wondered whether she would continue her discourse.

Then we heard the sound. It was a thunder unlike any heard on Earth, and it grew louder as the tornado moved closer.

I had a feeling that this whirlwind was the manifestation of a Gemstone Guardian and wondered how I would step into its consciousness. How does one communicate with a tornado? I thought I should feel afraid; yet my heart was still so full of Ruby's love, that there was no room for the fear to take hold. So I watched patiently with the others.

As the tornado drew nearer, we could see that it was actually a swirling mass of pink and translucent energy. It grew larger and larger, until it hid the entire horizon. Then suddenly it was upon us and we were enveloped by it. The thunder was deafening. White flashes of light within the pink whirlwind blinded me, forcing me to shut my eyes. Still, the wind and storm did not disturb my clothing or hair. Instead it moved through me, affecting me only on inner levels.

Then the center of the tornado hit. The impact of the silence and calm struck me more forcefully than the raging wind itself. Beyond the stillness could be heard the distant sound of a single note. This sound was not a hum, nor a siren, nor a flute; and yet it was all of these.

An inner voice asked me to open my eyes. When I did, I saw that the pink and white chaos of thunder and light now whirled around us. I also saw standing next to Ruby, in the absolute center of the calm, a man with dark hair and deep olive skin. He wore white and pink robes.

"Now I introduce you to the Guardian of Rhodocrosite," said Ruby, as she stood and stretched out her hands to this man. The two held hands for a moment.

"He can discuss more deeply the patterns that make up the physical and emotional bodies," Ruby explained. "Whereas Ruby gives an individual the power, love, and desire to change patterns, Rhodocrosite actually changes them."

Without warning, Ruby became a vortex of red energy. Then she disappeared.

The Guardian of Rhodocrosite waited for the group's surprise at Ruby's sudden disappearance to subside. A calm again settled over the listeners. Then he looked at me and said, You know what you must do to relay my words to the people of your planet.

I was still reluctant to enter his powerful aura. Then his eyes caught mine, and I felt a flood of reassurance similar to the calm which had embraced the group.

It will be all right, *he said. I gave my trust to Spirit, which told me that, indeed, all was well. I gathered my courage, walked forward to the Guardian and entered his aura. Then I turned so that I was facing in the direction Rhodocrosite faced. I kept my attention on the sound of Spirit, which I had learned to trust so completely.*

Greetings and welcome, *Rhodocrosite began. Then he turned to Michael.* I believe we have some focused business. I will do my best to answer your questions. You may begin.

"Can you give us a brief overview of your effects?" asked Michael.

Change. I cause change. But the changes I produce are not directed at the physical aspect. I am responsible for making changes in the emotional aspect of individuals. These changes often result in alterations in the physical aspect of those who wear me.

There was a long silence. We wondered whether Rhodocrosite would continue.

You did say "brief?" *the Guardian asked.*

"Yes, I did," replied Michael, somewhat apologetically. "Would you please give us more detail?"

Yes. When I am worn, I make changes. I do not wait until

an individual becomes strong enough to handle me. If a change needs to be made, I make it. I do not wait for an individual to get under an umbrella before I rain.

The vibratory rate of my sound does one thing; the vibratory rate of Rhodocrosite itself does another. The sound of thunder I carry destroys the patterns that restrict an individual from growth. It also cleanses any disharmony caused by the destruction. Then, the vibratory rate of Rhodocrosite rebuilds. These three functions—destruction of patterns, cleansing, and rebuilding—work together. I do not allow any work to be left undone.

My work can be compared to playing with a puzzle. When a puzzle which has been incorrectly put together is shaken up, the dust that has settled between the pieces flies into the air. Emotional patterns behave in a similar way. "Dust," or the residue of improperly formed emotional patterns, clogs the emotions and prevents them from being expressed. My thunder shakes up these patterns and cleanses the dust from them. Then I rebuild the puzzle, so that all the pieces fit together correctly.

"Can you tell us of your birth?" asked Michael. "Were you formed at the birth of the planet, did you evolve naturally, or were you brought here by others?"

I was not available on Earth until shortly after I became needed by the individuals living there. By shortly, I mean two or three thousand years. It took that long for my vibratory rate to expand into a physical matrix and to grow into crystals large and plentiful enough to be recognized and harvested by people.

"But how did this first occur? Did the Earth manifest you?" Michael prodded.

The Guardian laughed. I was wondering how I would explain this. You have the right idea; but before you can fully understand how this occurred, I must explain some things about your planet. The Earth has secrets, powers, and abilities hidden within it of which you are unaware.

Humans are very similar to the Earth. Once humans understand this connection, they will be able to understand and master the forces of their planet.

The Earth is a living entity, a living creature. Gemstones are also living beings, but a gemstone is made up of only one homogenous pattern; I will call it one type of "cell." Just like the humans who live there, the Earth is made up of billions of different cells. The Earth's cells are the gemstones, rock, and other elements of which it is made.

Why are humans so similar to the planet on which they live? Because they are born on the planet and have lived on it for thousands and thousands of years. Human beings and the Earth live so symbiotically, it is uncanny. Therefore, when people started to behave in certain patterns that were self-destructive, the Earth knew that one day this behavior would also become destructive to the Earth itself.

Everything the human race experiences is reflected in the planet, and vice versa. If you need to understand and cure a certain disease, look first to what is happening in the planet. In the future, physicians who dedicate their lives to discovering cures for diseases will need to spend many hours in the study of the planet's physics and "spirito-physics." Yes, I am speaking of a new science: "spirito-physics" or "spirito-mechanics."

They will study this, because every human disease is reflected in the planet. Because the planet is so big, it is easier to see which pathways need to be cleared to resolve a certain disease. It is also easy to see the relationship of these pathways to those in a human.

"Can you give us a specific example of the relationship between humans and the Earth?" asked Michael.

I am reluctant to speak. Yet I look to Spirit, and Spirit approves, to a degree. So I will speak of this, to a degree.

The disease AIDS is one example. If you are stuck in your attempts to reach a greater understanding of this disease, you must look beyond physical chemistry. Look to what is happening in the planet in a spiritual sense. When you look at the Earth this way, you cannot help but see the group consciousness of humans. You can see how humans and the Earth are related and the direction in which the two are going.

Also, you cannot help but notice patterns. Diseases do not just happen suddenly. They are the result of patterns. Every one of them—from the common cold to AIDS to the most elusive cancer—is the product of patterns.

Many patterns are the responsibility of the individual; hence the "New Age" philosophy that you create everything and are directly responsible for everything that happens in your life. However, there are many patterns that are not the direct result of one's own actions. They are the result of one's relationship with one's planet, society, and other factors over which we only have indirect control.

When specific locations in the body become the dumping pots for the body's toxicity, tumors are formed. Tumors are isolated encasements of toxicity; often the rest of the body will seem rather healthy—hence the idea that you can surgically remove the toxicity or cancerous tumor, and the body will be healed.

Look at the Earth now. Are there any spots on the Earth that are like cancerous tumors?

"Yes. Toxic waste or radioactive waste dumps."

I was actually thinking of some cities, where the toxic encasement forms a cloud of pollution which encompasses the city. Looking at the Earth from above, you will see that cities look like isolated pockets of toxicity, indicated by the cloud or dome of pollution which surrounds them.

Radioactive or toxic waste dumps are somewhat different, because their effect on the Earth is different. Instead of forming a surface dome of toxicity, they act like an injection of a harmful substance into the Earth's body. This is because the vibratory rate of radioactive or toxic waste is not limited by its containers, no matter what is used to encase it. The toxic vibratory rate seeps into the Earth. It is similar to the way humans might inject a toxic chemical into their veins with a syringe.

Usually when humans do this, at first they feel very good and even experience a heightened sense of awareness. Then what happens? They fall. Often this fall is harder than they consciously realize. Sometimes they do not even think they have fallen. However, their vibratory rate falls; and this is disastrous, because maintaining a high level of vibratory rate is essential. It is essential, because vibratory rate is life.

When radioactive toxicity is dumped into a certain area, for a short time the radioactive energy acts like a hallucinogen for the Earth. This is because of the nature of the radioactive material's vibratory rate. This vibratory rate is thrown into the surrounding cells of the Earth.

I was not going to speak about this. However, since you mentioned it, I must say that toxic waste dumps are more dangerous to the people of Earth than the most polluted city. Why? Because a drug addict is unpredictable. A cancer patient is much more predictable than a drug addict.

Once you start to inject hallucinogens into a planet, you do not know what that planet will do. Do you realize what only the slightest variation in a planet's orbit or in the tilt of a planet's axis will do to the climate of the planet?

The slightest falter or misstep in the Earth's rhythm will bring planetary disaster.

Perhaps the only reason I began to discuss this tangent is so that people will know what they are doing when they dump toxic waste into their planet. Perhaps that was the whole point of this. If I leave you with this awesome situation to think about, perhaps changes will be initiated to stop the injection of hallucinogens into the Earth.

In any case, diseases are caused by patterns. My role is to change the patterns that eventually cause disease. It is certainly a diseased individual, or group of individuals, who would inject their planet with a hallucinogen.

When your body needs a certain chemical, and it has enough ingredients, tools, and energy to produce this chemical by itself, it will do so. For example, when you eat something, the cells in your digestive system begin to produce acids and digestive enzymes that were not present before the food was ingested.

The Earth also has the power to manifest the chemicals or vibratory rates that it needs when and where it needs them. Hence, Rhodocrosite was not brought here; nor was it formed when the Earth was formed; nor did it evolve with the planet. The planet manifested it, just as a human manifests certain digestive enzymes when the need arises. When the need arose, Rhodocrosite was born.

"One more thing. Does the Earth have the ability to resolve the effects of radioactive waste dumps?" Michael asked hopefully.

Look at the human drug addict, *suggested Rhodocrosite.*

"Addicts often need to fall before they really come to grips with their situations," said Michael.

Or the ones who love the drug addict help the addict before he or she falls. When a drug addict falls, you don't know whether the fall will just be a fall, or whether it will mean death.

There are many forces who love the Earth planet enough to prevent the risk of it falling. Many individuals are even willing to sacrifice their lives to stop the utilization of radioactive substances. Besides, the use of these substances is based on primitive technology. Indeed, it is foolish; it is stupid; and it is ignorant.

People can die or risk their lives to try to make changes. Yet, in order for their efforts to be truly effective, they must work on the actual cause of the problem. They must work on those patterns that cause individuals to want to promote the use of radioactive substances and technology.

Spiritual or positive forces which intend to make any kind of major change must work subtly. They must be in the door and working before the individuals who need to change even know it. These forces must make their stronghold in the individual's consciousness before the individual even realizes he or she ought to resist.

This is also true for changing any disease or for altering the course of any condition that is becoming a disease.

The Early Years of Rhodocrosite

My effects during my early years on the Earth planet were exactly the same as they are today. I have always had the same purpose, function, and effects.

Rhodocrosite began in infant form at the end of the Age of Lemuria. Small crystals were found during the early part of the Age of Atlantis. They grew larger and more plentiful as the need for Rhodocrosite grew.

In general, the people of Atlantis did not recognize this growing need. They refused to accept that they were developing destructive patterns or to acknowledge that I had the power to change these patterns. If they had recognized these things the future of their civilization might have been affected.

Perhaps this is not surprising, since Rhodocrosite was young at that time and lacked wisdom. I lacked the understanding that positive missions should be carried out on a subtle level for their effect to be most powerful. Instead, I used the sound of my thunder for attention, thinking that people would want to change. This method did not work, because people did not want to change. Therefore I was not worn.

Of course, those wise ones who could see beyond the limitations of patterns, and who knew the importance of change, wore me and were greatly benefited.

After the destruction of the Atlantean continent, civilizations treasured Rhodocrosite for its beauty. People fashioned it into carvings. However, there were still a few wise ones who knew my mission. When they could, they discreetly used their influence to include high-quality specimens in royal collections.

Today, people's consciousness has risen far beyond that of the Atlanteans. Nonetheless, I find it interesting that people today mentally know what is good for them but react just like the Atlanteans reacted. They resist change. Although people know that a certain habit is not good for them, they find it extremely difficult to change. Enter Rhodocrosite.

At this time, the knowledge of my effects can be made available to the masses. It is my hope that the people will be ready to wear Rhodocrosite. You see, it is important for people's overall growth to have well-functioning emotional bodies, free of past impediments, accumulations, or emotional tumors. I can help individuals make their changes and rebuild a solid, efficient emotional foundation.

There is something else you should know. Your scientists may say that the Earth is so many millions of years old. That is because they measure time as a constant. Actually, time has slowed down since the early years of the planet.

Today, it may take several thousand years for a crystal to grow from point A to point C. A hundred thousand years ago, time on the planet moved much more swiftly. Crystals did not need the same number of today's years to grow from point A to point C. What might take a year to happen now, happened in a day back then.

Soon after the destruction of Atlantis, time on Earth began to slow down. A year started lasting almost a year. In other words, the Earth is much younger than you think. But time is an illusion anyway; so in the end what difference does it make?

Rhodocrosite Today

"What can you tell us that will help us understand your purpose? Please speak freely." said Michael.

I think I already have spoken rather freely, *the Guardian answered.*

Even though I said I work quietly and subtly, I have a

thunder that is deafening to the ears and a light that is blinding to the eyes. These are my tools. These are the forces Rhodocrosite uses to break up patterns.

By the way, it is not a coincidence that the Earthstone Rhodonite and I have similar names. Rhodonite was formed by the planet to help balance my power. While an individual is undergoing the great changes I can initiate, Rhodonite can provide a foundation of emotional and physical stability.

To understand how I work, it would be good to have an understanding of patterns. Patterns manifest in the physical body as actions and reactions. They manifest in the inner bodies as what appears to be very thin lines. If you look closely at these lines, you will see they are made of blocks positioned one after the other.

One block is a certain cause, the next block a response. The next block is a cause, the next a response, etc. The more times that you respond in the same way to a particular cause, the longer that pattern line will become.

As soon as you finish reacting to a certain cause, the circumstances surrounding the next cause will start to form, until a complete block is formed. As soon as a cause block is complete, it develops a magnetic charge which draws to it the response that is characteristic of that particular pattern line. The more times you respond in this characteristic way, the longer your pattern line becomes. The longer your pattern lines are, the more crucially they can affect the physical body.

Rhodocrosite affects the magnetic charge at the end of each pattern line, adding to it a small ball of energy which resembles a little sparkler. Once the magnetic charge of the cause block has changed, ideally, a different response is drawn to it.

Usually this new response is not drawn to the cause block immediately. Instead, the next time you respond to a particular cause, you will probably just find that you have a greater awareness of your actions. You will realize that these actions no longer feel like the most comfortable response you could make to that situation. It will seem like you have grown out of that response. Yet you will still respond in the same old way, despite the existence of your new awareness. It will be like wearing a shoe that fits a little too tightly but that you continue to wear, because you have not yet made the effort to buy another pair of shoes.

You might even respond the same way a second time; but

this time the shoe will fit even more tightly, and the response will feel even less comfortable. Hopefully, by this time you will be ready to buy another pair of shoes. "Buying a new pair of shoes" means deciding how you would like to respond differently the next time, and practicing that response over and over in your mind.

Here is an example: Your father has done a certain thing for years, and each time you have responded in a certain way. Now you plan to respond in a new and different way. Think of your father's actions, and mentally practice the new response you plan to give him. If you wish to heal yourself and your relationship with him, the new response should be more in harmony not only with yourself, but between you and your father, you and Spirit, and you and life in general. You should constantly be working toward establishing more uplifting patterns.

When you begin to react in a different way to a particular cause, you will form new pattern lines. Hopefully, these new pattern lines will be more uplifting and harmonious.

I do not affect all patterns, because some are as simple and insignificant as the way every morning for the past 36 years you brushed your teeth as soon as you woke up. Then before you did anything else, you washed your face and then brushed your hair. This same pattern, repeated again and again, is not affecting your health.

Rhodocrosite only focuses its energy on those patterns that have been highlighted by the mind. Your mind knows which patterns are adversely affecting you, because it has an expanded viewpoint. It can look upon the emotional and physical bodies and see their needs.

Rhodocrosite is a tool which individuals can use to change their lives. Of course, conscious knowledge of how to use the tool will make its effects much more profound. Also, the more willing to change the individual is, the easier it will be to for that individual to receive the benefits Rhodocrosite has to give. However, gemstones will work regardless of how aware the individual is of their effects or how willing the individual is to accept these effects.

Emotional patterns feed energy into emotional and physical conditions like laser guns. The amount of energy fed depends on the amount of feeling which connects the cause block to the response block. Whether this energy is positive or negative depends on the attitude which connects the blocks.

There is little feeling in the pattern of waking up, brushing your teeth, washing your face, and brushing your hair. Because there is little feeling, little or no energy is thrown into the physical body.

If the attitude attached to a pattern is one of harmony, goodwill, and happiness, the energy thrown into the physical body will be positive. If, when you were a child, your mother gave you a big hug every time you did your chores, a strong pattern full of wonderful feeling would have been formed. Therefore, this particular pattern line and the activities associated with it now throw wonderful, good feeling into the physical body. They have an uplifting influence on you.

On the other hand, if the attitude which connects the response block to the cause block is one of hurt, anger, fear, or anything negative, then this is exactly what will be thrown into the physical body. It will manifest as disharmonious energy.

If enough disharmonious energy is poured into a weak spot on the body, it will create physical disharmony. Of course, this physical disharmony will cease to be fed if you resolve and uplift the pattern lines and then create new ones with harmonious energy, good feeling, and positive mental attitudes attached to them.

To accomplish physical healing, the individual should also select and use appropriate physical therapies. Effective physical therapies will resolve the physical residue of the disease's disharmonious vibratory rate.

High-quality, translucent Rhodocrosite will have some cleansing effect on the physical body. However, one should not depend on it for direct physical healing. Rely on it for resolving the patterns that are feeding the physical disharmony.

* * *

Rhodocrosite has yet another effect. This is to make pattern lines more flexible or less stuck in certain places in the emotional body. When pattern lines are stuck, they restrict the life flow to the corresponding area on the physical body and thereby weaken it. When individuals wear Rhodocrosite, their pattern lines will begin to loosen until they move with the breath, just like the ribs do.

A pregnant mother's pattern lines will also affect her fetus. This is because a fetus is in a formative stage and therefore very receptive to change and other influences. Anything a woman can do to direct more positive influences into her life will only benefit her growing baby.

If a woman's pattern lines become less rigid, the growing baby will become more flexible, more open to change, and more able to deal with patterns he or she will create later in life.

Rhodocrosite Therapy

Rhodocrosite is easy to work with. All one must do is wear a strand of it in spherical form around the neck. Then its energy will radiate into the whole aura. There are no specific therapies for placing Rhodocrosite on particular parts of the body. It is best worn around the neck, since that is the most efficient way to touch the entire aura.

The faceted form of Rhodocrosite may light up patterns and focus energy toward them. However, one should only use my faceted form to direct energy at specific patterns if one is sensitive enough to see pattern lines and is a master of gemstone therapy. Faceted Rhodocrosite is not a tool to use if you do not know what you are doing. In contrast, the spherical form can be used safely by anyone.

It is best to wear Rhodocrosite at a length that falls near the heart. Other factors that affect how quickly, efficiently, and to what depth I work include: focused mental attention and the quality and size of Rhodocrosite used.

As far as quality is concerned, the richer is its pink color and the more translucent it is, the more powerful is the Rhodocrosite.

Also, the larger the Rhodocrosite is, the more powerful it is. One strand of six-millimeter spheres would help someone with relatively minor ailments, such as digestive problems or an organ that is not working as well as one might wish. For therapeutic uses, a 24- to 27-inch strand of fine-quality eight- or ten-millimeter spheres would be appropriate. My definition of someone needing therapy is an individual whose patterns are creating life-threatening situations.

A mental declaration that you are wearing Rhodocrosite

for a specific reason, such as to change the patterns that effect your digestive system, will strongly focus Rhodocrosite's activity on those particular patterns.

Otherwise, if no mental direction is given, the Rhodocrosite will work in a somewhat holistic manner. It will find the longest pattern lines that have the most amount of feeling and the most negative attitudes, and it will work on these first. However, there will be no specific focus; and in this case, since more pattern lines will be worked on, the changes themselves will seem less noticeable.

However, if you decide to wear Rhodocrosite to help a particular problem that is affected by only a few pattern lines—for example, some problem in your shoulder—then all of Rhodocrosite's energy will be focused on those few pattern lines affecting your shoulder. Also, the changes will be made much more quickly.

A condition that has, for example, only three or four pattern lines associated with it will change faster than a condition having ten or more pattern lines.

* * *

I do not really need to be cleansed. However, before another individual wears a gemstone, it is considerate to remove any residual energy that might be attached to the gemstone on a super-physical level. Any of the skin's oils remaining on the physical level of the stone should also be removed. Rhodocrosite only needs a brief rinse in hot and cold running water, followed by an hour in the sun.

* * *

When people's patterns begin to change, those people will become stronger. They will realize the great power they possess within themselves. Perhaps they will also realize that Rhodocrosite is only a tool. It is the force that mobilizes, encourages, and motivates. It is the individuals themselves who have allowed the changes to happen. When they realize that they have the power to change their lives and to change their emotions, patterns, and reactions, they will feel tremendous self-confidence. They will be flooded with great feelings of "I can do it! I have the power! I have the ability to master my emotional self and my physical self!"

As new emotional patterns are expressed, other individuals may react unpredictably in their surprise at this new behavior. If the wearer is affected by the behavior of others, my work will be disrupted. Therefore, I must protect the wearer from those outside influences which will interrupt or inhibit my work. This is necessary so that new emotional patterns can be physically expressed without fear of losing balance, or being weakened or hurt.

When a tornado comes, it breaks things up and dust flies. In other words, when people start to work on their patterns, their lives will start to change. They will start to react differently. Also, the feeling of self-confidence they gain from these changes will encourage them to do and say things that they have never thought of or said before.

This may create some level of disharmony—hence, the analogy of the flying dust. However, Rhodocrosite also brings a harmonious force into the aura of individuals who wear me. This force touches their families, the people they work with, and anyone else they are close to who might get caught in the possible dust storm. However, this harmonious force prevents the dust storm from ever occurring. It does so by clearing away any dust which becomes unsettled. Then it helps to rebuild the individual's life by helping the individual to create more harmonious and uplifting patterns.

Some people who wear Rhodocrosite will feel greater self-confidence almost immediately. This increased self-confidence may encourage them to behave in new and different ways. Others who wear Rhodocrosite may start to behave differently before this new confidence is felt. Therefore, these people may be a little unsure of themselves unless they continue to wear the Rhodocrosite. Wearing the Rhodocrosite continually will eventually build their self-confidence by keeping them connected with the life force or power within them.

You will know when this critical phase is completed. However, during this phase you should wear the Rhodocrosite all day. At night it can either be worn or kept close to you on your bed. Then it will continue to work, because it will still lie within your aura.

This critical phase may take two to six months. By then,

you will have regained greater balance. Enough pattern lines will have been resolved and enough new ones will have been formed, that it will seem like you are starting a new life. You will feel like you have a whole new framework; and you will have a new attitude about yourself and your physical condition.

Also, by this time—if other therapies have been properly supporting your physical body—you will probably feel very good and have made much progress in your physical healing.

In the next phase, wear the Rhodocrosite for at least a few hours every day. If this is not feasible, at least keep it next to your pillow or under it; or wear it to bed, so it can be working during the hours that you sleep.

Whenever Rhodocrosite is worn for therapy or to make great changes, it should be worn for a long period of time.

Rhodocrosite Tomorrow

"Can you speak about your future on the planet and how you will be assisting people? Can you give us a more expanded focus?" asked Michael.

Expanded focus! *The Guardian laughed.* That seems like a contradiction in terms! Yet one could say that the top of a tornado provides an expanded focus.

Although people may understand and know that they need to change, and that Rhodocrosite will assist them, Rhodocrosite will not be for the many. It will be for those who are truly and sincerely willing to change. Often these are the people who have a very special connection with Spirit and with Soul. This gives them a viewpoint higher than the mind provides. They see the whole purpose for changes and why mastery of the physical and emotional condition is so important. It is these people who will take the steps to wear Rhodocrosite and to use it as the tool that it is.

It is not my choice that Rhodocrosite is for the special few. Each individual will have to determine whether he or she is one of these select few. This is because it takes a lot of strength to go through changes, and often this strength must come from Spirit or Soul itself.

"Before we close, is there any other information you would like to share?" asked Michael.

I'm sorry, but nothing profound comes to mind. If you pay

particular attention to what happens when I leave, you may receive some insights.

I have spoken of the power of Rhodocrosite. Let it be known that it is with great love that I wield this power. It is a love for Soul's freedom. Patterns can enslave an individual. However, when patterns are worked on, brightened, and given perspective by Rhodocrosite, they can give people the lessons needed to become masters.

* * *

There is another who also has the mission of creating great change. We do not work together; yet our missions are parallel. This individual is the Guardian of what you call Purple Rainbow Fluorite. In order for you to understand the mission of this gemstone, it is best that you now interview the Guardian of Amethyst. Amethyst tends to come in his own time and in his own way, so I shall leave you now.

It has been an honor to be included in these interviews.

"May the blessings be," said Michael.

May the blessings be, *answered Rhodocrosite.*

I slipped out of his consciousness gently, as if I were being held and supported. Yet I wanted to hold onto this consciousness, for it was such a heightened one. I had clearly seen the pattern lines of which Rhodocrosite spoke. I had felt the Earth's pain when he spoke of radioactive waste dumps. And I had seen the profound relationship between humans and the planet. Indeed, they fit together like two perfectly matched puzzle pieces.

The other rim of the tornado was passing through us. I knew that this heightened awareness would be gone when the tornado's influence departed, and I was filled with sadness. Then Spirit reminded me that, by following Spirit and the light and sound within me, I could again reach these states of awareness and even go beyond them.

Then the tornado finally left. The sunlight returned, and the roar of waves and the song of birds could once again be heard.

"Let's see if Amethyst can top this performance," said one of the listeners. We all laughed and felt more relaxed. The experience had strengthened our group consciousness. Somehow, Rhodocrosite's presence had left us feeling as though we were all part of a team on a quest for greater knowledge.

8

AMETHYST

As the group sat and discussed when and how Amethyst might appear, the air grew cold. Clouds began to rise up over the cliff from the ocean below, and soon we were engulfed in a chilling fog. The sound that permeated the air also changed. The single note became all notes, from the lowest to the highest, sounding all at once. The new sound was sweet and full of power.

At first I felt uneasy about the changing scene. But soon a serene calm began to fill me, rising up from a source deep within my heart. It melted away my apprehension. In its place was the knowledge that everything was for a purpose, and that everything had its place and would occur in its own time. I knew that everything would be all right.

My perception of time also changed. I felt as though I had already experienced what was to follow. It was rather like being in a movie theater and getting ready to watch a familiar movie.

Behind me I sensed the presence of someone approaching. It was hard to distinguish this presence from the feelings inside my heart. I believe the others were having a similar experience, because when I opened my eyes everyone else was just opening theirs, too. Then I looked behind me. There stood the Guardian of Amethyst.

I recognized him from our first meeting with the Gemstone Guardians. He was an old man with white hair and a long white beard, which reached almost to his stomach. His robes were of the deepest, finest royal purple. He supported himself with a tall staff made of stark white wood. His eyes were also purple, but it was not until he placed his attention on us that a flood of life flowed from them, touching us all with love.

I have come to speak to you of the wisdom of Amethyst, for of myself there is little to say.

I did not have to ask permission to enter the Guardian's aura. I knew that Amethyst existed in the core of my being. All I had to do was place my full attention on that part of myself, and the words of Amethyst would flow freely.

Come, let us move from this place and find an area which will be more comfortable for us all, *the Guardian suggested.*

As we walked through the cool mist, we were again teased by illusion, for within moments we had traveled great distances. We found ourselves in a park where the sunshine was warm and the thick, green grass felt like a cushion. Many children played in the distance. Our small corner of the park, where we sat beneath a huge oak tree, was quiet and peaceful.

As soon as Amethyst sat down, he looked into the eyes of each of us, gazing deep into our Souls.

I have known each one of you and, indeed, each of you has known me. It is not necessary that you believe in past lives. Once you transcend your physical body, you will not have to believe. You will know that life does not end with the death of the physical body.

In a different time, in a different place, and in different physical bodies, each of you has worn Amethyst. You knew me when my power was in its prime and when Amethyst was at its greatest. That was in the Age of Atlantis. Now you have returned to learn more of Amethyst. Times are different now. I am no longer a youth and, indeed, my effects have changed as I have aged.

Now you have the chance to know me once again.

The Early Years of Amethyst

When the Earth was ready to support life, all the color rays were brought to the planet. It was by no coincidence that the purple ray was infused into the Quartz crystal, the most plentiful gemstone on Earth. That the purple ray was housed in Quartz, and therefore would be plentiful, hinted at the destiny of the planet and its people. It suggested that their destiny would be a spiritual one, or at least that they had the potential for great spirituality. Of course, what people do with their potential is up to them.

Today not all color rays enter the atmosphere in equal amounts. The indigo ray, for example, is weaker than the others. When I was born, purple was the weakest. The purple ray grew in strength as people evolved.

During the Age of Lemuria I was also popular. For the people of that era, my color symbolized their greatest spiritual potential. I reminded people that one day they would return to their true homes in the inner worlds. I also reminded them of all aspects of Spirit, including life, health, and wisdom. They wore me as an expression of their love for these things.

During the Age of Atlantis, men and women found that I could be used for spiritual unfoldment. However, they also discovered that by wearing me they could exert great power. Depending on the intentions of the wearer, this power could be the power of knowledge and wisdom, the power of healing, or the power of controlling others. Gradually the use of Amethyst for the purpose of having power over others became the most prevalent. Toward the end of this era, my ability to help individuals contact their higher Selves was forgotten by all except a few.

Since the Age of Atlantis, Amethyst has been coveted by royalty and nobility, powerful businessmen, church leaders, and the wealthy. I was not made easily available to the masses by these people, because I would have allowed the masses to see beyond the limitations put on them by their leaders. Indeed, with me the people's consciousness would have expanded to the point where the leaders' power over them would have evaporated.

Amethyst Today

Today many people are strongly attracted to Amethyst. They sense that the purple ray I carry will assist them in their spiritual growth and unfoldment. Yet times have changed. My power has gradually waned since the disappearance of Atlantis. It has greatly diminished in the past two centuries in particular.

Now my main focus is to provide people with the purple ray. The purple ray, with the Amethyst vibratory rate behind it, opens the circuit of energy flowing in through the throat chakra and out through the brow chakra. When this occurs, people become able to see into their inner worlds. This, in turn, brings spiritual unfoldment.

I must caution you that if an individual whose brow chakra is closed wears Amethyst, energy can build in the head. This can cause imbalances in the ego, which can lead to cravings for power. Ultimately these experiences lead to spiritual growth, since they give the individual an opportunity to master the mind. But do not use me to create such experiences. One most assuredly receives enough of these lessons in everyday life. To be sure the brow chakra is open before wearing Amethyst, simply place the Amethyst on the top of the head for 30 to 60 seconds before wearing it.

The people of Atlantis used me in the crystalline form. They knew how to harness the energy of the Amethyst crystal. Today the power of the Amethyst crystal is very weak compared to what it was in Atlantis. Now spheres are the best and most effective form of Amethyst for humans to use.

The consciousness of people today is different from what is was during the era of Atlantis. Today consciousness is rising planet-wide. People are becoming more spiritual and less connected with the Earth and with physical, material things. Of course, they are still connected with the Earth. However, during the Age of Atlantis, people were more physically oriented than people are today. Crystals were more in harmony with their vibratory rate. Today the situation is different. Now people are more in harmony with the spherical form of the crystal.

I have told you that at my birth the purple ray was weak on the planet, and that during Atlantis Amethyst was in its prime. Now you see me as an old man, and I say my properties are weakened. Does this mean the purple ray is weak on the planet? No, the color rays are available to everyone.

Every color ray must have a gemstone to collect its energy on a life-bearing planet. Gemstones are like catcher's mitts. They catch and contain the "ball" of light that is thrown by the "pitcher." The pitcher corresponds to the crystal on the mountain in the mental world where color rays are born from the pure white light of Spirit. Gemstones that bear the color rays maintain a connection between this place in the mental world and the planet. They ensure that the color rays are kept pure for the planet.

The crystalline matrix of Amethyst has not changed over

the thousands of years it has been on the planet; nor has the purple color ray. What has changed is the people of the planet. As the people change and grow, their needs change. It is the Earth's mission to provide the humans who live on her with what they need to support their growth. As you know, when humans' needs are met, the Earth's needs are also met.

To help meet the needs of the people, the vibratory rate of Amethyst, or the life inside of it, is changing. My energy is waning, because the crystalline matrix of Amethyst is not strong enough to support the increased flow of purple ray that will soon be required by the Earth's people. If I do not yield to a stronger carrier, a situation could occur similar to that which occurred between Ruby and the old carrier of the red ray. The crystalline matrix of the old carrier could not handle the increased flow of red ray that the people required. Ruby could. A great conflict arose, because the previous carrier did not want to yield.

God has blessed me with both age and wisdom; the two do not always go together. For me it has been a blessing. I know that even though my power is waning, life does not end with the death of the physical body. In the centuries to come—when Amethyst is just a museum piece, a memory, or simply a nice crystal—I know that my life will not end. Life goes on forever.

The new carrier of the purple ray will have a crystalline matrix so strong, that it will be able to bear as much purple ray as people require until the end of the planet's life. This new carrier will be able to fulfill the needs of the people, no matter how great their spiritual growth is or how much purple ray they need to assist them in that growth.

The difference in the amount of purple ray I have brought to this planet and the amount my successor will bring is very great. Because of this, the Earth has provided the gemstone that you call Purple Rainbow Fluorite to help people make the transition between the old carrier and the new.

There is another great evolution which is taking place along with the one I have just described.

For ages people have been very closed. Their means of communication allowed only a limited transfer of information from one town or city to the next, and practically none from one country to the next. At the same time, people were reluctant to change. People had hardened attitudes and opinions, because life was hard. In many ways, people reflected the properties and characteristics of metals. Even the gemstones they wore were always mounted in metal.

The power of crystals and gemstones is limited by any metal that bears or touches them. Metal will limit a gemstone's capabilities. Even gemstones that are in harmony with metal will have their scope limited by metal.

For centuries you have been living in an age of metal. As you are evolving toward the need for a greater amount of purple ray, you are also evolving out of what may be termed a "metal consciousness" toward what we shall call a "gem consciousness."

The metal consciousness is characterized by rigidity, closed-mindedness, reluctance to change, and reluctance to accept new ideas and new things.

Those of the gem consciousness will reflect the qualities and attributes of gemstones. They will be more able to accept the light and sound of the life force. They will be a giving people, just as gemstones are giving. They will have greater awareness of all aspects of themselves, since gemstones focus not only on the physical body, but on the emotions, mind, and Spirit as well. Therefore, the people of gem consciousness will gain greater self-awareness. They will also become more aware of the needs of those around them and of the harmony which must exist between all.

When a change is about to occur, people naturally cling more tightly than ever to that which is about to change. In the past several decades gold and silver have been worn more than ever before. However, one should not stereotype those who cover themselves with gold as being stuck in metal consciousness. Have compassion, for it is these individuals who are closest to making a change away from the limitations symbolized by gold and other metals. It is these individuals who are clinging most tightly to that which they know in their Souls they soon will be growing away from.

At the same time, there is also an evolution taking place away from limited technology toward an expanded technology. This supports the other two evolutions I just mentioned: the coming of a new purple ray carrier and the change from metal consciousness to gem consciousness. This expansion of technology is most evident in the way that communication is opening up. It is growing not only among cities and countries, but also among the inner bodies of individuals. Soon enough, it will exist between the planets themselves.

My purpose for humans today is to help them let go of Amethyst, of the metal consciousness, and of their attitudes regarding limited technology and communication.

It is not my duty, nor do I have the power, to help people make the change. However, I can help people let go of all that is old, all that holds them back, and all that it is their destiny to evolve away from. I can give this help on every level and in every aspect of life.

Unfortunately, the memory of me and who I was only causes people to cling more tightly to Amethyst. This is because some people's memories of Amethyst are clear, and because I was so powerful and such a significant part of the past. On the other hand, this attachment might be fortunate. Remember the spiritual principle I have given you: The closer that people are to making a great change, the more tightly they will hold onto that which they know, perhaps unconsciously, they will be evolving away from.

My purpose for the planet today is simply to be the carrier for the purple ray. I will be the carrier until my successor is mature enough to be given the rod of purple ray power and to accept it in a responsible manner.

Yes, my successor is available on the Earth today. It has great potential. Still, it must earn the right to carry the purple ray, because the responsibility will be an enormous one. It will not be my decision as to when this successor is ready. It will be the decision of several Guardians in the hierarchy.

You see, the life of a gemstone is reflected in its Guardian, since the Guardian has the responsibility of containing the gemstone's life force. Therefore, the Soul which has been given the responsibility of being the Guardian of my successor must go through spiritual tests to become strong enough to fulfill this responsibility.

When it has passed its tests and gained its strength and stamina, this Guardian will be ready to undergo the ceremony of being given the purple ray. When this individual accepts the purple ray, it will become the distribution point for every one of its crystals or gemstones on the planet, or wherever else the gemstone is found.

"Will this successor be available to the masses?" Michael asked.

In time. First it will be available to those who have earned the right or who have evolved to the degree that they can distribute or use this gemstone responsibly.

Those who have earned the right will become very attracted to this new gemstone. They will know in their hearts that they must own it, and that it will give them great awareness and great potential.

This gemstone should be worn without metal, for why limit something that is so purely of the gem consciousness?

* * *

The purple ray draws one's attention toward Spirit. Therefore, the gemstone that carries the purple ray must do everything possible to assist its wearers to focus their attention on Spirit.

For this reason I also have a strong balancing effect upon and between one's emotions, memory, mind, subconscious, and the physical body. When these are balanced and aligned, a greater flow of Spirit force can flow into the physical body. Spirit force is also the life force and the healing force. Once this force has flowed into the physical body, it must return to its source, which is God. Upon its return, the intention is that it will bring the attention of its wearers with it.

If I am worn over the heart, I can make a connection with the emotional body. Without this connection, my energy tends to flow directly to the head and mind of the wearer. With this connection, I have a general balancing effect on the emotions.

Specifically, I stimulate the area where emotions are born. This causes the area to become uplifted in consciousness. The upliftment brings a greater viewpoint, which in turn gives individuals a greater perspective on their emotions. Then this expanded perspective has the effect of calming or balancing emotional extremes.

Because whatever we send out returns to us, I have the effect of protecting individuals from their own negative emanations. As I promote balance in an individual, the emotions that the person sends out become less intense. Therefore, a less intense energy is returned to them.

If you are on the receiving end of someone else's negative emotions, you will be more protected. You will be more protected from the emotional imbalances of others, because your emotional body will be more balanced.

Amethyst's strengthening effect is cumulative. Therefore,

those who are easily imbalanced by others should wear Amethyst continually, so that this strength can build and grow. Then these individuals will be protected from further imbalances by their own inner strength.

My color reflects the highest aspect of the mind, which is also known as the subconscious, or that which is not open to conscious awareness. I stir this unconscious area, causing the mind to pay attention to it and become conscious of it. Ideally, the mind will also see beyond the subconscious to the area of Soul.

When the mind's attention is placed on its highest aspect, the energy that the mind once fed into its aberrations is refocused. This occurs only to the degree to which the mind's attention is placed on its higher Self. If focused there long enough, the aberrations will dissolve.

Amethyst Therapy

Perhaps the most significant therapy I can offer is to help people let go of anything that keeps them attached to a condition. For this, I simply need to be worn in my spherical form. In spherical form, I can affect all the inner bodies. This is especially important when working on letting go of anything.

Those who love to wear gold can freely wear Amethyst beads with their gold. Not only will it look beautiful, but the Amethyst will provide an understanding and supportive influence. It will help these individuals understand why they are wearing so much gold or why they cling so tightly to certain attitudes, feelings, or conditions. This understanding is important, because it will form the basis for these individuals to take further steps in their evolution. I do not push these individuals. I simply open up their understanding.

When I am in spherical form, my vibratory rate will affect each chakra differently.

Do not bother to place me over the lower two chakras. I have no effect there unless you are pregnant. In that case, lie on your back and place the Amethyst spheres where the uterus rises to its greatest height. This will uplift the child. It will create a greater connection between the fetus and the Soul that will soon enter its body. When the baby is finally born, this enhanced connection will cause the Soul to enter the body with greater vitality.

If I am placed over the stomach chakra, my vibratory rate will draw the body's energy to this point. I will draw resources from other, stronger areas of the body to assist the stomach area if it is weakened or in pain. Therefore you will find Amethyst spheres very helpful for soothing stomach aches, especially in children.

When worn over the heart, as in a necklace, I have the effect of balancing the inner bodies. I help people let go of all that is old. I help them understand why they are attached to certain conditions. I also collect some of the heart center's energy and use it to support the energy that naturally flows in through the throat chakra and out of the brow.

When worn around the throat, I increase the amount of energy flowing in through the throat chakra. This gives energy to the voice. Therefore, those who must address a group but are afraid to speak would benefit greatly from wearing Amethyst around the neck near the throat. This would also benefit those who lack the self-confidence to express themselves or who speak too quietly or with uncertainty.

When placed over the brow chakra, I help the head to release excess energy that may be building up and causing head pain. To release this pressure, hold the Amethyst over your forehead with either hand, or lie on your back and just allow the Amethyst to rest on your forehead. The Amethyst will open the door of the brow chakra. When it is opened, excess energy will naturally flow out.

As long as this flow of energy remains healthy, the brow chakra will remain open. When the brow chakra is open, energy will not be able to collect, build, and become stagnant in the mind. Stagnant mental energy often causes mental aberrations.

Those who are looking for a technique to let go of mental aberrations can place me at the top of the head over the crown chakra. This will encourage the flow of energy in through the throat and out through the brow or spiritual eye. This flow can also be supported by wearing the Amethyst around the neck.

* * *

Different shapes of Amethyst have significantly different effects. It is simply a characteristic of my vibratory rate that it reacts profoundly to the way Amethyst is shaped. In other words, Amethyst reacts differently depending on the way the life inside the crystal is allowed to express itself into the aura of the wearer.

The spherical form is the most gentle and harmonious. It is also the most powerful shape for allowing the purple ray to affect the wearer. This effect is greatest when the spheres are worn around the neck, because then the entire aura can be touched by the purple ray.

The rondelle form of Amethyst also has a profound cleansing effect on the organs over which it is placed.

When for years an individual has eaten foods that irritate the stomach, the stomach will produce scars and calluses to protect itself. Unfortunately, a callous stomach cannot digest food as well as it should. If the calluses become great enough, the stomach may not digest food at all.

Amethyst rondelles can be placed over the stomach to break up these calluses. The effect of this procedure will be disharmonious, but it is this disharmony that will cause the breaking up to occur.

Light purple Amethyst rondelles will have a sharper cutting effect than dark purple Amethyst rondelles; but the dark purple rondelles will cauterize after they cut.

Basically healthy individuals can place a strand of Amethyst rondelles over the stomach for fifteen to twenty minutes per treatment. Those who are very ill, and who require immediate work on the stomach's calluses in order to sustain life, should only use the Amethyst for five or ten minutes per treatment. A gemstone therapist may have to decide whether the stronger, lighter variety or the gentler, darker variety would be most in balance for the one who is ill.

The frequency and total number of treatments required will vary with each individual.

Those who have changed their diets and are now eating non-irritating foods after years of following an irritating diet can also benefit from this therapy. This is because the base on which the new cells are built will still have calluses and therefore may be causing underlying digestive problems. Although scientists say that every seven years all of the body's cells have been replaced by new ones, each new cell grows from an old one. Therefore, the quality of the old cells greatly influences the quality of the new.

The strength of this treatment can also be varied according to the way in which the rondelles are laid on the body. If they are laid so that the rows of rondelles form parallel lines, the cutting action will occur in only one direction. Naturally, the direction of the parallel lines can be changed with each treatment. On the other hand, if the rondelles are placed in a pile over the area in "spaghetti fashion," the cutting action will occur in all directions and more deeply. This is the most powerful way to apply the rondelles.

Because the dark purple Amethyst rondelles have such a mild effect, they will rarely need to be lined up in parallel rows.

You can change the variables of this therapy depending on the needs of the individual. For example, someone may be strong enough for the light purple Amethyst rondelles, but not strong enough to apply them in spaghetti fashion.

Whenever you complete a treatment, it is important to then soothe the area with the spherical form of Amethyst. Again, the placement of Amethyst spheres over the stomach area will call the body's energies to the area and promote healing. Of course, other soothing gemstones can also be used.

This therapy is most effective for the stomach, but can also be used for breaking up congestion in the spleen, pancreas, upper liver, or any other organs near the stomach. It has a milder effect on the kidneys.

* * *

People have looked to Amethyst for wisdom for thousands of years. I say this: Look nowhere for wisdom but within yourself, for within the core of your being is the source and fountainhead of the greatest wisdom that can ever be known.

We, the gemstones, are merely the tools. Many of us are tools which can help you to look inward to the core of your being. We can help you to recognize truth and help you to accept that what you learn from within is indeed true.

It is time for you to rest. Those who wish to return when the sun sets tomorrow evening will meet the one who serves as the bridge between myself and my successor. He is known as the Guardian of Purple Rainbow Fluorite.

Amethyst stood up and looked again into the eyes and Souls of each of his listeners. Then he walked down the path that meandered through the park.

9

PURPLE RAINBOW FLUORITE

The sun had just dipped below the horizon when I placed my attention on Purple Rainbow Fluorite.

The Guardian of Amethyst had told us that if we wished to meet the Guardian of Purple Rainbow Fluorite, we should return to the park where Amethyst had delivered his discourse. That is where I expected Spirit to lead me; but it was not to be.

Instead, I was guided to a place several hundred feet above a vast ocean. Below, I could see nothing but water in every direction. Above, the stars were just beginning to sparkle in the darkening sky. Michael's radiant inner form appeared next to me, and we waited for the Guardian of Purple Rainbow Fluorite to join us.

He approached us walking on the air. Brilliant streaks of white and purple light swirled around his body, forming a spiral. Within the white light flashed every color of the rainbow. The light hurt my eyes and forced me to look away, but I could not ignore the loud sound that pressed on my eardrums.

We have met before. You know me as the Guardian of Purple Rainbow Fluorite.

His voice was deep and soft; yet it rang and echoed in my head. I opened my eyes and saw that now the streaks of light flashed and spiraled around me. Somehow I must have entered his aura, but so subtly and quickly that I hadn't noticed.

My effect on the Earth human at this time is to assist in a fundamental change. It is a change in the way the physical body accepts the life force, particularly the purple and indigo rays. I prepare the physical body to accept a greater and more powerful flow of both these rays.

I have a two-fold mission. One is accomplished by the vibratory rate of Purple Rainbow Fluorite itself, the other by the vibratory rate of my color.

The vibratory rate of Fluorite enables the physical body to accept a greater flow of the indigo ray. This is a result of my vibratory rate's effect on the throat and brow chakras.

The vibratory rate of my color lets me help people let go of old patterns. This allows them to accept newer patterns with fewer limitations and thus gain greater freedom and spiritual responsibility. This part of my mission directly concerns the purple ray and the transition from Amethyst to its successor.

My purpose is to disrupt the old beaten path that the purple ray once took. This will enable the new carrier of the purple ray to make its own path without having to follow the same grooves taken by the present carrier, Amethyst. Imagine a hill of sand in which the purple ray flowing through Amethyst has carved deep grooves. The new carrier will not be able to follow these same grooves, because it will possess much greater powers and abilities. I come as the whirlwind to scatter the sand and fill in Amethyst's grooves, so that its successor can form its own path more easily.

The Early Years of Purple Rainbow Fluorite

My past should make little difference to you, since it is my purpose in the present that is so significant.

When the Earth formed, a certain destiny was mapped out for it. Of course, this destiny was flexible, but it provided a guideline for the life force to direct itself. The making of such plans is very important.

Destiny had preordained a certain window of time during which Purple Rainbow Fluorite would be planted into the Fluorite that already existed on the planet. The exact time of the implantation would depend on the progress of the people's evolution. When the right time came, the Fluorite was infused with the vibratory rate of the purple ray. This occurred in a way similar to that in which Lavender was introduced to clear Quartz.

I will be available only for a short period of time in Earth's history. When other races on other planets are ready for the transitions that Earth humans are now ready for, I will become available for them, too.

For the sake of comparison, let us say that if Amethyst's reign lasted ten years, my reign will last six weeks, and the reign of Amethyst's successor will go on for thousands of years. When I am replaced by this successor, I will become less and less available until I can no longer be mined.

Purple Rainbow Fluorite Today

To help you understand my purpose, we must discuss change and the way in which the color rays are changing.

People resist change. As much as they want change—in hopes that it will bring something better or more comfortable—there is still a fear that the change might not bring something better. There is a fear that the change will instead make life more difficult and uncomfortable.

When people are faced with change, whether they want it very much or do not want it at all, they will itch and squirm. Even if it is for their own growth and benefit, they will find excuses—consciously or subconsciously—to avoid the change. This is human nature, and it is why I am here.

I will make the change between Amethyst and its successor more gentle, less noticeable, and less recognizable as a change. A change made subtly will not be recognized as a change and therefore will not be resisted. I will make the transition to the new carrier less noticeable, because this change is too significant and important to be compromised by people's resistance.

That is on the grand scale. On an individual scale, Purple Rainbow Fluorite produces profound changes in the body.

In a healthy body, energy naturally flows in through the throat chakra and out through the brow chakra. Rainbow Fluorite strengthens this flow. It also raises the vibratory rate of the throat chakra, so that it will accept energies with higher vibratory rates.

As a result, the vibratory rate of the energies which leave the brow chakra will also be higher. This means that the individual's potential experiences beyond the brow chakra, or spiritual eye, will be heightened. In other words, one will have access to a greater arena of understanding, knowledge, and wisdom. In this way, one will gain the blueprints for greater spiritual experiences, either during dreams, meditations, contemplative spiritual exercises, or daily living.

This effect is fundamental and very important. It is why certain spiritual masters use the spherical form of Purple Rainbow Fluorite with their students. They place it in short necklaces around the necks of their students who need help making changes or in having clear inner experiences and remembering them.

Spheres of high-quality Purple Rainbow Fluorite must be used very carefully. It is fortunate that these spheres are rare, since they are exceedingly powerful. If people were to wear the spherical form, their awareness would be raised to vibratory rates so high, that the truths they would see in this state of awareness could shock and imbalance them. Therefore, it is best that a necklace of spherical Purple Rainbow Fluorite be used only by spiritual masters or by those who understand and can see imbalances before they occur. Rainbow Fluorite in cylindrical form has gentler effects. These effects are more controllable and appropriate for the average individual.

In the past, the indigo ray entered the physical body through the throat chakra. It entered this way for several reasons. One reason is that the indigo ray is extremely weak on the planet. Therefore, it could enter the body more easily through a chakra that has a naturally occurring inflow (as opposed to outflow) of energy.

The second reason involves Sapphire and Sodalight. Until recently, the indigo ray was carried by the earthstone Sodalight. However, because some people needed more indigo ray than Sodalight provided, Sapphire also accepted some of the responsibility of carrying the indigo ray in its darker, almost indigo-colored crystals. Sapphire energy naturally enters through the throat chakra. Therefore, those who were ready for more indigo ray could receive it through the throat chakra by wearing this darker variety of Sapphire.

I will let the Guardian of Sapphire tell his own story.

When I am worn, my vibratory rate will enable the physical body to accept a greater flow of indigo ray. I am now entering my prime, and people are ready to accept this change. At the same time, the indigo ray is now beginning to flow through its own gemstone and is therefore becoming more available.

People today are ready or preparing to accept the indigo ray through the brow chakra. This change heralds a transition that the indigo ray itself is experiencing. It is a transition from having an earthstone carrier, which is a physical, rock manifestation, to having a gemstone carrier, which is a light-bearing, light-giving, and more spiritual manifestation.

Individuals who accept the indigo ray through the throat chakra are oriented more toward the physical and the Earth. Those who accept the indigo ray through the brow chakra have a more spiritual orientation and less attachment to the physical. Those in whom the indigo ray seems to be entering both the throat and brow chakras are undergoing the transition; indeed, the indigo ray is entering both chakras.

I would like to clarify something I mentioned earlier. I said that energy naturally flows out of the brow chakra. If that is the case, how can a color ray enter the brow chakra? The answer is that in healthy bodies, the chakras breathe. They let certain energies in, and they let certain energies out.

Many of the energies that flow out of a chakra are those that have been used by the body and are no longer needed by it. They are excess. It is similar to the process of breathing. When you exhale, you expel both oxygen and carbon dioxide—that is, some air that is still useful and some from which all or most of its life force has been extracted.

The energies which flow out of the brow chakra may still contain some useful energy. However, the body has taken from it all that it can. It is now ready to let go of it and make room for fresher energy. On the "inhale," the chakra then accepts the energies that are harmonious with it and that will give it life and nourishment. By the way, it is the color rays which nourish and strengthen the chakras and make them function more efficiently.

I do not carry the indigo ray. My vibratory rate simply prepares the physical body to accept a greater amount and higher vibratory rate of indigo ray. I also prepare the body to accept the indigo ray's influence, which is to move the individual from a physical, materialistic viewpoint to a more spiritual one.

If you study the effects of Rainbow Fluorite, you will gain a glimpse of the capacities of the new carrier of the purple ray. For one thing, Rainbow Fluorite takes one's attention out of the physical body. This means that it draws your awareness away from your physical self until your attention is completely on the worlds within you.

These worlds have been called Heaven by some religions; but your experience is not limited by these realms of Heaven. You can soar on the purple ray beyond these realms, because the purple ray has the highest frequency of all the color rays. It is closest to the white light, which is the source of all life and which emanates directly from God. If you can follow the purple ray to these higher states of awareness, you will temporarily forget your physical body and, in a sense, be separate from it.

Because it is so powerful, the new carrier of the purple ray will be very rare in the first few centuries it is available. Therefore, even small amounts of it may be expensive. Later, as more of its effects can be accepted by people without imbalancing them, more of it will become available. People will be ready for it. At the same time, people will recognize the powers of gemstones, particularly the power of this new purple-ray bearer.

My reign on Earth will be very short, but that is fine. I have undertaken my mission on so many different planets throughout time. When my focus has left the Earth, it will move on to another planet.

"Why do the Gemstone Guardians speak so much of spirituality and spiritual growth?" asked Michael.

You ask a good question. If Rainbow Fluorite can do nothing but prompt you to ask questions such as this, my mission is working perfectly.

To answer your question: People are evolving. The next step in your evolution will transcend the physical. This step must be taken, because you have reached physical walls or limitations. You have the capacity to continue to grow physically. However, people's lack of understanding is making this physical evolution difficult. The food people eat and the air they breathe contain little nourishment or life energy. As a result, people's bodies are, in a sense, degenerating.

Still, it is your destiny to evolve; so if you cannot evolve physically, you must do it spiritually.

This is why gemstones are so important. Gemstones can assist people in their spiritual evolution. Increased spiritual evolution can enhance physical evolution by bringing about stronger, healthier physical bodies. Gemstones will awaken people to the limitations that they, as a race, have set on themselves and on their own physical evolution.

Rainbow Fluorite will prepare you to accept more indigo, which can give you a greater spiritual focus. It will also prepare you to accept a greater amount of purple ray, which will bring you greater wisdom, divinity, and spiritual inspiration.

* * *

If you want me to affect the physical body in the ways I have mentioned, you must shape my crystal so that the energy can flow around it and touch 360 degrees of the aura evenly.

The crystalline form cannot do that. The energy of that form can only reflect in the directions dictated by the faces of its crystals.

"What is your purpose for the planet?" Michael asked.

The planet is a living entity. Just like humans, the planet has an aura. It is also experiencing a transition concerning the indigo and purple rays, just as you are.

From my point of view, there is no distinction between the physical forms—be they planets or human beings—that Soul inhabits. You are all going through the same transitions. It is just your physical forms that are different. I see beyond the physical forms. I see the energies, the auras, and the changes you are experiencing. I see how I can assist you through these changes.

In crystalline form I am necessary for the planet, because the crystalline form is more harmonious with the vibratory rate or state of consciousness of a planet. The rounded form is more in harmony with the vibratory rate of a human.

* * *

Any effects that I have on the emotions or the mind are only the by-product of my primary purposes.

When one experiences physical changes, the emotions and mind are also affected. The mind will respond with an endless stream of questions; the emotions may experience turmoil; and the physical body will often get fidgety and irritable.

This is why Rainbow Fluorite is not worn by itself, except

when given by a spiritual master. One must combine Rainbow Fluorite with other balancing and/or uplifting gemstones. Such combinations make its effects more balanced and less traumatic on the emotional, mental, and physical aspects of the wearer.

Purple Rainbow Fluorite Therapy

To fulfill my twin purposes, the most effective place to wear me is around the neck.

I can also be beneficial if placed on any area of the physical body that is not healing as rapidly as you think it should. This could mean anything from a broken bone to a sore that will not heal, to a stubborn digestive tract that will not cooperate and digest food properly.

I will also help with any condition that is not responding to other treatments, including any treatments involved in a drug, gemstone, or other type of therapy. Healing techniques are often not as effective as they could be, because the physical body will sometimes reach a wall or plateau. Sometimes this plateau will seem endless. Such a condition needs a rise in vibratory rate, so that the individual's evolution toward greater health can occur.

For best results, the Rainbow Fluorite should be placed by itself over the area. This is the only time you should use Rainbow Fluorite by itself when performing treatments on your own. Keep it in place only for as long it feels comfortable. This is the only time frame I will give you. Remember my warning about the effects of Rainbow Fluorite by itself. The body will become itchy and fidgety and will want the Fluorite removed, because it will resist the changes Rainbow Fluorite initiates.

Often your mind will think that it wants a condition to heal, but another part of you will not. This will be the part of you that is relying on the condition, perhaps for all the love and attention you are getting because of it. Because your mind knows that it wants to move beyond this condition, it will tell you to put the Rainbow Fluorite over the troubled area to initiate the change; but your emotions will fight you. Therefore, keep the treatments short and frequent.

Using necklaces that contain both Rainbow Fluorite and

other balancing and/or harmonizing gemstones will also work for this treatment. However, their effects will not be as strong.

"Are there any other therapies you can share with us?" Michael asked.

Other therapies? My friend, what I have just mentioned covers practically anything—that is, anything that is not responding well or rapidly enough to other therapies.

Fluorite will assist other therapies. Fluorite therapy breaks through walls and resolves plateaus, so that the healing can progress to the next phase. All other therapies the individual is undergoing for the condition should be continued while the Fluorite is being applied.

The time it will take for the Fluorite to break through the walls preventing resolution of the condition will depend on the individual and how willing on all levels he or she is to make a change. It will also depend on the degree of disharmony present in the organ, or area and the degree to which that area is stuck.

The amount of Purple Rainbow Fluorite needed will depend somewhat upon the area involved. Twelve cylinders with an approximate size of seven by eighteen millimeters will work. However, twenty cylinders of this size would be much more effective. Lay them neatly over the area, one touching the other. Cover as much of the area as you can.

I only need to be cleansed in consideration of another wearer. Just rinse the Fluorite in running water, and wipe. Cleansing under sunlight may not even be necessary.

Purple Rainbow Fluorite Tomorrow

Purple Rainbow Fluorite may still be available in the distant future, but it will not be enlivened by its Guardian's concentrated focus for very long. When Purple Rainbow Fluorite is no longer needed, and the indigo ray and the new carrier of the purple ray are well established, my attention will leave this planet.

At that time, my effects will no longer be needed on Earth. The crystalline form may still exist, but my focus will be gone, and the crystal's energy will be greatly diminished. It will no longer be effective, because its effect will no longer be necessary. This process is similar to the way a fifth grader has little need for a first grader's school books; they just aren't necessary anymore.

I will not leave until I am no longer needed, and this may not occur for another three or four hundred years.

Rainbow Fluorite is for those brave and adventurous individuals who have the strength and stamina to make changes. It is for those who are aware of the importance of changes, for I strongly initiate change.

In your progress during changes, do not hesitate to ask questions. Do not hesitate to feel the emotions that may also be changing, and do not resist the fidgetiness of your physical body. The more you resist on any level, the more difficult it will be for the changes to occur. Flexibility on all levels will allow for smooth sailing.

Just remember to question and find your own answers as much as you can. The answers anyone else gives you will be limited by the state of consciousness of the one you asked. Find your answers in that infinite source of wisdom within you. Then you will know that the answer you receive will be true, for you will also learn to recognize truth.

For example, it is easy for the minds of most people to comprehend that there is an area of God where the pure white light and sound dwell. It is also easy to imagine a single stream of light entering a crystal on the top of a mountain and splitting into seven color rays.

People are comfortable with this idea, because they are familiar with the concept of hanging a crystal in a window to let the sun's white light separate into the colors of the rainbow and dance on their floors and walls.

Therefore, it is easy to comprehend how this great cosmic light is separated into seven rays of color and sound. It is easy to imagine these rays flooding the worlds below and creating everything below them: the mind, memory, emotional and physical worlds, levels, or bodies, or whatever you wish to call them.

However, to understand a greater explanation of this phenomenon, one must ride on one's awareness to a "place" where one can experience that time and space are illusions.

At this level of awareness you would see that there is no space. You would also see that there is no division between the source of the pure white light and sound and the color rays. All exists right here and now. And when the illusion of time and space are gone, all that is left is life force and different vibratory rates.

Don't worry if you don't understand this explanation. Rainbow Fluorite will cause you to think more deeply into life. It will cause you to question that which perhaps you have held sacred for lifetimes. It will also bring you to the point where you are ready for greater truth.

"From your point of view, why would the other Gemstone Guardians speak of the crystal on the mountain? Is this concept given just for the sake of simplicity or for providing a step in understanding?" asked Michael.

The image is a simple one, but it is given because it can be easily understood. And, in one point of view, this mountain with the crystal on its peak does exist.

Also remember that, if there are a billion different Souls, there are a billion different viewpoints and a billion different ways of looking at truth.

All I offer is the opportunity for you to become something far greater than what you are now. Perhaps you will look at Rainbow Fluorite as a challenge or as the gift for which you have been waiting for years.

* * *

The Guardian of Sapphire will meet you in a less spaceless space than this. It is difficult for me to feel comfortable in any one place, because I am too busy changing. If my surroundings are void, then there are no manifestations of any kind, illusory or not, to resist my changes. This area of emptiness above the ocean may have seemed an unusual meeting place in the beginning; but perhaps now you understand how appropriate it was for me and for the purpose of Purple Rainbow Fluorite.

"I thank you for sharing of yourself. May the blessings be," said Michael.

An unspoken flood of gratitude poured from this Guardian. As I felt these potent and formless words of thanks, I wondered if formlessness has more power than that which is formed, since forms by their very nature are limited.

I slipped out of his aura on this flow of gratitude as easily, gently, and swiftly as I had entered it. Then the formless form of the swirling mass of purple and white energy receded into the distance.

With nothing else on which to place my attention but the void around me, I realized how alone I felt there, despite Michael's presence. So I decided to return to my physical body to enjoy the presence and comfort of my family.

10
SAPPHIRE

We were lifted by a gentle whirlpool of energy to a place filled with mist. The mist quickly dissipated to reveal that we had arrived in a lush and grassy valley surrounded by towering mountains. I looked around. There did not appear to be an easy way to leave this narrow valley on foot.

Several others had gathered with us. While we waited for the Guardian of Sapphire, we enjoyed the music of the many brooks and streams that flowed into the valley.

We stood in a circle, silently feeling the energy of each other's presence. We seemed to be forming a group consciousness, an energy among ourselves which was becoming more unique and identifiable with every passing moment. Then this consciousness took on a life of its own and became a dome of protection which settled over and around us.

The sound of the valley streams grew louder, and we noticed a figure walking briskly down a mountain path. He was dressed in layers of robes and carried a tall wooden staff. He had an air of determination.

We knew that he was the Guardian of Sapphire. Even through his many layers of clothing he radiated the blue ray.

When he reached our circle, the Guardian looked at each of us. Then he removed his outermost, hooded cape. The man who stood before us seemed to be in his forties or fifties. His hair was still dark, yet his face was lined. The lines told of great experiences. They were not just the lines of old age; these lines had been earned.

Because he radiated so much energy, I was unsure as to how I was going to enter his aura. So I walked up to him, bowed my head, and inwardly asked for assistance. He understood and telepathically asked me to close my eyes. I had already left my physical body to come to this valley. Now, once again, I left a body behind. I met Sapphire in a radiant world where our forms appeared to be almost transparent and made of pure energy.

We embraced, and the next thing I knew was that I was looking at the listeners as though through Sapphire's eyes.

The time has come for you to know more about Sapphire.

My effects are not focused directly on the physical body. Any individual from any planet who takes on any form looks about the same as anyone else when the physical, emotional, and mental forms are dropped. You are all Soul. You are all masses of spiritual energy. Yet you are also individuals, personified by your experiences.

My purpose is to nourish the mind. Even the most brilliant minds need to be fed, or they will lose their vitality. I also balance the mind. This means that I put thoughts in order and perspective. When people's thoughts are in order, and they are thinking clearly, their lives also fall into order. This is because the orderliness of the mind is reflected in the emotional and physical areas.

Once there is order and discipline, doors will seem to open, and steps of opportunity will be presented. These opportunities will lead to even greater order and discipline, as well as greater spiritual and daily-life experiences.

The Early Years of Sapphire

I was planted along with the other color-ray-bearing gemstones by the great race of beings you have already heard about. Planting gemstones is an awesome responsibility; yet the experiences and freedoms enjoyed by these beings are equally awesome and great.

The Lemurians did not hold Sapphire in very high regard. A few large, clear, and bright specimens may have been treasured. Yet, it is my belief that the people were just not ready for the gifts I had to give. The Lemurians had no need for the gifts of Sapphire.

I was more precious to the people of Atlantis. Because I was still somewhat rare, I was enjoyed almost exclusively by the wealthy. The Atlanteans gazed into clear, light blue Sapphire; and the visions, thoughts, and dreams that were stirred were clear reflections of themselves. Those who had power and responsibility over a great many people could look into the mirror of Sapphire and see the truth of what was happening among the people.

I worked well as a mirror for the people of Atlantis, because the mental area of the Atlanteans was not well developed. Their lack of mental development may be hard to understand in light of the rumors that the Atlanteans had such great technology. Still, their focus was on developing emotional maturity.

Today people are working on mental growth and maturity. The lessons that people are experiencing today may seem to be emotional, but they are usually rooted in the mind. Although I can still be used as a mirror, the information reflected is not as clear. The reflection is not clear, because people's mental activity today tends to be scattered. This is why a greater understanding of the mind may be helpful.

"Excuse me," interrupted a listener. "Does gazing into a Sapphire have effects similar to those of gazing into a Quartz crystal ball?"

It is very different. Quartz is of the Earth; through it one sees things from a limited, physical viewpoint. Sapphire did not originate on the Earth planet. Therefore, through Sapphire one can see from a much higher viewpoint and encompass a much larger circle of truth.

The minds of the Atlanteans could have been broken if they knew that the ground upon which they lived would soon cease to exist. This is because, at that time, people held tightly to their material things. Those who survived the destruction of Atlantis were of a different fabric. The survivors knew about Sapphire. Their spiritual leaders allowed them to know and urged them to collect and wear Sapphire. They also encouraged them to keep the Sapphire a secret.

Sapphire was distributed as it was needed by those who would journey away from the Atlantean continent and survive its destruction. Those who could not afford it were assisted in obtaining it for their journey and paid what they could.

Sapphire Today

Now the time has come for individuals to know the truth about Sapphire, including my purpose, my effects, and what I can do for the individual.

I benefit the Earth simply through the blue color ray that I carry. The blue ray is necessary for the Earth's life as well as the human's. Remember, the Earth is a living entity. It also needs the presence of all seven color rays in order to exist.

For the human wearer, I have two missions: one that is directly related to being the bearer of the blue ray, and another that is the result of my vibratory rate. From one point of view, my two missions are parallel. From another viewpoint, they intertwine like grape vines that wrap themselves around each other.

Before I talk more specifically about my properties and effects, it will be good for you to understand something about the nature of the mind, since it is on this aspect of the individual that I have my greatest effects.

The mind affects the emotions and physical body more than you might think. The mind is very complex. Within it are contained many levels or areas, some higher and some lower. Thoughts are formed at the border of the highest level of the mind, the area where the mind touches the purely spiritual aspect of the individual.

Thoughts are formed continually. There is not a moment when a new thought is not born. That is why mental discrimination is a good quality to learn. This is the ability to choose which thoughts you would like to express, put your attention on, and give power to. It is also the ability to choose which thoughts you would like to ignore, so that they will just flow out into the ethers and never manifest or affect anything.

When I speak of "you," I speak of you as Soul. As Soul you are the owner of your mind, and you have the potential to master your mind. You, as Soul, have the ability and the power to discriminate and choose which thoughts you wish to have. This is an important choice, since your thoughts act as food for your emotions and your physical body.

Discrimination may be difficult to learn. However, it does not take much thought to realize the potential benefits of mind mastery, mental balance, or control of the mind. Because mental discrimination gives great power, with it one also assumes a great responsibility. This is because, when one possesses mental discrimination, mastery over physical and emotional conditions is an easy next step. And I mean all the implications of that statement. This is where Sapphire can be so effective and helpful. I teach discrimination in a very individual way. That is my goal and my intention. I am a tool which can be used to help individuals gain self-mastery.

Of course, self-mastery can be achieved without Sapphire. You can also pound a nail into a board with a rock to build a house. But using a hammer is so much easier. Sapphire is a tool which can be used to make self-mastery easier.

The self-mastery of which I speak is mastery of the mind, the emotions, and the physical body. To achieve this, that part of you which is bound and a slave to your physical body must be able to communicate with that part of you that is not bound to your physical body, emotions, or mind. This part of you is Soul, or the part of you that is really you.

When one chooses to use the tool of Sapphire to attain self-mastery, the first step I take is to bring some orderliness to the mind and thoughts. It is only when the thoughts possess some order and are somewhat under control, that one can even begin to work on the emotions or physical body.

It is as though your mind is thousands of square miles of open range, and your thoughts are the cattle which have roamed this range throughout the winter. Now that spring has come, it is time to round up the cattle. So the Sapphire "cowboys" round them up and put them into an enormous pen. Now there may still be some confusion among the cattle, but at least they are somewhat contained. Some order has been introduced, and they are no longer scattered.

I carry the blue ray, and with it I nourish the mind. The blue ray helps people to put their attention on the mind and the physical head. The blue ray enters the physical body through the throat. Then it rises and fills the head, nourishing the brain and the mind.

The mind usually uses all the blue ray "food" it is given. What the mind does not use flows out of the brow chakra. The more food it is given, the more that the mind grows and expands in the awareness of itself. And the greater the mind becomes, the more food it requires.

I do not think I have given enough emphasis to the importance of putting the thoughts in order and to the effects that orderly thoughts can have on the physical and emotional bodies.

When thoughts are in order, thinking becomes clearer. Memory also improves, because thoughts from the past become more available. Also, greater focus is given to the thoughts that are most important. The number of useless thoughts one has during the day is astounding. Sapphire promotes useful thoughts and useful thinking. When thoughts are in order, it is also easier to distinguish between pure and impure thoughts, complete and incomplete thoughts, and balanced and imbalanced thoughts—both in oneself and in others.

When the mind is balanced, that balance is reflected in the emotional and physical bodies. This is because the mind's function is to control these areas. When there is a dysfunction in the mind, without a doubt there will be a dysfunction somewhere in the emotional or physical bodies.

You have heard of the principle that thoughts can cure. This is no old wives tale; it is grounded in truth. The key lies in being able to determine which thoughts will act as medicine for a certain disharmonious condition and which thoughts have been feeding it disharmonious energy.

In order to apply this principle, you must also know which thoughts you must produce in order to cancel out and stop the flow of the disharmonious thoughts. You must also know which thoughts will resolve the condition and raise you to the next level of understanding or health.

When a physical body dies, in most cases the individual's emotional and mental bodies remain alive. My work is rooted in the understanding that life does not cease to exist when the physical body ceases to exist. Therefore, and perhaps unfortunately, my work is not directly related to preserving the physical body in all cases. As I open the understanding, individuals may conclude that the physical body has simply become a burden to them. On the other hand, they may come to understand what is needed to heal the physical body and the reason that they have a particular illness. They may recognize the lessons they must learn, and that perhaps those lessons do not have to be learned in the physical arena. Or, they may realize that one can retain the physical body and learn one's lessons on an inner level.

The mind is a fundamental part of who you are. Your

thoughts, attitudes, concepts, and ideas shape not only your physical body and all within it, but your physical surroundings as well.

Sapphire can open up all the levels of understanding I just described. The understanding I bring can cause fundamental changes in one's attitude, outlook on life, and consciousness.

The mental body and the emotional body exist next to each other. Some have described an area that lies between the two, called the memory. It is easy to regard the memory as a level different or separate from the mind, because its function is so distinct from other mental functions. However, the memory is really part of the mind. This is also true of the subconscious level. According to some definitions, the subconscious is that level which separates the mind from Soul. However, the subconscious is another area or level of the mind; it lies in the uppermost region of the mind, between the rest of the mind and Soul.

Thoughts and mental attitudes shape emotions and emotional expressions. If you think that a certain situation is one that will make you afraid, you will feel fear. If it makes sense to your mind that a certain situation should make you feel loving, you will feel love.

Sapphire directly influences the mind and the thought process. It puts thoughts in order, gives them clarity, and organizes them. Again, the mind greatly influences the emotions (perhaps more than it does the physical body). Therefore, when Sapphire puts the mind in order, the emotions naturally become more organized, more orderly, and more easily understood. It also becomes easier to express the emotions you want to express. In other words, you come closer to mastering your emotions.

* * *

The faceted, crystalline, and spherical forms of Sapphire all focus energy into the mental body. However, this is all that they have in common. The blue light that is reflected by the crystalline and faceted Sapphire nourishes the mind. However, in order to enjoy the resulting benefits on the physical level, the energy must be able to flow back and forth between the mind and the Sapphire. Sapphire in crystalline or faceted form cannot provide this effect. The return flow can only be achieved when the Sapphire is in a rounded form.

Faceted stones give their energy eternally and without discretion. The compacted light and sound energy contained in the Sapphire's crystalline matrix is forced to throw its energy in the directions dictated by the facets. There is no pathway for the energy to return to the Sapphire or to the body wearing it. This is also true of the crystalline form.

Faceted stones belong to the era of the metal consciousness. There is at least one exception, and you will learn of it in time.

If you can obtain one, a Sapphire crystal can become a very personal possession, because it has the ability to become intimate with its owner. A Sapphire crystal's energy can feel very good, because the crystal is an earthy, physical form and can relate well to the consciousness of the physical. The crystalline form can even help individuals understand from a physical viewpoint what the rounded Sapphire is doing for and teaching the wearer on the inner levels.

The rondelle form of Sapphire is even more effective than a perfect sphere. As energy swirls around a rondelle, it gains momentum. It slips over the side of the rondelle expecting to find more of the sphere; when instead it finds an inconsistency in the shape, the energy is then thrown into the aura.

* * *

Now I wish to clarify my mission regarding the blue ray and the way in which it nourishes the mind.

Today, with all the "garbage" thoughts that people let into their physical bodies, it is a wonder that they are not sicker than they already are. By garbage thoughts, I mean unconstructive and negative thoughts, as well as negative attitudes, opinions, and prejudices. I call these thoughts garbage, because they offer no upliftment. They only create an impulse that contributes to a downward spiral.

When an individual is on a downward spiral, he or she will be heading toward a physical death. Death may not happen immediately. However, as one spirals downward, one will be heading toward more unhealthy conditions and becoming further and further removed from the fountainhead of truth, the life force, and the healing force.

On the other hand, one can be very ill and be on an upward spiral. Upon that upward spiral the individual will be moving closer to the life force and, therefore, to a healing.

Unfortunately, a complete healing may not occur in the individual's current physical body. However, that person will at least be progressing toward a healing, and that is what is important.

When individuals allow mental garbage to flow through the mind and collect in the head, the physical brain and all the functions in the head become malnourished, strained, and stressed.

It is no wonder that, in general, people's eyesight and hearing are deteriorating. Although this is not a direct effect of garbage thoughts, it is the effect of the congestion and malnutrition caused by the garbage. Too many garbage thoughts clutter the physical head and inhibit these functions.

The blue ray is nourishment for the head. It also acts as a disintegrating ray on any negativity or disharmony (in other words, garbage) that exists in the head. This is parallel to the way that Emerald's green ray acts like a disintegrating laser on physical body disharmony.

It is wonderfully soothing to place Sapphire over the eyes. However, you should never place Sapphire crystals or faceted gems over the eyes. Use Sapphire ONLY in rounded form for this purpose.

* * *

It is best to wear Sapphire around the neck in a short strand of three- to four-millimeter rounded Sapphires. By a short strand, I mean one that is fifteen, sixteen, or eighteen inches long. This amount will not be too much for an individual.

Larger Sapphires in longer necklaces (for example, those that reach to the heart) will cause great mental confusion. Too much Sapphire will imbalance the mind, because it will make the changes occur too rapidly. This much Sapphire can have wonderful influences on the mental area; however, because the changes will happen too quickly, the emotions and the physical body will resist. They will rebel by creating situations where the mind will have to react in a scattered way.

A short strand of Sapphire in the size I described will have a strong effect. The blue ray enters through the throat chakra. The Sapphire vibratory rate rides on the blue ray and will therefore also enter the head through the throat. Because a short strand will be worn close to the throat and head, its effects will focus not only on the mental area but on the physical head as well.

This much Sapphire will immediately go to work on clearing the disharmony from your head. Eventually your eyesight will become clearer and your hearing more acute. This amount of Sapphire will certainly be more than ample. In fact, it will provide energy in excess of what is needed by the physical head. Therefore, there will be an outflow through the brow chakra.

Whenever a color ray flows through the brow chakra, one's attention flows with it, and one can become aware of things beyond the physical. When one's physical sight and hearing become clearer, so will one's inner sight and hearing. In other words, the light and sound of the life force that the Gemstone Guardians describe will become more real to you. This is because you will experience them for yourself. You will see the light and hear the sound for yourself. Therefore, you will know that what the Guardians have spoken of is the truth and is a reality, even though it is a reality beyond the limitations of physical sight and hearing.

If the Sapphire used for this purpose surrounds the neck, it can be small, because there will still be a good quantity of it.

The clearer the Sapphire is, the better. However, one should balance clarity with availability. Do not worry about or place too much emphasis on inclusions or spots or anything that prevents the Sapphire from being perfectly clear blue. It is true that perfectly clear blue Sapphire is more beautiful and can touch the inner bodies and have a clearer, purer effect. Nevertheless, the amount of Sapphire I am prescribing is very powerful; it will work wonders for you, regardless of inclusions. The only time you should avoid inclusions is when they overwhelm the Sapphire's ability to present the blue ray.

The closer that the Sapphire's color is to the blue of the rainbow, the more blue ray the Sapphire will carry. Therefore, the more effective it will be in raising the sight and hearing abilities and in clearing away any disharmony or garbage in the physical brain.

I keep using the word "garbage," because it is such a good analogy. When you have too much garbage down your sink, your sink gets clogged. When too much garbage piles up in your trash can, it overflows, smells, and attracts parasites. Too much garbage left anywhere for a long enough time will also attract disease.

* * *

Until recently, the vibratory rate of the people of your planet was just not ready for the true indigo ray. That is why the indigo ray was carried by the earthstone Sodalight, instead of by a gemstone, as are the other color rays. Because the indigo ray is one of the seven colors required for the life of the planet and its people, I have been helping to carry this indigo ray. You might say that I have been doing this as a part-time job.

This is one reason that the indigo ray appears to enter through the throat chakra in some people and through the brow chakra in others. Those whose vibratory rates or consciousness is more in harmony with the way Sapphire carries the indigo ray will accept the indigo ray through the throat.

A growing number of individuals have a vibratory rate that allows them to accept the indigo ray through the brow. Several decades ago such individuals were rare. Today, with the growth in consciousness and the onset of "gem consciousness" in the past twenty to thirty years, more people are being prepared to accept indigo through the brow. This also means that, in these individuals, the throat chakra is able to accept the blue ray in a purer way. Consequently, the blue ray can be a more effective tool for providing the benefits I have described.

There are some Sapphires that reflect the indigo ray more than others. These Sapphires appear to be a darker blue. Darker blue Sapphires carry the indigo ray along with the blue ray.

If the Sapphire necklace you choose to wear is of this darker variety, the influence will be more one of helping you to make changes. It will help you to shift your focus from a material viewpoint to one that is more spiritual. It will not have the profound effect on the eyesight, the hearing, or the brain that I have described.

If you are wearing Sapphire to remove disharmony in the head, to improve eyesight and hearing, or to resolve imbalances in the brain, the Sapphire should be worn constantly.

"How long does it take for Sapphire therapy to be completed?" asked Michael.

With Sapphire therapy, a point is never reached where it can be said that the therapy is finished. There is always another step to take toward greater health and visual acuteness. As your brain becomes more efficient and clearer, you will find that it can do more and more. Your brain has an enormous capacity that people today have not even touched upon; and, of course, there is always room for more mental order.

Mastery of the physical, the emotions, and the mind is not a single achievement that occurs like graduating from school. The self-mastery of which I speak must be won over and over again. There is no limit to the knowledge or wisdom there is to be gained. This is why in any group of bona fide masters, there is always a hierarchy.

If you just wear Sapphire for a short period of time and then take it off, you will still receive benefits. Then, whenever you start wearing the Sapphire again, it will begin to work and organize thoughts where it last left off.

However, if you are using Sapphire to clear the garbage away from your mind, it should be worn continually. It is analogous to the way, once you take out the household garbage, it seems to re-accumulate quickly; and the garbage truck never seems to come often enough.

By the way, Sapphire in rounded form will not do much good when placed anywhere on the body other than around the neck. The only exception to this rule, as I mentioned, is when Sapphire is placed over the eyes.

* * *

Sapphire will work on anything that is inhibiting the brain from working properly. I do not know enough about the human physical condition to give you specific names of diseases.

"Tumors, nervous conditions, blocked arteries, strokes," offered Michael.

Those words mean nothing to me. Think of garbage and

polluted waters. Think of the fluids in your brain and what diseases affect them; or think of how the fluids flow and what diseases result from pollution in these waterways of the brain.

"Basically, when people's brains are polluted, there will be pollution throughout their bodies, as well," said Michael.

Yes, but my concern is with the cause of the pollution. Gemstones work with cause. What caused the individual's brain or entire body to become polluted?

"Mental garbage," suggested Michael.

Mental garbage, indeed. The person's thoughts, attitudes, and concepts have polluted the physiology.

Every time you think thoughts such as, "Oh, I am so ugly, I am so fat, I can't do this, I'm so sick, I have this terrible disease, I'll never get well," you are throwing garbage into your system. You are perpetuating your disease and further removing yourself from the healing force.

This also includes every time you think a negative thought about someone else. Every time you think anything negative about anyone, it is you who are affected, because that negative thought must flow through you from your mind to your physical body. As it flows through you, it carries all the negativity with it; and that negativity is garbage. It collects first in your head and then circulates throughout your physical body. It collects in your head first, because your brain is the transmitter of thoughts to your physical body, just as the heart is the transmitter of emotions.

In your next body—whether or not you believe in reincarnation—you will not be moved any closer to the healing force than the point you have attained at the time of death. So death is no escape. It is only temporary pain relief. Eventually you must face what you have created for yourself.

Sapphire Tomorrow

In a sense, my mission for the future overlaps my mission of today. My future mission may arise from another, as yet unknown, effect of the blue ray, or it may come from another effect of my vibratory rate. At this time, I am not sure which it will be.

Rainbow Fluorite spoke of the many transitions on different levels that people today are experiencing. Sapphire will help people to make these transitions. I affect the mental area of the individual. I loosen concepts and attitudes that are hardened, crusty, and stone-like. Because they are so ingrained, these concepts and attitudes keep the individual stuck to a certain state of consciousness. Unless they are loosened, these concepts and attitudes will make these and other changes much more traumatic. The individuals who insist on holding onto their hardened concepts and attitudes will not be flexible enough to accept these changes.

Sapphire's energy will loosen the concepts and attitudes that are stuck in the mind. It will create more mental flexibility. Then, as the transitions occur, I will help individuals make these changes with more ease. Of course, these changes will occur whether or not the individual is ready, for destiny has ordained them.

I also help people to make these transitions, because I carry much of the energy required to make the leap or shift. The word "shift" is not strong enough. The transitions of which Purple Rainbow Fluorite spoke, and the transition between the metal and gem consciousness that Amethyst described, is actually a total reconditioning or transformation of the vibratory rate of the planet.

When these transitions are fully completed, and society is on its feet, I will be replaced by another carrier of the blue ray. When I am replaced, I will no longer carry the blue ray into the physical world. I will have relinquished this responsibility. However, I will have gained a greater understanding of the whole and will become a source of stability.

I also help people make transitions by nourishing the mind. This nourishment allows people to better comprehend the transitions that are occurring.

Although I need to be in the spherical form to aid people in making changes, I do not need to be used in the great amount I described before. I do not need to completely surround the neck. Wearing even one-and-a-half to two carats in one's aura, which is a small but significant amount, will help.

Do not expect the new carrier of the blue ray for many thousands of years. The only significance that the transfer to the new carrier has today is an upcoming event which I will discuss in a moment. Those of you with any insight at all may want to open your awareness to the possibility of witnessing it.

Because of the transitions that are now occurring, the time is right for the race of beings who plant gemstones to come and assist in the implantation of the seed of the blue ray's new carrier. The carrier itself will be needed in perhaps three to five thousand years. I am not sure exactly when the implantation will occur, since this is not under my control. However, the time is right for it to happen within this decade or the next or the next.

Chances are good that the implantation will not hit the newspapers. Those who wish to be invited to watch, and who have earned the right and have the ability to travel in a state of awareness beyond the atmosphere of the Earth, may look down upon the ceremony.

The process will not just happen in a moment. It will take several of your Earth's weeks, because this race of people must first research the planet. They must take more data, and they must research the Earth's channels and power points. They will do this by circling the Earth in their space ship and by scanning the planet with special instruments.

Then they will implant the vibratory rate of the new gemstone. I do not know whether the vibratory rate will be implanted in a gemstone that already exists or whether they will implant a new mother crystal matrix. In the latter case, a mysterious meteor may hit the Earth and implant itself beneath the surface.

Regardless of how the implantation occurs, the Earth will respond in some way. It must respond in order to balance the new vibratory rate that will be introduced. The Earth will probably respond in a unique way. It will not be your average volcanic eruption, hurricane, or unusual weather pattern.

* * *

My function and purpose is simple and basic. In fact, it could probably be covered in one page. It was the explanation and knowledge surrounding my purpose that I felt was important to share with you. It is important that you have a greater understanding of my purposes, my mission, and my effects when applied to the human body.

"It has been an honor," said Michael.

There is someone I wish to introduce you to. You will have

to follow me further down into the valley, for he is playing with the other children.

Although I am sure he is aware of his mission, I do not know what he will say. He is currently enjoying his boyhood as any boy would. You will know him as the Guardian of Indigo.

Of course, if you call him across the field by that name, he will not answer you. He answers to a common name. It is a name that perhaps sounds foreign to you, but one that is common in the country of his ancestors.

For now, good night.

I easily slipped back into the consciousness of my physical body. As I did, I had the distinct impression that time would stand still until we returned to this valley. Then time would resume and we would meet with the Guardian of Indigo.

11
INDIGO

Sapphire led us down the grassy slopes to a playground where many children were playing ball. We could discern no order to their play; there seemed to be no rules and no objective. Yet each child was playing with all his heart.

As the late afternoon sun began to set, we started to wonder why we were spending so much time watching these children. The sky darkened, and the children began to answer calls to return home for dinner.

When the game finally ended, one boy looked up and ran to Sapphire. He appeared to be about twelve years old and had dark hair and light brown skin. Sapphire patted the boy's shoulder good-naturedly. I sensed a feeling of pride in the gesture, like a father would have for his son. Then the boy turned to Sapphire with a questioning look in his perfectly indigo eyes.

"They've come to learn about your mission," said Sapphire.

I know. I guessed that, *said the boy.* Shall we tell them now and then go home to eat?

"Yes," said Sapphire.

OK, *the boy said and then quickly trotted up the hill. We followed him and stopped just outside the village at a spot where the sound of pots, pans, and dinner dishes from nearby homes would not disturb us.*

So, what do you want to know? *asked the boy, as we all found rocks to sit on.*

"Can you tell us how you affect humans and what your relationship is with Sodalight?" Michael asked.

Sapphire glared at Michael. His look silently but unmis-

takably reminded Michael that Indigo was a boy, and that he should word his questions appropriately. Michael got the message.

I think I understand what you want to know. You seem to have many questions. Let's sort them out one at a time.

They call me Indigo. At night I dream that I am standing in space. Below me is the Earth. Then a light flows through me and touches the rocks and crystals within the planet. In my dream the rocks listen to me, and I teach them how to become crystals.

When I wake up, I don't remember everything I have taught the rocks. I do remember that they listen, they learn, and they move. Yes, their molecules actually move under my direction.

The other thing I remember is the wonderful light that flows through me. I'm not sure where it comes from. It doesn't come from inside of me. It seems to come from somewhere above and beyond me, from an unknown place that I have yet to explore. It flows through my whole body, but especially through my eyes and my heart.

This is what I do when I sleep. Yet sometimes all I have to do is close my eyes, and I find myself in this place above the Earth.

I have heard of Sodalight. Sapphire is teaching me about all the gemstones on the planet. I know I have much to learn. I know that I'm special, because none of the other children get to listen to Sapphire's talks. But I like to keep our lessons quiet, so that people don't think of me as different. I think you understand.

"Do you meet with any others who teach you about gemstones?" Michael asked.

Yes, there are others. I get taken to a nearby temple that sits on a very high mountain. In the temple is a domed room. In the middle of this room rests the most beautiful, faceted Indigo gemstone I have ever seen. I feel like I know this gemstone, that it is my friend; and I study it. From this gemstone pours a very dark blue color that they call indigo. It flows into the room and beyond into the Earth's atmosphere.

There is a master there with white hair, a white beard, and white robes. I know he is a master, because he is the Guardian of the Temple. He stands next to me in front of this gemstone and directs my attention to certain aspects of it; he shows me how I should study it.

During my dreams, I teach the information I learn from these studies to the rocks. I keep the vision of this perfect Indigo gemstone in my mind as I teach, so that the rocks will see this image and know what to grow into.

"Are your dreams only about the Earth planet?" Michael asked.

Yes, for this is my home.

"How do you get to this temple?" Michael inquired. "The mountains surrounding your village seem too rugged for traveling."

I've never really thought about it. I'm just there! One moment I am here, either looking at the mountains or lying in my bed looking at the ceiling. The next moment I am there. It's not strange and it's not hard. It just happens. Sometimes all I have to do is think about the temple, and I'm there.

"Can you share some of the information you learn when you visit this temple—for example, what you teach the rock?"

I don't remember exactly what I tell the rock. All I know is that it's specific and involves patterns, numbers, sequences, and other things I don't understand yet.

As I study the Indigo gemstone, I learn about things that are hard for me to believe. They're hard to believe only because, in my heart, I know that these things are also about me. I know that somehow I am connected more closely with this gemstone than I think I'd like to be. But they tell me that a lot of freedom comes with responsibility. I guess when I'm old enough, I'll also understand what that means.

"Can you tell us some of the things that seem unbelievable?" Michael asked.

The boy paused, apparently lost in thought. You're a stranger here. We don't get strangers here very often. I know you'll be leaving soon, for life is hard for people in this valley. Strangers never stay long.

Although I've been told to expect visitors sooner or later, none have met me here before. I have been in classes in the temple where everyone gets a turn to lead the class; so I have spoken in front of people.

What seems unbelievable, *said Indigo, returning from his thoughts,* is that they say I am helping certain rocks in the Earth to become gemstones. They say that this will help the Earth and its people. This makes me feel very proud. It means that I can touch the whole planet and everyone on it, even though I am stuck in this valley.

Of course, I'm not really stuck here, because all I need to do is put my attention on the temple, or on any other place, and I am there. I don't know how many of my friends can do this. I haven't asked.

"What do your parents think of your experiences?" asked Michael.

I live with the Guardian of Sapphire. I call him Father. I don't think he's really my father, but he lets me share his dwelling. I think the villagers know that he really isn't my father. Still, it's nice to have a father, and he takes good care of me.

The villagers don't call him Sapphire; but you don't need to know his name. You don't need to know my name either. Teachings remain more pure when personalities are not involved.

"How old are you?"

Twelve, going on thirteen.

"Is there anything in particular you would like to do when you grow older?"

In a few years I will be old enough to go with other adults on long journeys outside of this valley. When traveling on foot, it takes several weeks before one comes to any other villages. Everyone who has ever returned from these journeys has such wonderful stories to tell. So this is what I look forward to doing.

My first duty, as Indigo, is for the planet. I've been shown what can happen when the planet is given more of the indigo ray. It makes the air cleaner, and it renews life. It allows the Earth to dream of what it would like to become. Then it allows the dream to come true.

It is only now that there is enough positive influence on the Earth to encourage it to dream of becoming something greater than it is. Then when the dreams come true, the Earth will be something greater. In that way, the indigo ray can be very rejuvenating.

I think this is what I, as Indigo, may also do for people. I have this idea that after I teach the rock to become a gemstone, I may teach people to become like gemstones. I may teach them to shine with the light that is already within them.

The more Indigo crystal there is on the planet, the more that the indigo ray can affect everyone who lives there. People should wear the Indigo crystal in a form suitable for humans and that can influence the entire aura. In my imagination, I see the Indigo crystal accomplishing this when it is in a round form.

When enough indigo ray enters people's auras, they will be able to see more clearly who they really want to be and what their true dreams actually are. If they continue to wear the Indigo, forces in their lives will work to make these dreams come true.

"Do you mean daydreams or night dreams?" asked Michael.

Indigo stood up, as if to emphasize his answer. I mean the dreams of the people: their ideals and goals and the ability to take charge of their lives and say, "This is who and what I want to be, and this is what I want to know and how I want to express myself."

When people wear the Indigo gemstone, the indigo ray will enter the aura and teach them what these ideals can be and what ideals are available to reach for. I think that this teaching aspect is the most important part of my mission. It seems that I'm getting practice right now.

I am a teacher. I teach the rock. And I will be a teacher. I feel that, in the years to come, I won't only be teaching in my dreams. Soon I will begin to work with people directly and teach them about their potential. Then, by wearing the Indigo gemstone, they will learn how to achieve that potential.

One time I got very frustrated, because I wanted to know more. I was instantly taken to the temple in the mountains. Somehow I found myself inside of that Indigo gemstone. Suddenly I knew everything about myself, about the inner worlds and the universe, and everything about the indigo ray. I knew about the white light, and the origin of the indigo ray, and where it leads. I wasn't ready yet for the knowledge. The information was so overwhelming, that I was sick in bed for two weeks.

The boy laughed. I'll never do that again! But it did teach me patience.

There's so much I have to learn, but from now on I'll just learn what they teach me. And they do appear to be intent on teaching me.

I seem to be good at absorbing information. It becomes a part of me. I'm not sure exactly where it is stored, but it's not all stored in my mind. They're always testing me to make sure my heart is open enough to store the information in a place where it is eternally retrievable.

You asked me about Sodalight. I have been taught a lot about Sodalight, and I have met this Gemstone Guardian. I know I've been avoiding speaking of him. It's just that he's the sort of individual I would like to forget. For some reason, our personalities clash, and he makes me feel uncomfortable. Sapphire says that it's because we are so alike in many ways.

When I was with the Guardian of Sodalight, I just wanted to rebel. I felt like the stereotypical teen-ager who just wanted to be uncooperative and disagree with everything he said. I've never acted this way toward Sapphire. He is more like a friend than a parent, and we get along very well.

I still don't understand why I acted the way I did toward Sodalight. Afterwards I felt foolish and wanted to apologize. Somehow I think he understood, because my actions didn't seem to surprise him much. In fact, I think he took my actions in his stride.

Anyway, one of the things our gemstones have in common is our ability to absorb. The way I absorb is going to change as the Indigo crystals grow further away from Sodalight. You see, the rock that I teach at night is Sodalight.

Indigo again returned to his own thoughts and said, Maybe that's why we didn't get along very well in person. It's different in the dream state, because there are no personalities involved.

"Is it true that Sodalight absorbs pollution and any kind of negativity from the Earth's atmosphere?" asked Michael.

Yes. However, when Sodalight is able to form more perfectly into crystals, the crystals will absorb something different. Their entire focus will be to support the purpose and function of the indigo ray. Therefore, the Indigo gemstone will absorb those things that hold people back from achieving their potential and their dreams.

Then I, as Indigo, will be used to benefit people physically, emotionally, and mentally. I know that I will be used this way in the future; I am not yet ready for these purposes now.

I've been told that I will grow to be a very strong man, and that the Indigo gemstone will also be strong. In the future you will call it a healing stone, because it will absorb any disharmony in the physical, emotional, and mental areas. It will absorb anything that is preventing its wearers from reaching their potential, as well as anything that is holding them back.

Actually, I think that the vibratory rate of the gemstone will make a disharmonious condition less stuck. Then more life force will be able to flow through the disharmonious area and spin around it. This will make the disharmony more apparent and therefore allow you to resolve it and be freed from it. Neither Indigo nor the life force will resolve things for you. You've got to do that yourself; but they will surely help.

This is what excites me. I'm looking forward to helping people more directly.

Of course, I personally might never help people directly, since I might never leave this valley. It might be like it is in my dreams when I teach the Earth—and that strange, powerful, and beautiful force flows through me and touches all the potential gemstones. I'm sure that, in the years to come, the same force will flow through me to touch those who wear the Indigo gemstone.

"What about the Indigo crystal that exists today?" asked Michael. "Is this Indigo different from the Indigo of the future?"

The Indigo available today is not yet transparent enough. The color ray hasn't quite set. The crystal still has more to learn, my friend.

Is there anything else you wanted to know?

"Yes, please," said Michael, always eager for the opportunity to ask questions. "Do you know of any specific therapies that the current Indigo gemstone can be used for?"

I don't know of any therapies.

I do have an Indigo crystal that is mine. I hold it whenever I go to the temple. I don't know whether it helps me to get there. They've told me that I must keep it with me at all times and watch it change.

"Is there anything else that you would like to share about yourself or your dreams?"

Only this: I have learned that when people are learning things that are new and very special, it is best to keep quiet. As the new information becomes part of them, and they know it to be true, it will touch those around them. It will touch people, whether or not they speak the information in words. When you speak the words, others have a chance to disagree. If you share the information without speaking the words, there will be no room for denial, conscious or unconscious. Others will think that they learned the information themselves, and therefore it will become their own truth.

"Perhaps that is how you will work with people," suggested Michael.

Maybe. You will learn more about Indigo by wearing it. You will learn this information in a nonverbal way, and then you will know it to be true.

Hearing about Indigo from me is just going to give you a chance to deny what I say, argue with it, or see my limited state of consciousness. I will admit that I'm a kid, but I'm growing. I know I've come a long way, and I know I have a long way to go. I know what I know. If you want to know what you know deep inside of you, you can do what I do. I just hold my piece of Indigo and dream while I'm awake. Maybe this technique will work for you, too.

"What shape is the Indigo that you carry?"

The shape of my Indigo looks something like a crystal. It isn't a true crystal, because Indigo has not yet become a true crystal.

If you want to help the Earth realize its dreams, work with the crystalline form. If you want to help yourself realize your own dreams, you must work with a crystal that has been rounded into the shape of the Earth or the sun. Then the crystal will become like the sun and radiate its energy into your aura and touch every part of your being.

I was going to invite you to supper, but I can tell that Sapphire doesn't think it would be a good idea.

"Thank you for sharing the information with us," said Michael.

I did my best. I hope you learned what you wanted to learn.

"Yes, and it was shared very well indeed."

Thanks.

"Until we meet again, may the blessings be."

Farewell. May the blessings be, *said the boy. Without any hesitation, he turned and started to make his way up the hill in the moonlight.*

* * *

Sapphire watched the boy momentarily and then said, "I hope this information will give you a greater understanding of Indigo. I hope it will awaken you to the forces, perhaps even the unknown ones, that work on your planet."

"It is very helpful," said Michael. "It gives me a perspective I didn't have before."

"Tomorrow evening you will meet with the Guardian of Carnelian," said Sapphire. Then he pulled his outer cape around himself and covered his head with its hood.

"Good night," he said, "and may the blessing be."

"May the blessings be," we replied almost in unison.

Sapphire waved to us in a half-salute and then followed the boy up the hill.

The group discussed where we might meet Carnelian. Then we decided to wait and let Spirit guide us, since we could only guess where in all the universe the meeting place would be.

We said our good nights, and one by one our forms disappeared from the valley. I returned to my physical body, which was resting peacefully in the bedroom.

12
CARNELIAN

I closed my eyes and imagined Carnelian's orange light; and in the next instant I heard music which moved and flowed like a strong wind.

When I opened my eyes, the Guardian of Carnelian sat facing me. She was clothed in yards of orange cloth, which was wrapped around her like an Indian sari.

She appeared to be in her thirties. The shiny, reflective quality of her skin reminded me of fine white porcelain. Her eyes were dark brown, but one could not miss the orange ray that shone from them.

Michael and two others joined us, and Carnelian and I stood to greet them. Carnelian seemed aloof, yet I felt comfortable in her presence. I sensed in her the characteristics of a loner, a quality I also recognized in myself. Soon she too realized that we had something in common, and a door seemed to open between us.

She asked me to stand next to her and enter her aura from the side. Never had this process required so much thought and calculation as it did now. Still, I was not able to take the step.

Then her vibratory rate changed, and she became less manifest and more obviously composed of energy. My body also underwent this transformation. Then, like two attracting magnets, we connected and I stood within her aura.

You wish to know more about Carnelian. There is not much to say, for I am a simple gemstone. The work I do is also simple. My mission is to be the bearer of the orange ray for the people of Earth. Carnelian is for humans and has little or no effect on the Earth planet. The Earth has its own ways of attracting the vibratory rate of the orange ray it needs.

The Early Years of Carnelian

During the Age of Atlantis, certain wise individuals noticed that the current carrier of the orange ray could not adequately nourish the people. They saw that a new gemstone was needed to bear the orange ray.

That is when I was given the responsibility of being the Guardian of the new gemstone that would carry the orange ray. It is a unique responsibility. I was not just shown a gemstone and told, "Here, this is your responsibility." Instead, I had to work with the minds of certain humans to inspire them to formulate a gemstone carrier for the orange ray.

This first Carnelian was like a mother crystal. It was formed when Spirit, the Guardian of the Earth, and I worked with certain individuals in their dreams and inspirations. Since the orange ray is so crucial to life, it was essential that its carrier be in absolute harmony with humans. What better way to make it harmonious with humans, than for humans themselves to have a hand in making it?

What may be called "little miracles" also occurred. It was as though an orange picture was being painted; yet it was not until I, as the Guardian of Carnelian, touched it with my orange ray that it came alive. Then it was no longer just a painted picture; it was a living picture. Like this, the Carnelian gemstone became a living vehicle for the orange ray.

The Atlanteans thought this first Carnelian was wonderful, and they traded it around the planet. When the Earth shifted and Atlantis was destroyed, this early Carnelian was buried in many places. Wherever it came to rest, it took hold and began to grow and reproduce.

The fact that people today synthesize Carnelian is only a curious reflection of how the first Carnelian manifested on the planet.

I also work on other planets. I teach the people there to fashion gemstones that bear the orange ray. Some planets have gemstones that bear the orange ray naturally. Since these gemstones are already in harmony with the people, I am not needed on those planets.

Carnelian Today

To understand the purpose of Carnelian, one should know about the color rays. The Guardian of Emerald introduced you to the color rays. Now I would like to give you more in-depth information about them.

Since the sum of all color rays constitutes the life force itself, all life is nourished by the color rays.

All individuals have one color ray in their make-up that they are most connected with. This ray can be used to balance deficiencies in the other color rays and heal the conditions caused by those deficiencies.

This ray may be called your "main color ray." It is your strength. It gives you energy. It provides a specific frequency of light and sound that enables you to grow beyond your current limitations. Your main color ray gives you the upliftment and strength you need to resolve all imbalances.

Michael, your main color ray is blue. Therefore, the blue ray is your strong ray and your healing ray. It can be used to open the doors for all the other color rays to enter every aspect of your physical and inner selves.

Everyone has a certain attribute that corresponds with the individual's main ray. This attribute is one of the greatest tools available to the individual. However, it can also be an insidious trap.

Since your main ray is blue, your mind is your strongest attribute and one of your greatest tools. In other words, you can use your mind and draw upon its strength to overcome any obstacle in life. On the other hand, if you use only your mind and place little attention on your other aspects, your mind could easily become your greatest obstacle.

If you wear the gemstone that bears the blue ray, the blue ray will shine upon your mind. It will teach you how your mind can be a potential obstacle. At the same time, the nourishment that it gives to your mind will strengthen it and make it less susceptible to becoming a trap.

One's main-ray gemstone can teach one how to work with one's strongest attribute and how to balance its power. You can then use your strongest attribute to help resolve the karma and learn the lessons presented by the deficiencies in the other color rays.

Those whose main color ray is red, consciously or unconsciously, draw on their heart center for strength. At the same time, the heart center and the emotions can be their greatest obstacles.

Those whose main color ray is orange rely on a certain vitality or energy that gives life to ideas and the cycle of cause and effect. The orange ray is a very powerful, life-giving energy. It teaches the balance between the positive, negative, and neutralizing forces in life. The trap lies either in not using this energy, which is so naturally available to them, or, in using this energy in an imbalanced way.

Those whose main color ray is yellow draw their strength from their spiritual potential. For example, if a difficulty arises in the life of a yellow-ray person, the individual can remember his or her spiritual potential. That memory will be the strength or magnetizing force needed to move through the difficulty. The clearer the flow of yellow ray becomes, the stronger will its magnetizing force be. However, there is always a balance. The pull toward spirituality is the individual's strength; the pull toward the worlds of limitation is the trap.

Those whose main color ray is green draw their strength from the knowingness that there is just as much God or Spirit in the physical world as there is in any of the inner, more "spiritual" worlds. In other words, consciously or unconsciously, they know that God exists here and now. Their strength lies in knowing that the only difference between the physical world and the spiritual worlds is the degree of the illusion of materiality. The trap lies in accepting that these worlds are separate.

Those whose main color ray is indigo draw their strength from their intuition, their innate knowingness, or their sense about things. Often this knowingness baffles them, because they cannot determine exactly where it comes from. They just know that what they know is the truth for them. Their trap is either in denying or disbelieving that which their intuition tells them, or, in denying that their intuition or innate knowingness even exists. This denial can result in confusion.

Those whose main color ray is purple draw their strength from the current of wisdom that flows through them and through all of life. Their strength especially increases when they become aware of this flow. The purple ray has a frequency higher than that of the other color rays. The trap for people whose main color ray is purple also offers them their greatest opportunity for learning. It occurs when these individuals expect to be greater than or above others. This attitude is an imbalance of the mind and can lead to serious mental aberrations.

There are many concepts about colors. Therefore, it is important to understand that those whose main ray is purple are not necessarily more "spiritual" than others; those whose main ray is blue are not necessarily more "mental;" and those whose main ray is red are not necessarily more "emotional."

I am simply describing where an individual's strength may be if the channel for that person's main color ray is open. Gemstones are powerful tools which can be used to open and balance this channel.

Wearing the gemstone of your main color ray provides continuous, pure, living stimulation for as long as it is worn. In some cases, it provides this stimulation as long as the gemstone is in the wearer's aura. Because the stimulation provided is alive and continuous, wearing gemstones is much more effective than wearing a garment or eating foods of one's main color. It is true that food, like gemstones, possesses life. However, once food is eaten, its color quickly changes.

There are some individuals whose main color is white. All seven color rays have the potential to give them strength. Their trap is the confusion that often results when they try to sort out and balance the influence of all seven rays. These individuals are grounded in the higher planes. They possess physical bodies only in order to carry out certain missions. It is only when they have mastered the balance of the seven color rays, that they gain the ability to leave the world of confusion. This is also when their missions or purposes become apparent. It is important to know that it may take many lifetimes before the confusion clears and their mission unfolds and becomes known to them.

These individuals are found throughout the world. However, the greatest percentage of them (although it is not a large percentage) live in the United States. This is because the people of this country are experiencing the most rapid spiritual unfoldment on the planet today.

At this time, Ruby is the carrier of the red ray; Carnelian carries the orange ray, Citrine calls the yellow; Emerald carries the green; Sapphire carries the blue; Indigo carries the indigo;

and Amethyst carries the purple.

"How can people find out which is their main color ray?" asked Michael.

That is an important question. Soon you will be trained in this process with the intention that you will then train others.

"How effective would it be to use colored paper or colored lights instead of gemstones?"

Colored paper or lights wculd not work as well as gemstones, because they are not alive. Gemstones are alive. It is their vibratory rates, or life energies, that enable the color rays they carry to profoundly affect the body.

Staring at colored paper, for example, or shining colored lights on the body will teach the body to recognize colors. The colors exist everywhere, and these therapies will teach the body to absorb them from the atmosphere. However, if you are looking for a strong, effective tool that will make profound changes in your life, you should wear the gemstone that carries your main color ray.

"I asked that question, because some people have the concept that the color is the essence of a gemstone. There is little or no recognition of the gemstone's vibratory rate."

If the color of a gemstone were its only essence, then orange plastic spheres would work just as well as Carnelian spheres; and, of course, they do not.

Remember, there is an intensely concentrated force of light and sound contained within the crystalline matrix of gemstones. In the case of the color-ray bearers, this light and sound has the vibratory rate of a certain color ray. For example, Carnelian contains the compact, compressed vibratory rate of the orange ray and the sound that the orange ray sings.

There is a point I wish to clarify: Whenever a Gemstone Guardian refers to a color ray, both the light and sound elements of that color ray are implied in the reference. For example, whenever I refer to the orange ray, I am not only referring to its color, I am also referring to its sound.

* * *

The original idea behind the concept of birthstones was to give infants some form of the gem that bore their main color ray. Certain children were given gemstones that were not color-ray bearers, but were otherwise associated with their destinies. Often these gifts were selected by masters of gemstone knowledge and wisdom. The birthstones established by the jewelry industry today do not necessarily have any correlation to a person's main color ray or destiny.

One of the greatest gifts you can give to an infant, a child, or an adult is the gemstone that bears that person's main color ray. It is also one of the greatest gifts you can give to yourself. Most effective would be a strand of spheres which encircles the neck.

* * *

"You mentioned that some Carnelian available today is not found naturally. Does the life force and the orange ray enter this Carnelian too?" inquired Michael.

Yes. The orange ray enters this Carnelian as soon as it is worn. More specifically, it enters when the Carnelian has been enlivened in someone's aura for an adequate period of time. A super-physical chemical reaction occurs between the gemstone and the individual's aura. This reaction allows me to infuse the Carnelian with the life-giving orange ray. It is part of my duty to make sure that this occurs.

The orange ray is a key ingredient for life, specifically for the life of the cells. Each individual cell bathes in glory when it is in the presence of the orange ray. Cells need all seven color rays for life. However, when given even a little extra orange ray, they react the same way you might react after a hard day's work when you get to soak in a nice, hot bath. You rest and relax; and although you continue to function, you let go of your troubles.

If you are in tune with the orange ray or feel harmony with Carnelian, the orange ray Carnelian provides will help your cells let go of their disharmony and disease. It is not necessary to have orange as your main color ray to be in harmony with Carnelian. Nor is it necessary for one's complexion or hair color to appear to be in harmony with the color orange for you to be in harmony with Carnelian. If you feel that you are in harmony with Carnelian, you probably are.

I work best for those individuals who feel harmony with Carnelian, whether or not their main color ray is orange.

Nevertheless, few people will be attracted to Carnelian unless they are in tune with its vibratory rate. Also, it is not a good idea to give someone a gift of Carnelian without knowing that the Carnelian will be in harmony with that person. Carnelian will almost always be in harmony with those individuals who have an orange coloring in their complexion, eyes, or hair. These people will be obvious. However, if someone who has a choice selects Carnelian, there is no doubt that the individual is in harmony with it.

Carnelian Therapy

When the orange ray is in the aura, its vibratory rate is breathed into the lungs and distributed throughout the body by the heart and the blood.

In addition to acting as a bridge for the orange ray to enter the physical body, Carnelian can assist with any physical situation that is being stubborn, persistent, or that is not reacting favorably to other therapies.

Carnelian will help if the cells involved in the condition are reluctant to release their disharmony. I will say to the cells, "Relax, and forget your troubles. Release your disharmony. Enjoy the bath of the orange ray, and enjoy life!" This effect will be magnified if I am placed over the disharmonious area under direct sunlight.

Gemstones whose missions involve the upliftment of human beings work on all the energy centers to create balance. My focus is on the higher energy centers. However, in order to do my best work, I must first resolve imbalances in the energy flows of the lower chakras.

This resolution involves creating a closed circuit, in which energy moves in a circular motion into the body through the base chakra and out through the sex chakra. This flow will become just powerful enough to feed and maintain life in these chakras. Then attention can be placed on opening and strengthening the higher chakras.

The lower chakras are not "bad," for every chakra has a purpose; and one chakra does not have a greater purpose than another. All are essential for life. However, if your goals and aspirations are of a spiritual nature, you will naturally want to place greater attention on the higher chakras.

Before physicians use the strong vibratory rates of gemstones to heal sicknesses caused by energy center imbalances, they should have a complete understanding of gemstones. Physicians should also know the mechanics of color rays, including their effects on the chakras, and the ways in which main color rays can be used to balance the other rays.

Toxicity is disharmony. Carnelian works on stirring and dislodging disharmony; then it absorbs the disharmony the body has released. Therefore, it is an excellent gemstone to use when you begin a cleansing therapy and want to focus on specific organs.

To help the cells in a particular organ release their disharmony, toxicity, or disease, follow this procedure: Simply place two or three strands of Carnelian (or enough to cover the area) over the desired area. Then allow direct sunlight to shine on it for about half an hour.

The deeper you want Carnelian's effect to penetrate into the organ, the more Carnelian you will need to use.

"Since Carnelian encourages cells to relax, would this treatment help someone who has a stiff neck or a tightness somewhere in the body?" asked Michael.

My work focuses on individual cells. Therefore, I may not be of much benefit if a stiff neck is caused solely by a lack of communication or cooperation between the neck's cells, rather than by a problem within the cells themselves. However, stiffness is usually caused by cells that are tight both individually and collectively. In such cases, I can help the cells to relax.

* * *

The emotions also relax in the presence of the orange ray. This relaxation manifests as calmer, more balanced emotions. When Carnelian is worn, it will have this effect on the emotions, regardless of the wearer's main color ray.

Negative emotions are not in harmony with the orange ray. Therefore, when Carnelian is worn, negative emotions are either dulled, dissipated, or canceled out, depending on the strength of the emotion and strength of the orange ray flowing through the individual.

The orange ray acts like a ramp on which positive emotions easily ride into the physical body. Carnelian also allows positive emotions to be more easily expressed.

* * *

Carnelian will sharpen, enhance, and stimulate mental functions. It will enhance clarity, accuracy, memory, and the ability to see things from a greater viewpoint. However, these effects will not occur immediately. First I stir up the clouds that prevent mental clarity. Next, I teach the body to metabolize these clouds. The more clouds that are metabolized, the greater and stronger the mental clarity becomes.

The individual gains strength as the body metabolizes and eliminates these clouds. This strength is required before the individual can accept mental clarity. This is because, once this clarity is established, it can change a person's life.

Sometimes when the mental clouds begin to be stirred, it will seem like mental clarity is actually decreasing. One's sinuses and lymph glands may also become clogged. However, this will be only a short-term effect. It will be the result of all the body's processes becoming involved in metabolizing whatever is inhibiting clarity.

It is best to wear Carnelian almost constantly, especially if it is being worn to increase mental clarity. Carnelian will open up the flow of life force. The longer it is worn, the stronger and more beneficial this flow can become.

It is also best to wear Carnelian by itself in a necklace. Whenever gemstones are combined, their energies create a particular focus that acts like a laser beam to fulfill specific purposes. Therefore, be very careful when combining gemstones in a necklace. There is an art and a science to properly combining gemstones, since not all gemstone combinations produce beneficial effects. Some improper combinations will scatter energy; others will negate the effects of the gemstones in the combination; and others will even have a disharmonious effect on the wearer.

Carnelian is most effective when worn around the neck. If worn around the wrist, for example, I cannot affect the energy centers. However, I can still absorb disharmony.

Wherever I am placed in the aura, I will work to stir and dislodge physical, emotional, and mental disharmony. After the disharmony is released, I will absorb it. Therefore, I should be periodically rinsed in hot, then cold, then hot running water. Then I should be left in direct sunlight for three or four hours for cleansing. If I am worn every day, this cleansing should done about once every two weeks. If the wearer is very ill, this cleansing should be done every day or every other day.

* * *

I will benefit anyone who is lacking in the orange ray. A deficiency of orange ray frequently manifests as an imbalance between lower and higher energies. This imbalance is often recognized when people's dreams, thoughts, and aspirations point in one direction, but their lives seem to lead in another.

When one wears Carnelian, the lower and higher energies in the body will become balanced. Eventually, the different directions or paths one is traveling will come closer and closer together. Then one will have much more energy, because one will be moving in the direction of one's choice and following only one path at a time.

Carnelian Tomorrow

My mission now and in the future is simple. As long as Carnelian is worn, I will continue to infuse it with the orange ray.

Before we end this discourse, I would like to reinforce the importance of the color-ray-bearing gemstones as tools to help in every aspect of life. When you wear your main-ray gemstone, your physical, emotional, memory, and mind aspects will be nourished with the light and sound of all seven color rays. As long as you have a physical body, your main-ray gemstone can be one of your greatest tools. This is because the color rays are life; and life is Spirit, or healing energy.

When you wear your main-ray gemstone, the doors will open for you to be healed and uplifted on all levels, and you will experience a greater creative flow on all levels. The ramifications of this are amazing; I will leave them to your own imagination.

* * *

I am sure you will not be surprised when I name the Guardian of Citrine as the next Guardian to be interviewed.

"Until we meet again, may the blessings be," said Michael.

Thank you for listening to my words.

"It has been an honor and a great privilege," Michael replied.

For me as well. May the blessings be.

I exited her aura in the same way I had entered. As soon as I did, her form disappeared and nothing remained but a swirl of pure orange energy.

We listened to the relaxing sound of the orange ray as we waited for the swirling energy to dissipate. Then an inner voice told me that this was the world of orange, and that the energy would never die down. We could leave whenever we were ready and return whenever we wished.

13
CITRINE

Citrine's energy was overwhelming. I felt waves of its vibratory rate surging from the top of my head, down my spine, and back up the sides of my back. It seemed to be readjusting and realigning my skull, all my vertebrae, and their surrounding muscles.

The flow of energy moving up my body became a stream of pure yellow light. It left my body through my crown chakra. My attention followed this stream as it flowed beyond the atmosphere and out into space.

I soon realized that I was riding this yellow current. Its sound was incredibly loud. I was heading toward a dark tunnel that appeared to be thousands of miles away. Apparently this tunnel was both the source and goal of the yellow stream, for I noticed an identical stream parallel to the one I rode flowing in the opposite direction.

I was impatient to reach the tunnel. I remembered a spiritual law which states that wherever one places the attention, one will be. I closed my eyes and imagined that I was standing at the tunnel's entrance. Seconds later I opened my eyes to discover that the tunnel was actually a massive hole in space, miles in diameter. The yellow current on which I rode was no small stream, but a huge river in which I was only a minute speck.

The yellow current carried me through the tunnel and into a world of brilliant yellow light. I leapt off the current, which continued to flow higher and higher into the sky.

I was greeted by a being clothed in a yellow robe. I knew

in my heart that this was the Guardian of Citrine. The Guardian's head was almost entirely covered by the oversized hood of the robe. Although I could not determine whether the Guardian was male or female, I caught glimpses of dark brown skin beneath the yellow hood.

Citrine led me past several golden domes. They were intensely beautiful, and I wondered what was inside of them.

They are traps, *warned Citrine telepathically,* Do not give them any attention!

Yet the domes were so beautiful and inviting, that I began to wonder what was illusion and what was reality. My heart told me to walk the path where the light and sound was most pure and intense; that way I would be safe. My curiosity about the domes faded when I realized the challenge of this exercise: the path of greatest light and sound was no wider than a razor's edge.

When we finally passed the domes, Citrine and I were met by my spiritual master, who is known by many names but is commonly called "Harold." I wasn't surprised to see him there. I welcomed his presence in this land where the line between illusion and reality was so narrow. Because of the brightness and abundance of pure yellow light, one could easily think that this place was the ultimate world, the true Heaven itself. But I knew that it was only a reflection.

Harold invited us to sit in a circle along with several other individuals. Then he stepped back to join two others who stood in silence a short distance beyond the circle. Although their faces were hidden inside the hoods of their robes, the light of their beings could not be contained, and seeped through the seams of their garments. It appeared that they wished to go unnoticed, though I couldn't help wondering who they were.

They are Gemstone Masters, *Citrine said telepathically when the Guardian saw me watching them.* You will learn more about them later.

Then Michael arrived and joined the circle, and I easily and swiftly slipped into Citrine's aura.

This discussion has a focus: to inform the people of Earth of my nature. Michael, I believe you have several questions.

"Would you begin by briefly describing your effects on the Earth human?" Michael asked.

It may be difficult to be brief.

I, as Citrine, assure the physical body—and, indeed, all the bodies—that it is all right to accept the yellow ray. In other words, I prepare all aspects of an individual to receive a greater amount of yellow ray. This is important, since the yellow ray in significant amounts is somewhat foreign to the physical body.

Once the body is prepared for the yellow ray, I act like a magnet to draw the yellow ray to it. The yellow ray flows to the physical body through all the inner bodies from the place where the ray splits from the pure white light and sound.

All of Citrine's effects support this purpose of preparing people for the yellow ray.

Citrine does not actually carry the yellow ray. Instead, I act as a magnet which draws the ray into the physical body. The crystalline matrix of Citrine is not strong enough to actually contain the high vibratory rate of the yellow ray. It is not strong enough to protect the ray from the coarse vibratory rate of the physical Earth world. To compensate, I carry the sound aspect of the yellow ray more strongly that the light aspect.

Citrine is not a very powerful gemstone, but it is a plentiful one. It exists simply in order to make the light and sound of the yellow ray available to the masses.

The Early Years of Citrine

Citrine is one of the vibratory rates that was brought to the planet along with the other original color-ray-bearing crystals. At that time, the Earth's vibratory rate was not able to accept an amount of yellow ray equal to that of the other color rays. Therefore, only a small amount of the true yellow-ray-bearing gemstone was planted.

You see, my mission was, and still is, to prepare the Earth and its people for the power of the gemstone that bears the yellow ray. That gemstone is currently very rare.

During the Age of Lemuria, Citrine grew up through the soil like clear Quartz did, although it was not as plentiful. Citrine was kept in people's homes, but was not worn.

In the Age of Atlantis, Citrine was used mainly for its communication abilities and its capacity to act as a searchlight.

When used properly, Citrine had the ability to make contact with extraterrestrials. When Citrine crystals were placed in a certain configuration, they sent impulses into space. The purpose of these impulses was to establish contact with those individuals who had placed their identification codes within one or more of the Citrine crystals.

Citrine was also used by extraterrestrials to keep records of their visits. They would place patterns of Citrine crystals in the Earth to mark where they had landed and where they should return. These patterns identified places where the travelers were welcome. They also contained information on what they had done in a certain area and how the people there had reacted to them.

Citrine was also used in these patterns to act as searchlights or beacons. They served a purpose similar to that of landing lights on an airport runway.

Although the general public of Atlantis was not aware of such things, some Atlanteans discovered the patterns of Citrine laid by the extraterrestrials. These Atlanteans formed their own patterns and were quite effective in attracting spacecraft to their areas.

I only mention this because I feel that it might be fascinating to your people. I also wish to emphasize the fact that crystals are tools, and that their functions go far beyond simply being objects of beauty.

Even during the Age of Atlantis, I worked to prepare people for the yellow ray. That purpose has been mine since the very beginning. The yellow ray prepares one for the coming of greater spirituality.

Every single one of my effects is related to my purpose of preparing people for a greater flow of yellow ray. My communication abilities prepared people by making them realize there were individuals living beyond the Earth planet. In this way, they recognized that something greater existed.

When Atlantis was destroyed, there was a disruption in the state of consciousness on the planet. Citrine's power was transformed. I am no longer the beacon or the communicator I once was. Now I search for disharmonies within the body, and like a beacon, I highlight these areas.

Still, there is something peculiar to the vibratory rate of Citrine that makes it easily seen from beyond the Earth's atmosphere. However, people should not expect to be contacted by an extraterrestrial if they wear just one or two strands of Citrine, or even if they place a large amount of Citrine crystals in their backyard and wait all night. My beacon power has greatly waned. On the other hand, if people want to experiment, they could wear eight or ten strands of Citrine and place their attention on their hearing. The most effective time to do this would be at dawn or dusk, when the sun's energy would not interfere. This might enable them to develop a communication with other individuals beyond the Earth planet.

By the way, you have the power to screen visitors by declaring that only those with honorable intentions are invited into your area.

Citrine Today

My purpose for the planet is the same as it is for the human. I simply prepare the aura of the planet for a greater force of yellow ray. The planet and its people will soon have to accept a greater amount of yellow ray, because that is part of their evolution. In other words, sometime in your evolution you will have to accept more yellow ray, and Citrine can help you to prepare for it.

The color rays are not equally balanced on the Earth. The balance is not equal on any planet, although on another planet it may be a different color ray that is most deficient. For example, on another planet there may be a lack of the red ray; and on that planet there might be a gemstone whose mission it is to prepare the people for a greater flow of the red ray. The particular balance of color rays found on any planet is determined by the needs of its people. It is determined by the lessons they must learn, the strengths they must gain, and the levels of awareness they must attain.

At death, when people's physical eyes close for the last time, they open inner eyes to behold a world of brilliant light. If they are not accustomed to consciously traveling beyond their physical bodies, they are often so taken by this light that they do not hear the sound.

People's fear of death can be greatly calmed, resolved, or even removed if they are able to glimpse beyond the veil of death. Then the inner sound they will hear and the light they will see will become familiar. Citrine can help an individual become comfortable, first with the sound and then with the light.

The crystalline matrix of Citrine is designed to carry the

sound of the yellow ray in such a way that it is more easily heard than the sounds carried by other color-ray-bearing gemstones. Sound is equally as important to life as light is; but the sound is often difficult to hear among the noises of daily living. Those who wear Citrine, and continue to do so, will find their ears becoming more familiar with the sound of the life force. This life-giving sound will become more real to them.

The more one listens to the sound, the more one's inner ears will be cleansed, and even more sound will be heard. Then one's ears may open to the different sounds of all the gemstones. Each gemstone carries its own music which is unique and enchantingly beautiful. If people are able to hear or imagine that they hear the sound of a gemstone when they wear it, its powers will increase by many fold. This is because the wearer will become more in tune with that gemstone's vibratory rate.

What I am saying is that Citrine not only prepares one for the yellow ray; it can also prepare one to accept the greatest benefits that any gemstone can give.

Actually, wearing a strand of Citrine along with a strand of any other gemstone will not increase that gemstone's powers. However, the individual's inner sight and hearing will be opened by the Citrine and will prepare the individual to become more in tune with the other gemstone. Then that gemstone will be able to work more effectively for the individual and in greater ways than it did before.

Possession of greater spiritual sight and hearing carries with it a certain responsibility. Before Citrine will work on opening people's spiritual eyes and ears, its light will bring into their lives the lessons they need in order to earn that responsibility. To accomplish this, the Citrine must be rounded in some way. The crystalline form does not have the effect of enhancing spiritual sight and hearing.

In general, the most effective learning occurs when lessons come from every direction and are somewhat unpredictable. When lessons are predictable, people will often find loopholes or ways to avoid the lessons. Light reflects off of Citrine spheres in a predictable way. Therefore, spheres will not be as effective as the rounded—yet irregular—form you call "chips," since light reflects off of chips in an unpredictable way.

The faceted form of Citrine can also be effective for this purpose. Faceted Citrine gemstones would have to be mounted in gold and placed around the neck, one next to the other.

However, this would be impractical.

Wearing crystals of pure yellow Citrine will prepare only the physical body to accept a greater amount of yellow ray. However, you are not just a physical body. Those who wear the rounded forms of Citrine have, in effect, graduated from the crystalline form. They have realized that they are responsible for more than just a physical body, and that more than the physical body must be prepared for the yellow ray.

There is nothing wrong with wearing Citrine crystals. They bring an awareness that there is something more. However, once that awareness dawns, it is only natural that the individual's state of consciousness will be ready to graduate to a rounded form of the crystal. Then the gemstone will work in areas beyond the physical. It will teach people about the worlds that lie within them. Wearing crystals is a necessary step, but it is not the ultimate. The physical state is not the ultimate. There is something more, something greater. In fact, there is much more.

Crystals are just stepping-stones. Wearing gemstones in the rounded form will cause an individual's state of consciousness to grow and expand. This expansion of awareness will then lead people to appreciate greater ways that the crystalline form can be used. They will realize how important the crystalline form actually is, and what a wonderful tool it is for physical applications.

Once the wearers of the rounded form realize the potential of the crystalline form, use of the crystalline form will lead them to greater physical technologies. These new technologies will then provide people with more time or the right conditions to develop even greater states of consciousness. These greater states will then be supported by the rounded form.

I find this relationship between the crystalline form and the rounded form of gemstones very interesting, indeed.

"How does Citrine specifically affect the physical body?"

I am able to highlight or identify areas of disharmony on the body. When worn alone, I can focus the body's attention on these areas. If the Citrine is worn along with a strand of another gemstone that can affect the disharmonious areas, I will focus that gemstone's energy specifically upon these areas.

If Citrine is used for this purpose, it need only be worn along with the other gemstone for a few days. Then it could be worn for one or two days once every two to four weeks, depending on how rapidly the changes are occurring or how quickly you want them to occur.

Wherever Citrine is placed on the body, it has a stirring effect. This is especially true when it is placed over the energy centers. This means that Citrine will greatly benefit any chakra that is tightly shut, locked or stuck. Its vibratory rate will gently massage the area and stir it open. Some individuals call this stirring effect "unwinding."

If the Citrine is held on or over the body with the left hand, there will be more of a calming, relaxing effect. If held with the right hand, the stirring or unwinding activity will be emphasized, and the area involved will be stimulated to move into proper, natural alignment.

The body is a living organism. It does not want to be out of adjustment, since misalignment cuts off the flow of life force that keeps it alive and gives it spiritual sustenance.

Although they are key ingredients for life, you are sustained by much more than food, water, and air. Your body accepts many energies through the chakras. It cannot live without food, water or air; nor can it live without the energies that flow into the chakras. If all your chakras were tightly shut, you would die.

As the body ages, it grows more out of alignment and—as we all know—it draws closer to death. Citrine can allow the body—at any age—to relax to the point where the life force can rush in, take control of the individual, and move the physical body into a more healthy alignment. With this improved alignment, the life force can continue to enter the physical body at the higher rate.

Individuals who are particularly sensitive may experience somewhat uncontrollable movements or unwinding as the body reacts to the Citrine's energy and moves it into greater alignment. These movements are usually not uncomfortable. Those who are less sensitive will still experience the alignment, but it will be more gentle and will occur more gradually.

Citrine Therapy

To achieve head and spine alignment, follow this procedure: Lie down and, with your right hand, hold the Citrine on top of your head over the crown chakra. Then gently move your head back and forth or in a circular motion. This will help to relax your muscles, stretch them, and make them more supple. Let your mind relax and let go of thoughts. Feel the movement in your head and neck, and follow it. Let your head move as it wishes.

Soon your movements will be guided by the Citrine's energy. It may seem like the gemstone has taken control; your head, neck, shoulders, and back will begin to move, stretch and twist. Once they seem to be moving on their own, you can remove the Citrine from your head; but keep it somewhere on your body if you want the unwinding movements to continue.

When held at the crown chakra, Citrine's energy will flow down the spine and then back up the sides of the spine to collect in the neck and head. The spontaneous movement of the head, neck, shoulders, and back will only begin when enough of this energy is collected. This should occur within minutes. The more deficient or blocked the yellow ray is in an individual, the longer this will take. Some individuals may need two strands of Citrine, but it is best to try one strand first.

If the Citrine has been on your head for a while, and then you remove it, you may notice that your head feels heavier, even though the weight of the gemstone has been removed. If you replace the Citrine, the head may feel lighter again. This effect is caused by my vibratory rate and the effect of the yellow ray on the body.

This therapy will work better and more quickly if you prepare for it by wearing Citrine beforehand, perhaps even for several days. However, with those individuals who are more sensitive or flexible and not as stuck or rigid, it will work even without this preparation.

Individuals may try this therapy on one another. Therapists may also wish to incorporate Citrine into their work. When practicing this therapy on someone else, follow the same basic procedure as described above. Hold the individual's head in your hands. With the Citrine in your right hand, gently move the patients head until the Citrine energy seems to start directing your hands. At that point, allow the Citrine energy to do its work.

It is important to trust your feelings and to trust Citrine. Since Citrine is naturally aware of disharmonies in the body and can see the entire body's condition, it will only initiate changes that the body can handle.

Nevertheless, you can regulate the power of Citrine by transferring it to your left hand whenever you wish to slow the changes down.

After the Citrine is removed, the body will tend to follow its old patterns and will eventually fall back out of adjustment. This tendency can be inhibited if the individual keeps the Citrine somewhere in the aura, ideally around the neck.

If you have chronic structural imbalances of the neck and head, it will be best to keep the Citrine at the top of the head for as long as possible. You could wear it under a hat or fastened around a bun of hair.

* * *

Although the yellow ray is one of the seven color rays that splits from the pure white light of Spirit, it is the only color that reflects the realms of God and the source of all life. Because I reflect the source of life, when I am held at the crown chakra I enhance the connection between the life force and the physical body.

A different effect occurs when Citrine is placed over the brow chakra. The yellow ray in its pure form meets the consciousness of the individual at the brow chakra. I clear away obstructions in this energy center and make the body aware of the yellow ray. I also act like a magnet. I attract the yellow ray to the body, and I attract the individual's awareness to this chakra.

When the individual's awareness and the pure yellow ray come together, they acknowledge each other. Once acknowledged, the yellow ray becomes a part of the individual.

This will occur regardless of the condition of the brow chakra. If it is closed or stuck, the yellow ray will still shine through the door to make the connection in the physical body. Of course, if it is open and functioning normally, one's awareness of the yellow ray can be much greater.

If you hold Citrine over your brow chakra, you will know that your awareness has connected with the yellow ray when you can easily imagine the color yellow, when you can see it on the inner screen of your mind with your eyes closed, or when you can distinctly hear its sound current.

Your entire physical body can greatly benefit from this treatment if you use the following technique to distribute the yellow ray throughout your body: Once you become aware of the yellow ray, imagine that your attention is like a freight train that has been filled with yellow light. Then move your attention to each part of your body and allow it to deposit some of the yellow cargo as it moves.

You may find it helpful to move your hand over your body and place your attention on the area covered by your hand as it moves. As long as the Citrine is on your brow chakra, and your awareness remains connected with the yellow ray, the vibratory rate of the yellow ray will be deposited anywhere in the body on which you place your attention.

* * *

"How does Citrine affect the emotions?" Michael asked.

All emotions are the result of something that I call a "cause point." This is something that initiates an emotional response. My function is to shine my spotlight not on the cause point, but on the "effect point," specifically the first effect point. The first effect point is the immediate mental reaction or first thought you have directly before you have an emotional response.

For example, a cause point might occur when your wife cleans the sink with your toothbrush. The first effect point would be your thought, "Hey, I have to brush my teeth with that!" This would be followed by your emotional response—probably anger.

I shine my spotlight on this first thought or effect point. This spotlight gives you a clearer view of what is happening before you respond emotionally.

If you were wearing Citrine when this cause point occurred, your first effect point would be highlighted and, in effect, brightened up. Then, instead of having a negative thought, you might think, "Big deal. I can either wash out my toothbrush or get a new one." You might also think, "Well, perhaps she had an overwhelming desire to clean the sink, but didn't have a scrub brush." Such thoughts would tend to defuse an angry reaction before it occurs.

I take no responsibility for the emotion or the strength of the emotion you express. I simply highlight your first effect point. With the awareness of the first effect point, your emotional response becomes more controllable.

By the way, you might still choose to become angry just to convey to your wife that you never want her to use your toothbrush to clean the sink again.

Emotions often become out of balance in those who have a deficiency of the yellow ray. If these individuals wear Citrine, they will become aware—although subconsciously, perhaps—of an emotional balance point within themselves. In this way, Citrine can greatly benefit those who react in emotional extremes or who lack an emotionally balanced nature.

* * *

"I don't understand how color ray deficiencies can occur, if indeed the color rays are essential for life," commented Michael.

Each of the inner bodies has energy centers, just as the physical body does. Ideally, all the chakras in all the inner bodies line up, one on top of the other, over the chakras in the physical body. The color rays of the life force flow from their source to the physical body through the chakras of the inner bodies.

Unfortunately, no one is perfectly balanced on all levels. One chakra might be shifted to the left; another might be shifted a little to the right. These shifts occur for many reasons, including various experiences, imbalances, hang-ups, blockages, or diseases. If a chakra in an inner body moves too far out of alignment, the flow of the color rays is affected. The corresponding chakras in the bodies "below" that inner body will suffer from a life force and color ray deficiency.

"There is a belief among some people on my planet that each color ray of the life force enters the body through a different chakra—that red enters the base chakra, with the other rays following the order of the rainbow up the body," Michael said.

Actually, all the colors enter each chakra. However, there is a color that enters each chakra more strongly than the other colors. It is difficult to give you a universal answer to this question at this point in history. This is because the colors that predominantly enter certain chakras are moving to different chakras. In other words, the color rays that once entered certain chakras most forcefully no longer do so. This change is a result of the transitions people are now undergoing.

As people are evolving toward greater spirituality, energies are moving up, away from the base and sex chakras. These two chakras are still very important and are crucial to life; they are not becoming ignored by the light and sound rays. However, they are being nourished only to the extent that they can maintain their flow and therefore support the higher chakras.

Whenever a color ray enters a chakra, that area of the body is enlivened. The base chakra symbolizes the grounded or physical state of consciousness that people are moving away from.

The stomach chakra has always accepted the yellow ray as its primary color ray, and will continue to do so. However, the stomach chakra is no longer as far down on the body as it once was. In some people it has already moved closer to the stomach organ; in others it is in the process of moving up; and, unfortunately, in others the change has not yet begun to take place.

The Earth is in a transition of great magnitude, depth, and significance. For the transition to be well-established, these changes must occur slowly.

* * *

To cleanse Citrine, all that is necessary is to place it in the sun for several hours after a brief rinse in hot or cold running water.

Citrine Tomorrow

I will continue my mission of preparing people for the yellow ray for centuries. It is as though my work will never be done: As soon as some individuals are prepared, others will be born who will also need the experience of being prepared.

My mission will stay the same. However, as people change and grow, the effects of Citrine that support my mission may change. How my effects will change is hard to predict, because it is hard to anticipate how people will choose to grow, how fast they will grow, and in what direction.

Before we end this discussion, I would like to say that you do not need Citrine to prepare yourself for the yellow ray. You do not need gemstones for anything. However, if you have a goal and any wisdom at all, you will use the tools that Spirit brings to your awareness. The tools that Spirit makes available to you are there to help you attain your goal.

If you want to achieve your goal in this lifetime, I highly recommend that you use the tools with which you feel most in harmony. I suggest that you use the tools that feel most comfortable to you for the particular space and time that you currently occupy.

I, as Citrine, am available to assist. I am available to give. The gift has only to be accepted.

"Is there anything else you wish to share?" asked Michael.

It makes no difference whether I am male or female, who I am, where I come from, or what I look like. My purpose has nothing to do with my personality. You should not place attention on these details; when my experience of being a Gemstone Guardian is completed, and I have learned the lessons I need to learn from it, another individual will step into my place. Another individual will become the Guardian of Citrine, because the lessons and experiences that go along with this job will be needed by that individual.

This transition can occur at any time. Therefore, who I am is immaterial. After all, you do not wear the Guardian; you wear the gemstone.

* * *

The next Guardian you will meet will be the one whose duty it is to experience and learn all the lessons required of being the caretaker of the gemstone Aquamarine.

Thank you for meeting me here.

I slipped out of Citrine's aura easily. The Guardian immediately readjusted the bright yellow hood to cover his or her head more completely, knowing that I would probably want to sneak a look.

Harold moved into the circle and motioned for everyone to stand. Then, without hesitation, he walked away. I knew that he was going to the world of Aquamarine or to the place where we would find the Guardian of that gemstone. He did not look back. We all knew that if we wanted to meet Aquamarine, we had to follow him without delay.

14
AQUAMARINE

Harold led us out of the land of golden yellow and through a tunnel of enormous, transparent veils that shimmered with iridescence as we passed. From there we entered a lush countryside where the colors of the thick grass and the abundant trees, flowers and streams glowed brightly. The landscape before us was unusually rich and seemed to vibrate with life.

We walked over a gentle hill and came to a small river. There we sat in a semi-circle in front of Harold. After a few moments he walked behind us and out of sight. I could still feel his presence, but now my attention turned to the melodic sound of the water tumbling against the rocks in the riverbed. Soon I realized that the air itself also had a melody—a vibrant, golden hum. The more I listened, the louder it became.

Then a woman approached us. Her light blue aura was so brilliant, that it seemed to be made of the gemstone Aquamarine itself. The Guardian appeared to be in her twenties; she had light blonde hair, which was shoulder length and very thick. Her eyes were pale blue.

She looked at me and gave me the telepathic message that she would not speak until everyone could hear her. We both understood that it was not until I entered her aura that my physical voice could speak, word for word, what she wished to say.

Greetings to all who have come and to all who may read of this experience in the future. Each of you can come to this place and be here for this discourse at any time. Time is flexible here, and those who live here are not bound by it.

My work is on the inner aspects. I have little direct effect on the physical body. I know the inner worlds well, and my mission is to share this awareness with those who are in harmony with Aquamarine.

Each of my children, each Aquamarine crystal, reflects the inner ocean—that vast area of liquidity, knowledge, and wisdom within each individual. I connect people with this inner ocean, so that they may become aware of its knowledge and wisdom.

My work is subtle and quiet. Rarely do I rage in a storm. I do so only when the one who is attracted to Aquamarine needs to be cleared of the dross that inhibits my mission and stands between the individual and the ocean within.

I have been manifested by Spirit as a source of spiritual nourishment and nutrition. I bring upliftment, but not in the way that Lavender does. My effect occurs directly as a result of the awareness I bring. This is an awareness of the truth and the reality of every level of existence: physical, emotional, mental, and spiritual.

I also open the awareness to the ways in which the realities or truths on these levels seemingly conflict with one another. I bring awareness of these paradoxes, which exist only because the laws of nature are different on each of these planes. Realities are different, the focus is different, the state of consciousness is different on each of these levels.

The Early Years of Aquamarine

I appeared on the planet Earth, not just as a product of the Earth's evolution, but as the result of a grand evolution which occurs on all levels.

First I was manifested in the land of pure Spirit as an idea. Then I manifested on the mental level, then on the emotional level, and then in the physical world.

The area of pure Spirit is the fountainhead of the life force. It is also the source of another stream of energy, which also flows through the mental and emotional worlds to the physical.

As it flows through these worlds, it changes color and consistency. In the mental world, this stream is often referred to as the Healing Waters, the Nectar of the Gods, or the Fountain of Youth. This stream sometimes flows underground and at other points gurgles to the surface; some of its springs are held sacred.

In the emotional world, it becomes somewhat more material. The people there fashion it into bowls in which they keep precious things. It is also worn as jewelry and made into ornaments that people look upon to remind them of the source of life.

When this stream finally reaches the physical world, it manifests as the gemstone you call Aquamarine. A crystal or gemstone is the only physical manifestation that can contain the intense force of light and sound characteristic of my vibratory rate.

Although both I and the life force originate in the land of pure Spirit, the life force originates in the very heart of God. When the life force flows through the inner worlds to the physical, it can return to its source through its own momentum. I do not have the same momentum. I can only return to my source when those who own and wear Aquamarine are uplifted, grow, and unfold.

Therefore, it is important that I am worn by as many people as will accept me. I will stir within them memories of my source. These memories are the first steps toward greater spiritual awareness.

Although Aquamarine had already manifested in other areas of the physical world, it was not available on Earth until there were people who needed it. Aquamarine was not manifested there until the people had lost their natural connection with their inner worlds and needed a reminder. When the Aquamarine was to be planted on Earth, certain messengers from the emotional world directed my vibratory rate toward the Earth; actually, it was shot like a laser beam.

The planet willingly accepted Aquamarine. The Guardian of the Earth understood its importance and knew of its life-giving qualities and its ability to increase the awareness of all living entities. Since the Earth wore the Aquamarine before its people did, this greater awareness was first experienced by the planet.

During the Age of Lemuria, people wore the crystalline form. Because of its lack of brilliance, Aquamarine was not considered valuable.

During the Age of Atlantis, I had strong physical-healing powers and was very plentiful. Since my powers were subtle, the royalty and rulers saw Aquamarine as a gem appropriate for the masses. Because my color resembles that of the ocean, people thanked the ocean for my existence, as though I came from there. They even wore me during their ocean voyages for safety and good luck. They did not understand that my color was meant to be a reminder of the ocean within themselves.

Most of the Aquamarine disappeared beneath the surface when Atlantis was destroyed. Over the years, legends grew up that were based on memories of Aquamarine's powers and abundance. It then became a stone of mystery, valuable and desired by those who collected riches.

Aquamarine Today

As the seasons have passed and times have changed, my focus has shifted away from direct physical healing. I now promote inner awareness.

In order to experience greater physical healing, people today must focus on their inner worlds. People often think that their physical diseases have physical causes, when in fact, physical diseases actually have inner causes.

Although my work is subtle, Aquamarine is more powerful than it appears.

It is the vibratory rate of Aquamarine that is most important. Just having the Aquamarine vibratory rate in one's aura will begin to open one's awareness on all levels. However, it is also true that the presence of deep color in the Aquamarine increases its strength by many fold.

To more fully understand Aquamarine's effects, we can compare the individual to a mansion with many rooms. The floors of the mansion are like the inner levels of the individual; and each floor contains many rooms. Aquamarine works to open more and more windows and doors in the rooms of this mansion. (By the way, the doors and windows I open are not the chakras.)

When the doors to these rooms open, my vibratory rate turns on the lights within them. Then I move through the mansion, turning on more lights in more and more rooms. In other words, my light and sound shine on your inner bodies and bring increased awareness in more and more areas. This process gives you a greater insight and a fuller comprehension of who you are and what your potential is.

Now, when the awareness opens, the truth that is revealed may be too much for the physical mind to accept. This is because the conscious memory opens much more slowly than the unconscious or the inner awareness does.

Because I open the awareness so powerfully, many people will not feel comfortable wearing Aquamarine. This discomfort will occur in individuals who are not yet ready to accept any more truth about themselves than they are already trying to digest. These people will want to take off the Aquamarine. If they do not remove it, their bodies will become fidgety.

As an individual becomes more comfortable with the increased inner awareness, this period of resistance, fidgeting, and crankiness will pass. It will pass, because the awareness also brings greater balance, control, and self-understanding.

When individuals gain a greater understanding of themselves, doors will begin to open for them on all levels. They will start to have a better understanding of life, and this will allow them to work in greater harmony with themselves and with all of life. Relationships will also become stronger and more harmonious. If one belongs to a spiritual path, one's understanding might grow beyond the limits of one's religion. One might then be compelled to look elsewhere for spiritual succor and sustenance. In other words, one may want to look for a spiritual path that always offers another step to take.

Aquamarine will benefit most those who are on a spiritual path of awakening. It will assist those who want to know more about themselves, their destiny, and their potential. I will be especially beneficial for those who have reached apparent plateaus in their spiritual unfoldment, for I can awaken them to new vistas and allow them to grow to much higher levels.

I have patience; I am gentle, calm, and understanding. At the same time, I am painfully honest, truthful, and clear. Yet my patience regulates my honesty. For example, when I am worn, I show my wearers only enough about themselves to spur their growth. When this growth raises their vibratory rate, I show them more. Again they will grow and reach yet a higher vibratory rate, and again I will show them more.

I will continue this cycle for as long as I am worn. The amount of truth I show people at each stage is only limited by the depth of my true color. Therefore, the stronger my natural color is, the more I can give.

* * *

Aquamarine is found in varying shades of blue-green and light blue. The blue-green variety has unique qualities in addition to the ones I have described.

The blue-green Aquamarine has a stronger physical-healing effect than the light blue variety. Aquamarine's vibratory rate uplifts. When my vibratory rate is combined with the color green, which supports physical healing, this upliftment focuses on the physical body. Its effects are greatest on any organ through which substances, especially liquids, flow. These organs include the heart, liver, spleen, and bladder. If blue-green Aquamarine is worn long enough, the upliftment it offers will transform the organ.

For this purpose, Aquamarine should be worn around the neck. Then it will focus on uplifting the area of the body that has the lowest vibratory rate.

The blue-green variety also has the property of easing physical and emotional pain, especially the pain of grief. This effect occurs as I brighten people's auras. When the aura is brightened, one's outlook is also brightened, because one must look through one's aura.

"Aquamarine is often treated to enhance its color. How does this treatment affect your properties?" inquired Michael.

Aquamarine's color is sometimes enhanced with heat and sometimes with molecular bombardment, a process which you call irradiation.

There is nothing wrong with heat treatment. It will not inhibit my mission; but nor will it make my vibratory rate any stronger. Heat-treated Aquamarine only looks stronger because its color has been darkened.

Irradiation of Aquamarine is a sad occurrence, for it results in the death of the crystal. It destroys the life, or the vibratory rate, of the gemstone and replaces it with an extremely disharmonious vibratory rate.

When irradiated Aquamarine is worn, this disharmony will be thrown into the aura. Because Aquamarine's focus is on the inner aspects of the individual, the destructive emanations of irradiated Aquamarine will affect the mind first. It will disrupt mental processes, viewpoints, and concepts, and it will distort one's view of reality. Then it will disrupt the mind's harmony and relationship—first with itself and then with the emotions and the physical body. Then the emotions will also become disrupted and distorted.

* * *

During the Age of Atlantis, Aquamarine in crystalline form was strong medicine for the physical body. The crystals used for this purpose were two to five inches long.

At the destruction of the continent, nearly every crystal was broken or buried. The Aquamarine crystals that formed subsequently, and that are available today, contain a different vibratory rate. They do not have the same powerful physical-healing effect as did the crystals of old.

Today, Aquamarine crystals are best kept in people's homes. It is most effective to keep them in that part of the home where you spend most of your time—for example, near the bed or in the office where you work. The Aquamarine will lighten the atmosphere and make the air more vibrant, clean, and pure. It will also bring healing energy to the room. This healing energy will be focused toward the physical level. This is because the Aquamarine crystal, like any crystal, focuses its effect on the physical level for the benefit of the Earth.

The energy radiated by the Aquamarine crystal will be felt; and it will have a positive effect on any individual who spends some time in the crystal's aura. A three-inch crystal will radiate energy in a radius of several feet.

When the crystal is cut into any rounded form, its attention immediately focuses on the wearer's inner aspects. This is the form that supports my mission for the human.

The key to Aquamarine's effectiveness is mass. The greater the mass worn, the stronger will be the effects. Therefore, a strand of rounded Aquamarine worn around the neck will be much more powerful than a single crystal or faceted gemstone. This is simply because, in order to surround the neck, a much larger quantity of Aquamarine will automatically be used.

The faceted form will not be of much help to people today. In order to be worn, a faceted gemstone must be mounted, contained, or confined in a metal. Whenever a gemstone or crystal is contained in a metal such as gold or silver, its effects are also confined and become very limited. If the Aquamarine vibratory rate is worn in a form uninhibited by metal, it will have no limitations. It will function in the full spectrum of its capabilities and will touch every part of the wearer's inner aspects.

Nevertheless, I would like to mention a way in which a certain type of faceted Aquamarine can be used beneficially. To practice this technique, one must use a fine-quality, Emerald-cut or rectangular-cut Aquamarine weighing at least two or three carats. Be sure that the Aquamarine you use has not been heat-treated or irradiated.

Begin by wearing a strand of Aquamarine uninhibited by metal, for several days. Then gaze into the uppermost flat surface, or the "table," of the faceted Aquamarine as though you were looking into a crystal ball. Allow your mind to wander. This technique will bring an awareness and understanding of what is occurring in your emotional and mental levels; or it might allow you to become consciously aware of what the Aquamarine necklace is highlighting on those levels.

Before you try this technique, be sure that you are open, receptive, and ready for truth. This technique will work. If you are not ready for this information, you will not accept it or believe it to be true. You might even deny what the Aquamarine has shown you about yourself, or you might deny that this procedure even works. But it will work, even for those who are not clairvoyant.

I will explain the mechanics of how this technique works.

The necklace has been filling your brain and inner levels with vibratory rate ever since you started wearing it. The faces of the faceted Aquamarine are directing its vibratory rate out through the table of the gemstone. When you gaze into the faceted gem, its vibratory rate enters your eyes and touches your brain. This vibratory rate then connects with the vibratory rate coming from the Aquamarine around your neck. Once these two vibratory rates are connected, the truths that the Aquamarine necklace have been unfolding in your inner worlds will come into your conscious awareness.

* * *

I brighten and fill people's inner aspects with greater light and sound. This allows them to become aware of things that might be hiding in the shadows and recesses of the mind, emotions, and memory.

It is up to my wearers to regulate how much truth they want to see. They can do this by regulating the amount of

Aquamarine unrestricted by metal that they wear. Clasps do not have an inhibiting effect, because clasps do not encase Aquamarine spheres like the prongs of a ring encase a faceted gem.

To experience my effects, one can wear Aquamarine around the head, neck, arm, or waist.

Everyone will react differently to Aquamarine, because everyone accepts truth in different ways and to different degrees. To some, the truth may seem harsh and brutal. These individuals might become rather cranky as they resist the truth, but they will only be resisting themselves and their own growth.

After a while, these individuals should relax. This relaxation will be due partly to the vibratory rate of Aquamarine's color. The deeper the natural color is, the stronger this relaxing influence will be. My color helps people to let go of their resistance and stop holding themselves back. When people relax, they can accept the truth more easily, because it can flow more easily into their conscious awareness.

Aquamarine Therapy

I do not directly heal the physical body. However, when a person's state of consciousness is uplifted, his or her body will change. In some cases, when this upliftment of consciousness occurs, the forces that caused a certain physical condition will cease to exist.

Aquamarine can also give you the awareness of what has caused a specific condition. People often place the blame for their conditions on something in the environment or on something someone else did. It is easy, for example, for people to blame a certain cancer-causing agent or some chemical that they ate or breathed.

However, the truth is that if it were not for your own inner patterns, circumstances, and state of consciousness, you would not have developed your condition.

In your inner worlds you have set up the circumstances that have brought about your condition. You have done this simply because you need the experience of having your condition in order to grow and to master the lessons that accompany that condition.

Every physical situation is the result of inner conditions,

blockages, or patterns. These inner patterns act like signposts. They direct Spirit to lead you to your physical situation, because you, as Soul, need this experience. You need to experience the effects of your creations: what you have caused by certain actions, reactions, thoughts, emotions, or other situations in your past. These actions, etc. create the signposts for Spirit to lead you to the experience of your physical condition.

Let us say, for example, that in this lifetime you are a miner and that you contract lung disease. It will be easy to blame the lung disease on your occupation. You might blame it on management for poor working conditions, or on your father and grandfather for being miners and convincing you to uphold the family tradition.

However, the only thing for which you can honestly blame others is being the vehicles through which Spirit worked to give you the experience that you have set up for yourself.

The reason you are having this experience is that you must eventually take responsibility for the effects you have caused. In other words, you must reap the karma for the signposts you have created throughout your lives. This experience of lung disease—or any experience—could be resolving all kinds of karma. At the same time, it is giving Soul the opportunity for its mind, emotions, and physical body to learn the lessons involved in resolving, curing, or perhaps even dying from this disease.

You can use Aquamarine to help understand what these signposts were or what actually caused a particular condition. To do so, place a strand of Aquamarine over the affected area, and keep it there for as long as possible.

The chip form of Aquamarine will be effective for this technique, but may be uncomfortable on the skin. Solve this problem by placing a layer of cotton cheesecloth or thin cotton cloth between the chips and your skin.

If you wish, you could practice this technique at night. At that time, your resistance to truth is lowered, and you can get your answers and gain the awareness needed through the dream state. Write your dreams down in the morning, and interpret them as best you can. It is important to use your own meanings for dream symbols and not those given by someone else. Someone else's symbols and sense of reality will not be as true for you as your own.

There is nothing wrong with telling your dreams to someone

else, because that person's viewpoint may add to yours. However, do not accept another's interpretation of your dream, unless it feels comfortable to you. Only the dreamer has the right and the authority to accurately analyze the meaning of his or her own dreams.

If you use this technique, you should write down your night dreams, daydreams, and intuitive insights. If you don't, you will forget them. They will be harder than usual to remember, because your physical consciousness will resist the knowingness you experience at the time of your dream or insight. Once you know why you have a condition and can acknowledge and accept the reasons, you will be halfway to a cure.

Aquamarine will not remove symptoms; it will help you to understand why you have them.

You can safely place Aquamarine on any part of the body, including the head, for as long as it feels comfortable. The longer you wear it, the clearer your awareness of the reasons for a particular condition will become.

Pregnant women can also place an Aquamarine strand over the uppermost portion of the uterus. This will help them come into contact and become more aware of the Soul that will enter the body of the fetus body when it is born. If they sleep with the Aquamarine over the uterus, they may even dream of previous lifetimes they shared with their soon-to-be-born child.

Any physical-healing effects that people attribute to Aquamarine are only memories of the effects I had in crystalline form during the Age of Atlantis.

However, it is true that when I am worn in rounded form around the neck, there may be enough mass to strengthen the movement of fluids in the body. I do not strengthen the heart to pump the fluids or strengthen the kidneys to process them. I only affect the charge of the fluids and enliven their movement.

I have no other physical effects. If I did, I could not focus as strongly as I do on the inner bodies. With focus there is strength. This principle is well illustrated by a laser's powerful focus and its resulting force.

My focus is on inner awareness. The by-product of greater inner awareness can be improved physical health. This is similar to how the by-product of my vibratory rate on the physical body is enhanced movement of fluids. In other words, this enhanced movement is not my focus; it is just a side effect.

* * *

There is another way to use Aquamarine. This involves focusing its ability to bring greater awareness to an activity or creation of your choice. I say "use" Aquamarine, verses "wear" it, since one wears jewelry. Aquamarine is not just jewelry; it is a tool, and one uses a tool.

Let us say that you are an engineer, and that you are designing some type of mechanism. If you wear a strand of Aquamarine around your neck and are willing to become awake to the inner levels where ideas, thoughts, and inspirations are born, the Aquamarine will open your awareness to the possible designs appropriate for the mechanism you are working on.

This technique can be helpful if you are experiencing problems with the design. The Aquamarine can give you a broader viewpoint, which might then give you the insights needed to solve these problems. It can also help you move past creative plateaus or blocks.

This technique will work for anyone who deals with the creative flow, including healers. For example, it will be useful for a physician who has a patient whose symptoms or condition is unclear or not responding to therapy. Aquamarine can help if the physician is unsure about what to do next.

The next time the patient in question has an appointment, both the patient and the physician should wear a strand of Aquamarine. The physician should explain the powers of Aquamarine and why they are wearing it. Then both the patient and the physician should focus their attention on opening their awareness to what should be done for the patient.

When Aquamarine is used for any of these applications, it should not be worn continually. If it is, the focus will be lost. For example, artists should only wear the Aquamarine when they are painting. They should remove it if they are disturbed for some reason, such as a need to go to the bathroom, answer the phone, or get a snack. This requires discipline; however, it is necessary to maintain a pure focus—in this case, on the artwork in progress.

Students could wear Aquamarine during a particular class. Of course, it would be foolish to wear Aquamarine for more than two classes in a row, because the focus would be lost as the awareness was opened in too many different directions.

Remember, focus is the key to enlivening Aquamarine's

greatest power and effectiveness.

* * *

I am eternally young. I bring youthful energy wherever I go. It is a characteristic of youth to want to know things, to understand, grow, and have greater awareness.

It is my mission to help people evolve and unfold. In the physical world this often means helping people to complete certain cycles within a physical body. In no way does this mean that I hasten the death of the physical body. On the contrary: when death comes near I can lighten the load, shine the way, and make the experience calmer and less fearful. Therefore, one of the greatest gifts one can give to a dying individual is an Aquamarine necklace. It will help to ease the transition.

Aquamarine Tomorrow

There is no end to the growth and achievement of greater awareness. Therefore, there will be no end to Aquamarine on this planet. As long as there are people on this planet, there will be Aquamarine.

As the awareness of people all over the planet expands, people will recognize those things on the planet that are powerful forces for healing. People will become aware of gemstones. Gemstones are the strongest, most concentrated containers of the healing force, or life force, on this planet. Once people know how to unleash and use this healing energy, they will make huge advances in the fields of medicine and the healing arts, as well as in their own spiritual growth.

Gemstones will accelerate the growth of awareness and spiritual unfoldment. Once you awaken to the powers of the gemstones and use them to accelerate your unfoldment, you will become aware of even greater uses for gemstones. This, in turn, will accelerate your unfoldment even more.

I, as Aquamarine, present a challenge. I present a door through which one can go to see the truth about oneself. Aquamarine is only for those who have the courage to walk through the door and confront themselves. Aquamarine is for those Souls who are brave, whether or not they are consciously aware of it.

I feel that I have said enough. I have not said all, but for now I have said enough.

You must return to the physical world now. Too much work and too much attention out of the physical body is not in balance. Therefore, the next Gemstone Guardian you meet will be one who has a very physical focus. You will know him as the Guardian of Green Tourmaline.

I can introduce him only by name, for we are from two different worlds. Spirit will make sure that you find each other when you are ready to meet him.

"It has been an honor to hear your discourse," said Michael.

It has been a pleasure and a joyful opportunity for me to clarify some misconceptions about Aquamarine. I thank you for this opportunity. It is time that Aquamarine is used on your planet for its proper purpose. It is time that its potential is realized, and that its key of focus is put to use.

In awareness, may the blessings be!

"May the blessings be," Michael replied.

I slipped effortlessly out of her aura. She smiled graciously and very gratefully; I had never seen such pure gratitude before. It was mixed with love and understanding. If Aquamarine teaches these qualities, then she is surely a special gift from the planet to its people.

The listeners remained silent, enjoying the beauty of the countryside. A feeling of companionship, understanding, and love for all life permeated the air.

I looked around and suddenly realized that, ever since Aquamarine had begun to speak, the wildlife had moved closer and closer to our circle. Several deer were grazing close to us and a badger—who had nonchalantly waddled up to the river—drank only a few feet away from where we sat.

Rabbits, squirrels, foxes, birds, and many other woodland creatures had also gathered around us. They appeared to have been listening and enjoying the sweet feeling which radiated from Aquamarine's aura.

I returned to my physical body with reluctance. Yet I drew consolation from the thought that this place exists somewhere within me and—as Aquamarine said when she first began—I can return whenever I wish.

15
GREEN TOURMALINE

I looked within and placed my attention on Tourmaline. Immediately I felt a surge of its powerful energy. Although this energy felt very uncomfortable, I knew I must find its source. Cautiously I allowed the energy to lead me there. Moments later I found myself next to a tall, tropical waterfall.

I stood in a small clearing next to the fall, surrounded by lush jungle foliage. A cloud of green spray rose from a pool at the base of the towering column of water.

There was something unusual about this waterfall. I studied it more carefully and soon realized that the column of water wasn't water at all. It was a Green Tourmaline crystal! And the mist that rose from the pool below wasn't water vapor, but a cloud of Tourmaline's vibratory rate rising into the atmosphere. The pool itself was a seemingly bottomless hole filled with nothing but this mist, which swirled and folded into itself.

Suddenly someone appeared at my side. It was the maroon-robed spiritual master who had accompanied Michael and me during our first meeting with the Gemstone Guardians.

Four others, including Michael, also appeared. Then the Guardian of Tourmaline arrived. He came by a footpath that seemed to lead from behind the waterfall.

The Guardian appeared to be in his fifties. He wore a dark green, long-sleeved robe that hid what seemed to be a tall, slender, and muscular body. His hair was dark forest-green with streaks of gray, and the features of his face were hard and angular. He had light green skin that looked surprising healthy, despite its unusual color.

Then I knew why the spiritual master was there: I personally did not feel in harmony with Green Tourmaline. The presence of the master made me feel protected and sure that I would not become imbalanced by the great power of this Guardian. I had to overcome my reluctance to enter his aura by focusing on completely relaxing; even then it was difficult. Nevertheless, I suddenly found myself within his aura.

I give power and strength to those whose molecular structures have a vibratory rate of a certain nature. Only the male vibratory rate has this nature and is compatible with Green Tourmaline.

It is foolish for women to wear Green Tourmaline alone without the gemstone you call Pink Tourmaline or Rubellite. If a woman wore a necklace of only Green Tourmaline, her masculine nature would eventually overwhelm her feminine nature. One imbalance after another would manifest. Her emotional strength would be crushed, and eventually hormone imbalances would occur. The addition of Pink Tourmaline would cancel out most of Green Tourmaline's power—unfortunately, most of Pink Tourmaline's benefits would also be nullified.

I will strengthen the vibratory rate of every molecule within a man's body.

A man must wear Tourmaline consistently—every day or every night—to experience its greatest healing effects. After wearing a strand of rounded Tourmaline around the neck every day for a month, the effects should be unmistakable.

My mission is to balance the male and help him to reach his full potential. I broaden the viewpoint of any man who wears me and maximize the life force flowing through him.

If a woman wears Green Tourmaline, I will withhold my power. However, I can only do so to a certain degree. I cannot hold back completely.

Green Tourmaline may appear to protect a woman. However, the protective energy that a woman may sense is coming from the Tourmaline itself as it tries to protect her from its own vibratory rate. I will never give a woman the strength I give a man. I am too busy holding back my vibratory rate from her. I do this because I do not wish to imbalance any human. My purpose is to uplift and be beneficial and healing.

Nevertheless, I am a gemstone that must be used with respect, self-discipline, and understanding. I must also be used without ego, vanity, or concepts regarding my effects on women.

"As a Gemstone Guardian, are you aware of all Green Tourmaline, and the way each Tourmaline gemstone is acting with the person wearing it?" Michael asked.

No, I am not. Gemstone Guardians are to gemstones what your brain is to all the cells in your body. Your cells give your brain information about their needs, and your brain directs the life force to the cells as they need it. In a similar way, every Green Tourmaline crystal relays information to me, and I direct life force and nourishment back to each crystal. However, both of these processes occur on an unconscious level.

You do not know what every cell in your body is doing. Generally, your attention is called to particular cells only when they are experiencing some great challenge or disharmony, or when they are trying to accomplish something noble. This is also the case with Gemstone Guardians and the gemstones for which they are responsible.

It is the nature of gemstones to know the one who wears them, just as it is your nature to know the people with whom you live. The longer you live with them, the better you get to know them.

"How does the gemstone get to know its wearer?"

I shall answer this question in simple terms.

Your aura contains all the information about your physical body, emotions, memory, mind, unconscious, and—to a degree—Soul itself. It also contains information about how your non-physical aspects relate to the physical body.

This information is stored in the aura in patterns or sequences of vibratory rate, sequences of light, and varying densities and concentrations of energies. They contain specific information about the past, present, and future. (By future, I mean the potential future as it is being created by conditions in the present. If you change the conditions in the present, you will change your future.)

The energy or vibratory rate that radiates out of a rounded crystal fills the aura and touches these patterns and sequences of information.

With some gemstones, the vibratory rate then bounces back to the gemstone, carrying this information with it. This is how these gemstones learn about the wearer.

Tourmaline is slightly different. Tourmaline in rounded form knows all of its vibratory rate intimately. It is as though every "molecule" of vibratory rate that is thrown into the aura is still a part of the Tourmaline. It still has a connection with the gemstone around your neck.

Essentially, what occurs is that the gemstone around your neck expands itself to the size of your whole aura. It is as though the gemstone itself fills your aura. Its relationship with your aura becomes like your brain's relationship to the cells in your body or a Gemstone Guardian's relationship to the crystals which it is in charge of. The Tourmaline gemstones around your neck know fully and consciously what each "molecule" of their vibratory rate learns when it is in your aura.

The Early Years of Green Tourmaline

Tourmaline crystals are not as old as Quartz crystals, although Tourmaline in all its color manifestations formed as the Earth was forming.

The Green and Pink Tourmaline symbolize the positive and negative forces, and how both of these forces must be present for physical matter to manifest. They also represent the male and female energies, and how both of these energies are required for life to exist. Green Tourmaline is the carrier for the male energy, the north pole, and the positive force. Pink Tourmaline is the carrier of the female energy, the south pole, and the negative force.

The neutral force is the third ingredient required for manifestation. This third force was not strongly manifested in the Tourmaline crystal. Although it is hinted at in clear Tourmaline, it is not carried by it. Besides, there may be no such thing as true clear Tourmaline. If it were chemically analyzed, some molecules of the Green, Pink, or another color would probably be detected.

Clear Tourmaline that contains a small, perhaps unnoticeable, amount of green can be worn by a woman. This form might be dilute enough simply to give strength to her masculine aspect. Still, it is not the ideal vibratory rate for a woman. She should look to the Pink Tourmaline, which works in harmony with her, like the Green Tourmaline works in harmony with men.

During the Ages of Lemuria and Atlantis, my rounded form

was not used. If it were, and men had become aware of its powers, Green Tourmaline would probably have been misused.

Therefore, we should focus on information that will help you to understand my purpose today.

Green Tourmaline Today

The crystalline matrix of Tourmaline was chosen to carry the masculine and feminine energies, because Tourmaline is very strong, resilient, and steadfast. Masculine and feminine energies were contained within crystals, so that the men and women who would eventually inhabit the planet would have an energy source that would make each sex independent and strong.

The masculine and feminine energies are scattered throughout space. Tourmaline crystals in the Earth—even those that are deeply buried—attract these energies. Green Tourmaline acts as the Earth's receiver for the masculine energy. This energy flows toward the crystal, filling the Earth's aura with a defined vortex of masculine energy. Pink Tourmaline draws the feminine energy, although its vortex is different.

I feel that you should know that in the past there were much larger quantities of bright, emerald-green Tourmaline on the Earth than there are today. This variety of Tourmaline is the strongest and therefore carries the greatest and purest form of masculine energy. The dark green crystals abundant today are not as strong. This is because much less light can flow through them, and their color is not as pure and bright as the green of the rainbow.

When one sex is dominant over another, there are lessons to be learned by both sexes. There are important lessons for Soul to experience on both sides of the situation. Now, in the past several decades, a very curious thing has occurred. Both sexes are demanding equality. One might think that only the female sex is demanding equality, but this is not so.

The domineering sex often dominates only to hide its weaknesses. It does not want its weaknesses to be apparent. It wants to hide its vulnerability, so it pretends to be strong. This impulse is natural for men, because their physical bodies are naturally much stronger than women's. This physical strength is due to the vibratory rate of their molecules.

So it is that men are also striving for equality, whether or not they are conscious of it.

The secret is that the equality sought by both sexes is not the equality between the millions of women and men on this planet; that is only the outward appearance. What is really happening is not the "battle of the sexes." It is the war between each individual's feminine nature and masculine nature.

Whether you have a female or male body, both masculine and feminine energies exist within you. It is just that one type of energy is greater than the other, depending on the sex of your physical body. The true conflict is occurring between these two types of energy within you.

As I have said, during this century both sexes have begun to demand equality. There are probably many reasons why this highly unusual behavior is suddenly occurring. You may not believe that what I am about to tell you has anything to do with it; but remember that the amount of Green Tourmaline on the planet directly affects the balance of masculine and feminine energies. It does this by affecting the amount of masculine force that exists there.

During the past 700 years, the finest quality Green Tourmaline has been taken from the Earth by individuals from other planets. The Tourmaline they have taken possessed the brightest emerald- green color and, therefore, the strongest effects.

The situation has been similar to that of a farmer who does not know the boundaries of his property. Let's assume that you are a farmer who lives on twenty square miles of land with no fence around your property: you probably wouldn't know exactly where your property ended and your neighbor's began.

Let's also assume that you once had crystals growing on your land, and that you did not understand their value. Your neighbor, on the other hand, understood that they were very valuable indeed. Now, if your neighbor took these crystals from your land, you probably would not consider it stealing. For one thing, you are not aware of your exact borders; therefore, you could not be certain whether the land where the crystals grew is really yours. For another, you do not think that the crystals have any value.

One day you hire a surveyor to clearly stake your land and

mark its borders. You learn exactly where your borders are, and you claim all the land within them as your own. You also declare that all resources on this land are yours to harvest, reap profits from, and use for your own benefit.

Then, if your neighbor took the crystals growing on your property, you would consider it stealing. This is because he would now be taking without permission something that belongs on land you have claimed as your own.

It is time that the people of Earth do the same. It is time that you claim your planet as your own. You need to do this in order to stop its resources from being plundered by those from other planets.

Now, I am neither for nor against this plundering. However, it is my duty is to benefit man (and woman, indirectly) in any way I can. Therefore, I must tell you that it is time you recognize and claim the Earth as your own planet. If you accept it as yours, those from other planets who have honorable intentions will not intentionally steal from you.

It is similar to the situation that you, as the hypothetical farmer, experienced with the crystals on your land. Your neighbor had no intention of stealing; and since you were not sure of your boundaries, it is fair to say that even though your neighbor took the crystals, he did not steal them. Again, this is the case only because there was no conscious claim made on the boundaries of your land.

You Earth humans need your resources. You may think that you have plundered the Earth. However, what you have taken from the Earth is perhaps ten percent of what people from other planets have taken.

To stop this plundering by outsiders, enough Earth humans must consciously take possession of the Earth planet. To do this, you must consciously claim, "This is my planet, my home, and my land." This should not just include the boundaries of your backyard. It should include the entire planet. If enough people adopt this attitude, the Earth will be protected from those with honorable intentions. Then, if these outsiders still want what the Earth has, other avenues of negotiation will have to be opened.

How does this help you to understand my purpose? It does so only indirectly. I give men motivation, courage, bravery, and self-confidence. I give them these qualities, so that they can become confident and strong enough to allow other feelings to develop and to be expressed. These qualities also help them to strengthen their weaknesses and become more balanced. In other words, their masculine and feminine natures are allowed to work in greater harmony with each other.

One begins to change his life by staking a claim such as, "This is my life. I have the power to take charge of it, and I am going to take charge of it. But I need help. Green Tourmaline can help, so I will wear Green Tourmaline. This will be one of the tools I use to attain self-mastery."

One can stake a parallel claim for one's planet: "This is my planet. I choose to be the master of my planet. But I need help. I need the help of a certain percentage of the other individuals on this planet. Then we, as people of the Earth, can work together. We as a whole can exist in greater harmony."

* * *

I promote balance on the physical, emotional, mental, and spiritual levels. However, the way I do this is very different from the way other gemstones with balancing effects do this.

I promote balance by strengthening the weakest link in the chain. First I fill your aura and gather information about all your aspects. Then I identify and focus my energy on the weakest area of your physical body. Next, I move to your weakest emotions and finally to the weakest part of your mind.

If you wear Tourmaline for at least a day, you may feel physically stronger. This might lead you to believe that Tourmaline only works on the physical level. Actually, Tourmaline works on the physical level first; it is not until the physical body has achieved a greater degree of balance, that I start to focus on the emotions. Therefore, if you continue to wear Tourmaline, you will find that you also become emotionally stronger and then mentally stronger. Tourmaline works in stages. First the physical body is brought to what we shall call "stage one." Then the emotions are brought to stage one, and then the mind. At that point, Tourmaline's focus returns again to the physical body to bring it to "stage two." The emotional body is then brought to stage two, and then the mind. The process continues in this way.

The first movement in the physical body from "zero" to stage one will probably take the longest to accomplish, because physical matter takes a long time to change. Therefore, Green Tourmaline's focus is frequently on the physical body.

Before the weakest link can be strengthened, it must be recognized. It takes a lot of courage to recognize one's weaknesses and to face them. Therefore, when men first put on Tourmaline, my initial response is to give a feeling of strength, courage, and self-confidence. This occurs as soon as Tourmaline touches a masculine aura.

As soon as Green Tourmaline touches a feminine aura, the Tourmaline pulls backs its energy. The female body also recognizes that the Tourmaline is not in harmony with it and starts to put up resistance. This resistance appears to be an aura of protection. Indeed it is, for the body is protecting itself from an invader: a disharmonious vibratory rate. Therefore, the aura of protection that a woman feels when wearing Green Tourmaline comes from two sources: from the Tourmaline itself as it tries to protect the woman from its energy; and from her own defense mechanisms.

When people encounter disharmony and must engage their defense mechanisms, they are faced with a choice between "fight or flight." The protective aura that a woman creates when she is wearing Green Tourmaline is the fight response. This response is designed to last for only short periods of time. However, if a woman wears Tourmaline continuously, her fight mechanisms will be compelled to work constantly and will quickly become exhausted. Once these are spent, imbalances will occur. Unfortunately, those women who have not had the self-discipline to listen to their bodies and who continue to wear Tourmaline will experience these imbalances.

I, as Tourmaline, am providing you with knowledge about a powerful tool. Power is a double-edged sword; you have the option to use it to great advantage or to misuse it to great disadvantage. You are given this freedom and the responsibility to exercise it.

* * *

In most cases only the highest quality Green Tourmaline is chosen to be cut into faceted gemstones. Therefore, relatively small specimens are often quite expensive. Usually these small amounts do not possess enough mass to initiate the healing effects I have described.

For men, it is not true that the greater the mass of Green Tourmaline worn, the better. For women, I would say that it is better to wear a greater mass. This is only because it will allow them to get the message sooner that the Tourmaline does not feel right for them and that they should stop wearing it.

By the way, a woman should not worry that she will experience imbalances if she wears a faceted Tourmaline, for example, in a ring. The amount of mass appropriate for a ring would not be great enough to affect her negatively.

* * *

Green Tourmaline crystals that are touching the Earth draw masculine energy from the universe, in a vortex or whirlpool toward them. If you place Green Tourmaline crystals in the soil of your potted plants, they will also have this effect, so long as the soil is from the Earth and not a synthetic compound. However, it would not be wise to place a Green Tourmaline crystal in a potted plant without doing the same with a Pink Tourmaline crystal, perhaps in another plant. That way, both masculine and feminine energies will collect in your household atmosphere. Tourmaline crystals that are not touching the ground or the soil do not have this effect.

Hopefully, once people realize the effects of the rounded form of Green Tourmaline, they will no longer feel a need to wear the crystalline form. However, they can still receive benefits from Tourmaline crystals by placing them in the Earth or the soil and enjoying the energies that the crystals bring into their homes. Their plants will like it, too.

If men wear the crystalline form of Tourmaline, they will feel a certain energy. However, from my point of view, that energy will not be particularly definable. Those who wear Tourmaline crystals might experience some residual effects that come from my ability to attract masculine energy. However, if men wear the crystalline form, I will not be able to reach into their auras and affect their inner aspects.

Tourmaline crystals naturally form into long, thin rods of various thicknesses, and can be used as instruments for non-invasive surgery applications. In these procedures, the crystals are used to direct light, and do so very powerfully. These surgical procedures probably lie beyond your present level of technology. However, to satisfy your curiosity, I will give you some information about their application.

Now, just holding a Tourmaline crystal over an area of disharmony would not be effective for this application. It would be like holding a bottle of medicine over an area rather than taking what is inside the bottle.

The best way to infuse the energy of Tourmaline crystals into specific locations of the body is to attach a power source to one end of the crystal. Then the surgeon can perform the operation above the skin without causing the trauma that comes from the use of a scalpel.

Those who use Tourmaline for non-invasive surgery think about health in a way that is very different from the way most of Earth's medical professionals think. Most of Earth's physicians at this time follow the precept that, if there is something wrong in the body, it should be taken out.

Those who perform Tourmaline-laser surgery do not often perform invasive surgery, because they understand that the body can heal itself. They know that sometimes it just needs a push and some degree of enlivenment. Tourmaline will do this. It will give the body what it needs to take care of itself. It will give the cells the power and the strength to regain their harmony.

Again, I do not believe that this technology is available yet. However, you do have the ability to apply Tourmaline using the same principle. The sun can be used as the energy source.

Green Tourmaline Therapy

To use Tourmaline on specific areas of physical disharmony, place a strand of rounded Tourmaline over the area. Then allow the sun to shine directly on the Tourmaline. This is most effective for organs, since it is usually disharmonious organ functions that compromise one's strength before anything else does.

It is not necessary to also wear Tourmaline around the neck while practicing this therapy. However, wearing a Dark Green Aventurine necklace would be very effective. Then the organ would be attacked from two areas: from inside the body by the Aventurine and directly through the skin by the Tourmaline.

The Tourmaline will powerfully transform any disharmonious molecules.

"For what specific disharmonies are you most effective?" Michael asked.

Disharmony is disharmony, no matter what name you give it. I can be particularly effective if the disease has a focus in a particular area. Then I can be placed directly over that area. Otherwise, I have to be worn around the neck.

When Tourmaline is placed over a disharmonious area, layer after layer of disharmonious molecules switch the direction in which the vortex of their vibratory rate is spinning. The vortex of disharmonious vibratory rate spirals in a certain direction. If the direction of the vortex is switched, the vibratory rate will spin in the opposite direction and become harmonious.

I am not saying that the molecules will become healthy. I am saying that they will no longer be disharmonious for the body. In order for the molecules to become healthy, the individual would have to change his patterns. He would have to learn how to give his cells the nourishment they have probably been lacking.

Aventurine will also be helpful in maintaining the harmony of the cells after Tourmaline has switched the direction of their vortexes. You see, when the Tourmaline is removed, it is easy for a vortex that has switched to a positive direction to switch back to a negative, disharmonious one. Aventurine will inhibit the return to disharmony.

Again, one would wear Aventurine at the same time that the Tourmaline is being placed over a disharmonious area. The Aventurine will infiltrate the organ and support the cells that have just had the direction of their vortexes switched. This will be useful, because once a cell switches from disharmony to harmony, Tourmaline moves its attention to the next cell. It does not continue to support each individual cell.

One would wear the Aventurine for support. At the same time, one would hopefully begin to support oneself. This support might be nutritional. Greater nutrition will help make the cells healthier and stronger. The improved health of the cells will then strengthen the harmonious vortex and help it to maintain its new direction without the presence of Tourmaline. For this purpose, one should also continue to wear the

Aventurine between the Tourmaline therapy sessions.

After enough disharmonious cells in the physical body have been made harmonious, Tourmaline's attention moves to the emotional body, since disease is always reflected there. The way Tourmaline works on the emotions is similar to the way it works on the physical body. Although it is best to keep Tourmaline over the disharmonious organ, it does not have to be kept there in order for it to work on the emotions surrounding that organ's condition; it could be worn around the neck.

Once a certain plateau is reached in the emotional area, Tourmaline turns its attention to the next inner level: the mind.

Before we continue, I'd like to say more about the working relationship of Green Tourmaline and Aventurine. Both are very effective gemstones for physical healing. However, they are two different tools with two different actions.

Some individuals' conditions require force and power to be healed; others need a more gentle effect. Green Tourmaline works with force and power. Compared to the force and power of Tourmaline, Aventurine's work is quite gentle.

However, too much healing force and power can make some people "explode," especially if they are already pent-up dynamos of stress and tension. An individual who is extremely tight in most aspects of his physical body will benefit from wearing Aventurine before wearing Tourmaline. It will help the cells begin to open up.

One can be very tight and very weak at the same time. Someone who is weakened in this way can wear a short strand of Tourmaline, a longer strand of Clear Quartz, and an even longer strand of Aventurine.

"Wouldn't that create a conflict between the powerful force of Tourmaline and the gentle force of Aventurine?"

No. The two forces will be balanced by the presence of the Clear Quartz between them. With this combination of gemstones, the Aventurine will make the physical-healing changes, and the Tourmaline will give strength. Of course, even if Quartz is not present, no conflict will be created by wearing Aventurine around the neck and placing Tourmaline over a specific area, since both strands will not be around the neck.

* * *

Now, regarding the effects of the two types of rounded Tourmaline: the chip form is more forceful than the spherical form when it is placed over an organ. The spherical form works in a more balanced, soothing way; the chip form has a more cutting, penetrating action. Both forms work on one layer of disharmonious cells at a time; but the chip form reaches into deeper layers of cells and works in a more haphazard way.

The spherical form does not move its attention from one cell to the next as rapidly as the chips do. Spheres keep Tourmaline's energy focused on a cell for a longer period of time after it makes its vortex switch. This extra attention imparts to the cell some of Tourmaline's strength. It also supports the vortex switch and helps it to continue moving in the more harmonious direction.

The changes initiated by the chip form will occur faster than those initiated by the spherical form. The chips compel Tourmaline's energy to move onto the next cell as soon as the vortex switch is made. Therefore, it would be especially wise to wear Aventurine when using the chip form of Tourmaline over a specific area.

The "poultice" therapy I have been describing can be applied anywhere on the body. For best results, the Tourmaline must be kept in your aura constantly, especially if you are very ill. If you cannot keep the Tourmaline taped to the area constantly, wear it around your neck during the times it cannot be taped.

Men should not wear more than one strand of Tourmaline. Even one strand might not be comfortable enough to wear 24 hours a day; some might only want to wear it for half a day, or only at night. For some, even this might be too much.

Those who feel that Tourmaline is too powerful for them, or get headaches if they wear it constantly, should remove it as soon as they feel any discomfort. Then they should put it back on the next day.

"Can a woman benefit from wearing Tourmaline over a specific organ?"

A woman's cells will experience the vortex-switching effect. However, the Tourmaline should only be placed over the disharmonious area for about one hour per day. During that hour, her defense mechanisms will be in full swing. Therefore, in considering whether to use Green Tourmaline, she should balance her need for the Tourmaline treatments with the potential depletion of her reserves. For therapeutic uses, a woman should consider using the Pink Tourmaline instead.

* * *

"Should Tourmaline be cleansed after being worn or used for therapy?" Michael asked.

Tourmaline should definitely be cleansed before being worn by another patient. Sunlight is the best cleanser. If the sun is very strong, fifteen to 30 minutes of exposure to direct sunlight would probably be sufficient.

Sunlight does wonders for Tourmaline, and the sun acts on it quickly. Placing Tourmaline in the sun will give it extra energy. If placed in the sun before being used for any application, including the poultice treatment, the Tourmaline will work more effectively and with greater strength.

* * *

There will be a few women who crave Green Tourmaline, because they have specific imbalances in their masculine and feminine energies. Wearing Green Tourmaline for a short period of time may correct these imbalances.

Despite what a woman may read about the terrors of Green Tourmaline, if she craves it, it will be admirable if she listens to her inner voice and wears the Tourmaline. However, she should continue to listen to her inner voice. When that voice tells her that she has had enough, she should remove the Green Tourmaline. If she ignores her intuition and continues to wear it, her strength and balance will be compromised.

When she is finished with the Tourmaline, she should give it to a man she is living with. When the man wears Green Tourmaline and its vibratory rate fills his aura, that vibratory rate will affect the woman's aura as well. It will support in an indirect, secondary way the changes that it began to make in a primary way when she was wearing it herself.

Many disharmonies occur because of problems people have in their relationships with their mates. These problems can be caused by many things, including alcohol, the kids, money, or another woman or man.

Whatever the cause, the best therapy for ailing relationships is to have the man wear Green Tourmaline and the woman wear Pink Tourmaline. When the man wears Green Tourmaline, its vibratory rate will fill the atmosphere in the house. Therefore, it will fill and affect the woman's aura as well. This will nourish the woman's masculine aspect. Since she herself will not be wearing the Green Tourmaline, she will experience a secondary effect which will benefit her greatly and create no disharmony.

When the woman wears Pink Tourmaline, her feminine nature will be greatly nourished. She will learn from the Pink Tourmaline how to work with the masculine part of herself and how to balance her feminine and masculine aspects.

At the same time, Pink Tourmaline's vibratory rate will touch and affect her mate's aura. Pink Tourmaline is a strong protector. When its vibratory rate enters an aura, it transforms it into a shield. When the man begins to feel this natural protection—consciously or not—he will feel safe and therefore comfortable enough to work on balancing his own feminine and masculine natures.

Pink Tourmaline opens lines of communication between masculine and feminine and thereby creates balance. When a man and woman each wear the appropriate Tourmaline, each is affected by the vibratory rate of the Tourmaline worn by the mate. The result is an opening of communication between the man and the woman, and an increase in balance between the masculine and feminine energies that exist within each of them.

Therefore, if a man and woman have any problems in their relationship that they want to resolve, they should try wearing Green and Pink Tourmaline.

However, if the individuals want to separate and end their relationship, the woman should wear Green Tourmaline, and the man should wear Pink Tourmaline. If they do this, I guarantee that the marriage will be over within weeks. The man and woman will not be able to live with each other.

"Can you tell us about the naturally-formed combination of Green and Pink Tourmaline known as 'Watermelon Tourmaline'?"

This is a complex situation, but I will only give a simplified explanation at this time. When the environment in which the crystals grew was one that supported masculine dominance, the Green Tourmaline grew around the Pink Tourmaline, thereby creating the "watermelon" effect. (By environment, I mean the chemical composition of the air and rock in which the crystals grew.)

On the other hand, when the environment supported a condition in which the feminine energies dominated, the Pink Tourmaline surrounded the Green. Of course, there are also environments that support the existence of harmony between these energies. In these locations, Green and Pink Tourmaline grew side by side.

* * *

"How effective are gem elixirs?" inquired Michael.

I can assure you that the powers and effects of the elixirs currently being made with Green Tourmaline are almost nonexistent, compared to the effects of wearing the Tourmaline itself.

Green Tourmaline Tomorrow

One of the reasons I have shared this information about the qualities of Green Tourmaline is to see how Earth humans react to such knowledge. Are they self-disciplined? Will they take the responsibility to use this powerful tool properly? Or will they just ignore the gift and let it sit unopened in the box?

Any man—even the healthiest man on Earth—can benefit from wearing Green Tourmaline, because there is no such thing as perfect health. There is always something out of balance somewhere or some weakness on some level. As far as one's health is concerned, there is always another step to take.

However, once people have attained some degree of health, their attention will turn away from their physical problems and toward a greater understanding and awareness of themselves. This will eventually lead to self-mastery.

Before one can be a spiritual master, or a master of Spirit, one must be a master of one's physical body, emotions, memory, mind, and unconscious. I help individuals to master their physical bodies and their inner aspects; look to the spiritual masters to learn about spiritual mastery.

* * *

If you walk down the path that I took to get here, and then continue past the point where I manifested out of the waterfall and over to the other side of the mountain, you will find a waterfall of pink and gold. There you will find the Gemstone Master Rubellite. Rubellite is another name for Pink Tourmaline.

I will lead you there. Before I do, have you any more questions?

"I only wished to know if there was anything else you wanted to share," Michael replied.

There is still much to share about Tourmaline. The therapies I described are important and can be used in many ways. There are other specific ways in which Tourmaline can be used, but they will wait for next time.

"Thank you," said Michael and the others, almost in unison.

May the blessings be.

As difficult as it was to remain in Tourmaline's aura, it was equally as hard to leave. Even after I finally wriggled out of his aura, I still felt his powerful effects. I believed that they would be with me for many hours.

Without saying another word, the Guardian walked down the footpath. We knew that we were expected to follow. I waited until everyone else filed behind him, trying to get as much distance between us as I could. When the others could barely be seen through the foliage, I started to walk down the path. The maroon-robed master followed behind me.

I decided not to hurry, since I knew they would not start until I arrived. Instead, I let my senses drink in the balmy, fragrant, tropical beauty that surrounded me.

16
RUBELLITE

(Pink Tourmaline)

The scene surrounding the second waterfall was almost a mirror image of the one we had just left behind. The mysterious pool, the lush foliage, and the small clearing were all there before me again. The only difference I could detect was the color of the crystal waterfall and the mist rising from the pool. The mist was pink, and the mammoth crystal itself was a combination of light and dark shades of pink mixed with pure golden light.

The Guardian of Green Tourmaline had waited with the other listeners until I arrived. He introduced the Guardian of Rubellite with a simple nod of his head. Rubellite returned his nod, and then the Guardian of Tourmaline retreated down the path.

Rubellite was dressed in layers of sheer, pink fabric; it draped her body like the cascading waterfall behind her. She was about six feet tall and appeared to be in her late thirties. The Guardian had suntanned skin, rich golden eyes, and brown hair, which fell just below her shoulders.

She smiled and reached for my hand. As I took her hand I knew I would slip instantly into her aura and the discourse would begin.

Greetings, everyone. You may call me Rubellite. Rubellite is the name given to the finest quality Pink Tourmaline, the gemstone for which I take responsibility.

"The Guardian of Green Tourmaline referred to you as the 'Gemstone Master Rubellite.' Is your mission different from that of the other Gemstone Guardians?" Michael asked.

I will speak of the Gemstone Masters, because I have great

respect for them. However, I can only do so because I have not yet been fully initiated into this order of Masters.

You have already met several Gemstone Guardians. You have learned that they do not all come from one place, nor are they all the same age. You have also discovered that not all of the Guardians are required to devote all of their time to the gemstones for which they are responsible. Some Guardians, whom you have not yet met, are even in charge of more than one gemstone.

What we Gemstone Guardians do in our spare time, if indeed we have any, is entirely up to us. I believe it is the same with you.

My personal interests lie beyond the energies, powers, effects, and properties of the gemstone Rubellite. Although Rubellite is my focus, I am deeply interested in all gemstones. I am interested in their purposes, their effects on different people from different planets, and the ways in which they can be used.

Although each discourse you hear will comprise one chapter in your book, there is enough additional information available on each gemstone to fill an entire volume. As you research each gemstone more deeply, you will discover that the discourses you are hearing are actually introductions, for the Gemstone Guardians have been speaking in general terms.

I am in training to be initiated into the order of Gemstone Masters. I have declared this intention, for it is my personal direction of unfoldment. It is the way I choose to be a co-worker with Spirit.

The Gemstone Masters do not work as the Guardians work. You might call these Masters the keepers of the gemstone knowledge, since their purpose is to collect, record, file, and keep safe all the knowledge and wisdom available regarding gemstones. This includes all the knowledge from all the universes and worlds where gemstones manifest.

Part of the Gemstone Masters' duty is to constantly keep this information up to date. As gemstones grow, mature, and evolve, their properties and effects change. Similarly, as people experience their own individual and collective growth, their reactions to gemstone energies change.

When an individual has earned the right and proven that he or she can be responsible for the information a Gemstone Master imparts, that individual will be given certain knowledge by these Masters. It will seem as though the individual has gained this awareness on his own, because the Masters will not communicate directly. That is not their way; the Gemstone Masters take no credit for their work. They are beyond ego or vanity. They work with complete humility as co-workers with Spirit.

It is not the purpose of these Masters to change people's attitudes, concepts, or opinions about gemstones; nor is it their purpose to raise people's consciousness about them. These things will occur in time. Therefore, any individual who says he or she has "channeled" a Gemstone Master has not communicated with a master of this particular order.

The Gemstone Masters work directly with Spirit. They know what gemstones really are. I will tell you what gemstones really are, but know that my description is only superficial.

Gemstones are embodiments of the light and sound of God. You also encase the light and sound of God in your physical body. However, a one-carat gemstone can carry a thousand times more light and sound than your entire physical body can. This is simply because the crystalline matrix of the gemstone can handle more concentrated energy than the cellular matrix of your physical body.

Just as there might be a Gemstone Guardian who has a physical body and lives on your planet, there might also be a Gemstone Master with a physical body living there.

When these Masters are working, they often wear a black robe and a black hat. You might call this outfit their uniform. The color black reminds them to be neutral and not partial to any one color or gemstone. By the way, the colors that gemstones carry are not given to them by accident. Each gemstone has a particular color, because that color supports its mission.

Since the color black tends to absorb all colors, it also reminds them that it is their duty to absorb and gather information. The presence of the black uniform presents an interesting opportunity for those who meet a Gemstone Master. Unless one can let go of all concepts surrounding the color black, one will not be ready to learn or accept what these Masters have to offer.

It was an honor to be called a Gemstone Master. It was Green Tourmaline's way of recognizing and affirming my direction and my potential.

During my spare time, when my attention is not on Rubellite,

I focus on learning and teaching some of the information that the Gemstone Masters have gathered. I assist them in their research. Therefore, to some I might already appear to be a Master of Gemstones. However, as I said, I have not yet achieved full initiation into this order. So I consider myself an apprentice.

"Can you tell us why light and sound have been contained in crystals?"

Gemstones provide a concentrated focus for light and sound in the physical world and in all the other worlds in which they have manifested.

If there were no gemstones or crystals, planets would not be alive; and if planets were not alive, they could not support life. One can compare crystals to a human body's organs. Like organs, crystals carry out specific functions that are necessary to keep planets alive.

Rock and metal are so physical and dense, that there is no way for the life force to penetrate a planet that is made of nothing but these elements. It will become a living planet only when it is given crystals and a Soul. It gains its Soul in the form of a Guardian for the planet. Only then does it possess the three key elements needed for life: light, sound, and Soul.

The more of these three elements that are available to you, the more of life you can experience. This is why gemstones are available to humans. Gemstones offer them the opportunity to gain a greater connection with their Souls and a greater amount of light and sound, which are the components of Spirit.

Actually, it is not correct to say that you have a Soul. You are Soul. You, as Soul, have a mind, emotions, and a physical body. The point of having these physical and inner aspects is to gather experiences, learn lessons, gain strength and stamina, and become aware of Spirit. These lessons and experiences will then allow you to fulfill your true purpose, which is to regain the awareness that you are really Soul and to realize that you do not live just to follow day-to-day routines.

Eventually, you will gain the awareness that you live to become a co-worker with Spirit. I have chosen to do this by working to become a Gemstone Master. Others can do this by becoming artists, engineers, teachers, homemakers, salesmen, or even people who are chronically unemployed.

As Soul, you originated in the heart of God. One can say that you "flowed down" to Earth and as you did, you collected a mind, emotions, and a physical body. As Soul, your ultimate goal is to return to the heart of God.

It takes a great amount of experiences, stamina, strength, and lessons learned to gain the impetus, motivation, or power needed to turn around and flow back to the heart of God. Flowing away from God is easy. It is like flowing with the force of gravity. However, just as a rocket needs a tremendous amount of fuel to defy gravity and leave the Earth's atmosphere, people need a tremendous amount of "fuel" to return to the heart of God.

Gemstones are points of concentrated light and sound "fuel." They can act like booster rockets, giving you the extra energy you need to help lift you in the direction of your goal. How a gemstone does this depends upon its mission, purpose, and effects.

Not all gemstones can give this boost or extra "fuel" to help Soul return to the heart of God. Only those gemstones that are beneficial to man and woman will do this. All the Gemstone Guardians you are interviewing for this book have only beneficial effects in mind for their wearers. However, there are some gemstones whose duty it is to keep your attention on the physical.

These gemstones often cloak their negativity, so that people with shallow insight will only see positive benefits from wearing them. Of course, if people saw the true nature of these gemstones, they would be shunned and not mined. Because they must be mined in order to carry out their missions, these gemstones create a false front.

In a crude and harsh way, these gemstones temper men and women. They make people strong, but only through experiences which are ultimately negative. These gemstones keep people on a downward spiral. If and when their wearers finally become aware of the ways in which they have been affected, they will also discover that they have gained strength. However, this is only because awareness is strength.

In this rather harsh way, the wearers of negative gemstones will come to understand the power of gemstones and will remove the negative ones from their lives. Then they may look to a spiritual master, uplifting gemstones, or another focus of light and sound to help them change the direction of their lives. This will help them to evolve in an upward spiral toward the heart of God. There are many ways or paths which reach into the heart of God. Gemstones do not take the place of religions; nor do they take the place of spiritual guides or spiritual masters. If I have given you that idea, I apologize. It is the wrong idea.

Gemstones are not "the path" or "the way." They are only tools, though powerful ones. Their power is often proportional to the wearer's state of consciousness. The more spiritually aware you are, the more powerfully the gemstones will work for you. And the greater your consciousness is, the more you will be able to determine which gemstones give experience, strength, and stamina in a negative way, and which ones provide these things in a positive, uplifting way.

The purpose of gemstones is not to heal just the physical body or make it feel better. When worn, the gemstones will gather information about all your inner aspects. They will know that a certain condition requires not only physical therapy, but mental and emotional therapy as well. Gemstones work holistically in the truest sense of the word. Their work involves your whole being, the life force which gave you your being, and the energies that created your conditions.

There is no other therapy that can promise this—unless, of course, it includes gemstones, or is one that involves working directly with the light and sound of God.

When I become initiated into this order of Gemstone Masters, I will not be able to speak as freely as I just have. As an outsider of sorts, I still have the right to speak freely about gemstones and Gemstone Masters. On the other hand, I have only been given information that can be freely shared. When the initiation occurs, I will be given wisdom, information, and knowledge so vast that I might not know what needs to be shared, what can be shared, or what should be shared.

You can well imagine that one of the prerequisites of Gemstone Mastership is mastery of the law of silence. Besides knowing when to keep silent about certain information, masters of this law know how to teach in silence. Indeed, it is much more effective for information to be taught silently. Then individuals are not just given information by an authority with whom they can agree or disagree at their whim.

When teaching is done silently, individuals learn through their own direct experience. Then they truly know what they have learned, and no one can take that knowledge away.

"When you become a Gemstone Master, will you no longer be the Guardian of Rubellite?"

Yes. Another will be given the experience of being the Guardian of this gemstone.

"How many individuals have been initiated into this hierar-

chy of Gemstone Masters?"

It is a relatively small order. I have never counted; and perhaps no one will ever know exactly how many are involved. You were correct to call this order a hierarchy, because the Masters who have belonged to this order for the longest time are the most wise and have access to the most information. They are also the most silent.

"Do these Masters store information in crystals?"

It appears as though the information is kept in large books similar to scrapbooks. The information is impeccably neat and well organized.

In order to extract information stored in crystals, a certain process is involved. It is easier to scan the pages of a book or the titles of many books; there is no need for an information-retrieval device.

Nevertheless, the actual material of which the pages are made is illusory, for it is very close to being pure light and sound. It is just for the sake of convenience that it manifests in a form which looks like a book.

These books have manifested only for recording purposes and for those of us who are apprentices. Often, when the Gemstone Masters need to know something, they expand their awareness to the level of infinite all-knowingness and get the answer. This source is beyond any physical manifestation, be it in the form of books or crystals. My fellow apprentices and I are still unable to access this source of infinitive wisdom easily.

The Early Years of Rubellite

Tourmaline crystals take a long time to grow. They are built carefully and precisely. As each molecule is added, it is done so with an understanding of Tourmaline's responsibilities.

It was not until the Age of Atlantis that Tourmaline crystals had become large enough to be recognized, appreciated, and used. I was not as popular as Green Tourmaline, since it was not yet time for my missions to unfold.

I have two missions. One is to provide protection by effectively transforming the aura into a shield. This shield protects people from any external disharmonious influence, whether it be mental, emotional, or physical.

This mission does not include protecting you from your own

inner disharmonies. If you already have a certain disharmonious vibratory rate within you, it is difficult to protect you from external forces of the same disharmony. For example, if you have greed within you, I cannot protect you from greed. I can protect you most effectively from those disharmonies that are foreign to you.

My second mission is to give woman the power, awareness, understanding, and ability to realize her full potential. I help her to realize how her feminine and masculine natures coexist and interact; and I help to bring her masculine and feminine natures into greater harmony.

My two missions intertwine. This is because women need the protection of Rubellite when they are undergoing the changes required to accept their new self-awareness.

In the Age of Atlantis, civilization was not yet ready for all women to have this awareness. If women had gained the awareness I bring, history would have been different. Men might not have kept the dominant role.

Rubellite Today

It is only in recent times that equality has come to be recognized as a virtue. Only now is it something that both sexes, but particularly women, are working toward.

The equality for which men and women are striving is not equality between the sexes. The true equality they seek is the balance between the masculine and feminine energies within both men and women. Once this inner balance is achieved (or at least approached), the harmony between the sexes will increase. It will occur naturally.

I am not saying that when a balance between masculine and feminine energies occurs, there will be no conflicts between men and women. I do not mean that everyone will be in agreement with each other, and that marital spats will be a thing of the past. Not at all. Men and women will bounce their energies off each other for eternity; it is the nature of their vibratory rates and their magnetism to do so.

It is also interesting to note that the closer people come to achieving a harmonious and balanced male-female relationship (both within and between men and women), the more quickly the effects of any disharmony will return to the sender.

For centuries, the feminine aspect of the domineering male was suppressed and therefore weakened. Yet, because the male's feminine aspect is part of him, by dominating the female, he only weakened himself.

Also, while the male was dominating, the feminine and masculine aspects of the female were learning to become strong. This strength was learned in a way similar to the way negative gemstones teach strength—the hard way. It is true that sometimes this kind of lesson is remembered best; but it is certainly the most painful.

And so it was, that while man was weakening himself, woman was slowly, slowly becoming stronger.

I could speak for hours on this subject. However, that is not the purpose of this discourse. Besides, I feel that I have already given you enough information to upset many people's concepts about male-female relationships.

Now let us take what I have just discussed and apply it directly to Rubellite.

Centuries of suppression have taught many women that the masculine aspect of her is wrong; or it has taught her that males in general are wrong, shortsighted, egocentric, and not really as strong as they think they are. And I am sure that if you included three or four blank lines, many women who read this list will be happy to fill in more adjectives.

I notice that the men in this audience did not find that humorous.

Woman consists of both masculine and feminine energies. Therefore, until she releases her concepts about male energy, she will not be in harmony with herself. Rubellite will help her to do this. I will help women to achieve an understanding and communication between their male and female aspects.

It is probably no coincidence that I, as an individual, was given the responsibility of being the Guardian of Rubellite. This is simply because I may be the first woman ever to be in line for initiation into the order of Gemstone Masters. If there is a woman who has already attained this initiation, her vow of silence is impeccable. I have not yet met her, nor have I heard of her. I am doing something that, as far as I know, no other woman has done. I know that, in addition to all the requirements demanded of any applicant, it takes something extra for a woman to do something like this.

I also know that if woman can master both the feminine

and masculine aspects of herself, there is nothing that she cannot do. She will only be limited by how far she wishes to go.

Women who reach this state of strength, self-confidence, balance, and power also tend to see more of the whole picture of life. They begin to see that one of their greatest blessings is the power of motherhood and the preservation of the family. Some realize that they can best use their power and abilities to preserve the family, rather than to enter society and assume a typically male role. By the way, there is nothing wrong with taking either avenue.

The woman who reaches this state of consciousness should also have the awareness to keep quiet about her strength, just as the Gemstone Masters keep quiet about their strengths and their wisdom. Practicing the vow of silence is often the mark of one who is truly wise and strong.

It is the male's purpose to carry the strength of the family's group consciousness throughout the generations. This manifests as the custom of passing family names from father to son and of women taking their husbands' names. Similar customs are practiced in societies other than those on Earth.

It is the female's purpose to provide the force of change. She broadens the family's group consciousness and therefore strengthens it. When daughters marry, they step away from one family unit and enter another family's group consciousness, broadening it and strengthening it as they enter.

If a woman refuses to take her husband's last name or chooses to change her last name after she has taken her husband's name, it is an indication of imbalance.

Yes, I know that this statement may ruffle some feathers!

Rubellite can give a woman the self-confidence to stand on her own as her own individual being, separate from her husband. Yet, in the realization of her powers and her recognition of the importance of family preservation, she may see the importance of having one identity, or name, for the family unit.

When you wear an identification bracelet, the bracelet is not you. It is only something you wear for identification. Likewise, when a woman wears her husband's name, it is not her. But she can use the name to identify the group consciousness she is forming in her family. One family name strengthens the group consciousness of the family unit.

In any case, a name is only a temporary identity. Who you

are as Soul will not change if your name changes. However, names can be tools. For example, if you wish to release an old identity and take on a new one, you are free to change your name. If you are not sure of your identity, you might change your name often. This is what I have done. You have known me by several names including Pink Tourmaline and Rubeen; and now I am called Rubellite. I have come to realize that it does not matter what my name is or what people call me. I am who I am.

* * *

Rubellite will not imbalance men in the same way Green Tourmaline will imbalance women. When worn by a man, Rubellite will have the same protective qualities that it has for a woman.

Wearing Rubellite will also allow a man, consciously or unconsciously, to recognize his feminine nature. Often, when this happens, a man will not like what he sees or will not be able to accept it—especially if his feminine nature needs attention and healing.

Therefore, one of the greatest gifts that a man can give himself is to give Rubellite to the woman he is sharing his life with. As the Rubellite vibratory rate fills the woman's aura, it will also affect his aura. This way, Rubellite's influence will not be as overpowering for the male as it would be if he wore it himself. Therefore, it will be easier for him to balance and heal his masculine and feminine qualities.

The aura of protection around the couple created by the Rubellite will enable the man to feel safe enough to allow the healing changes within him to occur. This will happen even if only the woman wears the Rubellite.

* * *

I protect Rubellite's wearers from all external disharmonious thoughts, emotions, and energies, including electromagnetic radiation and microwaves. Now I would like to explain how I can protect those who wear Rubellite.

You have been told how the white light splits into seven

color rays just above the area known as the mental world. You may be surprised to learn that, even though I manifest in several shades of pink, the color-ray vibratory rate that flows through me is actually blue.

The vibratory rate of my crystal pulls the blue ray into the physical world with such force that the pink ray of the emotional world is pulled along with it. This force is so strong that particles of pure white light are also pulled into the physical. By the way, the pink color ray—which gives Rubellite its predominant color—is a dilution of the red color ray.

When people wear Rubellite, the light rays that are strongly pulled toward it collect in the aura. This makes the aura so strong that it is practically impenetrable.

When individuals are protected from external disharmonies, they have the freedom to be braver and more adventurous than they would otherwise be. They also have the freedom to think new thoughts and feel new emotions.

Also, because of the added protection, they will more easily be able to travel in consciousness to places within themselves. Even if they physically travel to foreign countries or to foreign parts of their own country, they will be protected from the stresses of travel. No matter where they are, they will be protected from the energies and influences that are foreign, disharmonious, and potentially harmful to their bodies.

* * *

I must also warn you about Rubellite. Its power should not be underestimated.

Rubellite should not be worn in a strand by itself unless the wearer will be doing something potentially life-threatening. When worn alone in these situations, I can be used as a tool for protection. Then the wearer will not need to focus his or her personal strength on self-protection and will be able to focus entirely upon the task at hand.

In other words, I should be worn alone only during circumstances in which your natural defense mechanisms might be so overburdened in their attempts to protect you, that your mission would be compromised.

Rubellite's energy enters the body through the lower four chakras and sometimes through the throat chakra. It only exits in a gentle outflow through the brow chakra. Even a single strand of Rubellite worn around the neck would bring more Rubellite vibratory rate into the body than the body could express through the brow chakra.

Therefore, if an individual wore a strand made entirely of Rubellite, the pressure of its vibratory rate would build in the head. It would distort the balance of mental energy and accentuate negative thought patterns. If the individual continued to wear this much Rubellite, the emotions would soon experience the same imbalances.

Therefore, for everyday use and protection—and to experience all the other benefits I have described—Rubellite should be combined with other gemstones in a necklace. However, one must be sure that these other gemstones do not impede, confuse, interfere with, or cancel out my work. By the way, Green Tourmaline should not be included with Rubellite—or with any quality of Pink Tourmaline—because it will have these negative effects on my work.

The strongest and highest quality Pink Tourmaline—namely, Rubellite—is that which appears brighter, has fewer inclusions and less cloudiness, and whose color is darker pink or somewhat purple. Rubellite that is darker pink or somewhat purple contains more of the blue ray. The more blue ray contained in the Rubellite, the stronger the Rubellite is. This is because a greater presence of blue ray draws the other color rays into the physical level more quickly and strongly.

The effects of any rounded form of Rubellite are more gentle and balanced than those of any other form. They are also stronger. This is because, when the Rubellite is rounded, its vibratory rate can be evenly distributed throughout the entire aura.

A faceted or crystalline Rubellite will not have protective effects that are as reliable as those of a rounded Rubellite. The facets will build and reflect energy only in the directions dictated by the facets. To be most effective, a shield must cover the entire body. A shield that exists in only a few areas of the aura—for example, only in the front—does little good if you are attacked from the back.

My protective properties can also have a secondary, healing effect on the body.

Often a particular part of the body is prevented or inhibited from healing, because it is being bombarded by outside influences. These influences may include the energies of the thoughts, feelings, attitudes, concepts, and prayers that friends and family may be directing toward the person or the diseased part of the person's body. Not only must the affected part of the body focus on healing, but it must also contend with these outside influences. Despite good intentions, these influences may or may not be positive, welcomed, or in the best interest of the individual.

If the individual wears Rubellite, the affected organ or area will be able to relax its defense mechanisms. It will be able to place its full attention and energy on healing, cleansing, or rejuvenating itself.

Rubellite Therapy

When Rubellite is placed on specific areas of the physical body, the effects it produces will be the result of both the vibratory rate of Rubellite and the vibratory rates of the color rays within it.

When Rubellite is placed along the spine, several effects occur very quickly, and one after the other.

First, an aura of protection surrounds the spine. This allows it to relax from worry about outside influences. It can then turn its attention to clearing pathways: first to the brain, and then from the brain to the rest of the body. After these pathways are cleared, the spine can work on any disharmonies that exist within it.

Because blue, pink, and white light are pulled toward Rubellite with such great force, any disharmonies in the spine will be dissolved by the vibratory rate and the intensity of the light. As this occurs, the spinal vertebrae will align themselves into a more harmonious position.

One should not use Rubellite over the spine for more than thirty minutes. The length of the average treatment should be fifteen minutes. If the spine has severe or chronic problems, only five-minute treatments may be appropriate. Too much light and too rapid a change may imbalance a weakened spine.

If I am worn around the neck, the light will enter the entire aura. If I am worn over a particular organ or part of the body, the light will focus only on that area.

Remember, this light will not just affect the physical body.

As it is pulled to the physical from its source, the light will move through the mental and emotional areas, as well. If Rubellite is worn around the neck, the entire mental and emotional areas will be affected. If, on the other hand, it is worn over a specific area, the light will affect the thoughts and emotions that directly correspond to that area.

This means that when you place Rubellite over a specific area of disharmony, its light will dissolve the disharmonious energy related to that area on all levels. This is significant, because physical disharmonies are usually caused by disharmonies on inner levels. In other words, Rubellite's light will eat away at the causes of people's conditions, as well as their effects.

Rubellite can offer individuals true changes after only several treatments, because the causes—as well as the symptoms—are affected.

* * *

Rubellite can also be used to break up congestion.

Here is an experiment you might wish to try. Gently hold a strand of Rubellite in your hand, with the Rubellite facing your body. Hold it anywhere from three to ten inches away from the body. Then move your relaxed hand (with the Rubellite in it) up and down in front of your body. You may notice that the Rubellite wants your hand to stop over certain areas.

Then, if your hand is relaxed enough and your intuition is open, you will find that the Rubellite encourages your hand to move in a circle. Soon you might find that the Rubellite encourages your hand to circle in the opposite direction or move to another area of the body. Do not be surprised if the circles change directions often.

What is occurring is that the Rubellite is unwinding the tension in whatever organ or part of the body over which it is circling. Tension is somewhat like a combination lock. Rubellite's circular motion reflects the sequence needed to open the lock. To release the tension, the Rubellite might have to turn a certain number of times to the right, then to the left, and back again. Rubellite knows the "combination" to the area over which it rests, because the clockwise or counterclockwise motions are needs being dictated to the Rubellite by the body.

If Rubellite touches the skin, the unwinding motion will occur inside the body.

Using Rubellite in this way will help certain areas come into greater harmony with the rest of the body. For example, let us say that your body has an overall toxicity level of what we shall call "five," and that one particular area of the body has a toxicity level of "six." Rubellite will bring the level-six area into greater balance with the rest of the body by bringing it closer to the toxicity level of five.

* * *

Because of my specific mission regarding women, I have a particularly strong effect on women's reproductive organs.

A healthy woman can place one strand of Rubellite over her uterus to tone it up or to relieve cramps.

I cannot assist women who are infertile for physical reasons, such as the lack of a uterus or ovaries. However, I can greatly assist women who possess all of their reproductive organs and are infertile for unknown or unexplainable reasons.

Before you begin this therapy, determine exactly where your uterus and ovaries are located. Then lie on your back and place a strand of Rubellite on the skin over the ovaries, fallopian tubes, and uterus. Spread the Rubellite so that it covers as much of these areas as possible. It will be best to cover only these areas, because then there will be greater focus.

The blue, pink, and white rays entering these areas will be extremely helpful. This is not only because of their effect on physical disharmony, but because the rays will also highlight the reasons for the infertility. These reasons are there for you to face, accept, and resolve—and they may not necessarily be physical. Simply gaining the understanding and knowledge of its true causes will help you to resolve your condition.

If you place Rubellite directly on the skin, it will also work to unwind the tensions and stresses contributing to the infertility on the physical level.

It is very difficult to cure infertility with diet, because the causes are usually not physical. However, I am not dismissing the possibility that dietary measures might help.

In this era, the causes of physical conditions are no longer solely physical, like they might have been in the past. The causes are often mental and emotional; and they usually manifest physically.

Before you begin the next stage of this treatment, find out from your physician exactly which part of your reproductive system is most responsible for your infertility. Is it the left ovary? The uterus? A fallopian tube? Rubellite can assist if the condition is due to a clogged fallopian tube, because this is not the same type of physical impairment as not having a fallopian tube at all or not having a uterus.

The reproductive organs of a woman who is not pregnant are located in a relatively small area. Before you begin the treatment, mentally divide the area into three sections: left, middle, and right. If the left ovary or fallopian tube has been identified as the culprit, place the Rubellite over the left section of your reproductive organs for three consecutive treatments. Then place it over the middle section (the uterus) for one treatment, and then over the right section (the right ovary and fallopian tube) for one treatment. Continue to repeat this sequence of treatments.

If a uterine condition is responsible for the infertility, place the Rubellite over the middle section for three treatments, then over the right section for one treatment, and then over the left section for one treatment. Again, continue to repeat this sequence. Follow a similar pattern if the right ovary or fallopian tube is causing the greatest disharmony.

After a few of these sequences, it might be beneficial to alter the pattern. Start giving three treatments to the most critical section and two treatments to each of the other sections. Or you could give two treatments to the most critical section, and then one treatment to each of the other sections. This will allow the entire reproductive area to be exercised more frequently and evenly.

If you do not know which section is causing you the most grief, place the Rubellite over a different section for each treatment. For example, first place it over the left section, then the middle, then the right, and repeat.

Treatments should be given every day and should last at least fifteen to thirty minutes. However, this is only a guideline. Rubellite is very strong, and I do not know what quality of Rubellite you will be using. The more intense the color is, the stronger the Rubellite will be. The stronger the

Rubellite is, the less time you will need for each application. You could keep the Rubellite on for up to an hour if you wish, as long as there is no discomfort.

If at any time you experience any additional pain or discomfort, immediately remove the Rubellite.

For best results, apply the Rubellite where direct sunlight can shine upon it. If you cannot go out in the sun for every treatment, apply the Rubellite over the entire reproductive area when you are able to be in the sun.

It is not necessary to wear the Rubellite around your neck when you are not applying it to the skin over your reproductive organs.

You can either start trying to get pregnant as soon as you begin this therapy, or you can wait until you have been practicing it for some time. Waiting for at least a month would provide time for the physical changes to take place. Continue the therapy while you are trying to get pregnant.

This therapy is one that you can apply to yourself. However, a physician may want to keep track of your progress and give you suggestions about where to place the Rubellite.

Although I used infertility as an example, any disharmony in a woman's reproductive organs can be particularly benefited by Rubellite. The reproductive organs are more sensitive and respond better to this application of Rubellite than do any other organs.

However, a woman can also use Rubellite in the same ways that a man applies Green Tourmaline. And, of course, a woman can wear Rubellite along with Aventurine if she has a physical condition she wishes to resolve.

Gemstones are not to be used in place of physicians. Gemstones are tools. If I had a certain condition which was limiting me from attaining my goal, I would certainly see a physician with whom I felt comfortable. At the same time, I would use my intuition to select the most powerful tools I knew of to help me resolve and remove the obstacle.

The most powerful tools I know of—and that are available on the Earth planet—are gemstones.

Some may argue that drugs are more powerful than gemstones. Drugs appear to work faster and provide results almost immediately. My question is: Do they work on the actual causes of the problem? Furthermore, do they help the individual resolve these causes? Or do they only work on symptoms?

Remember, most gemstones work on the actual causes of conditions.

Herbs are different from either drugs or gemstones. First, they are more easily obtainable, since anyone can grow an herb. They grow much faster than gemstones, but their life spans are also much shorter. The life span of a gemstone will exceed your lifetime. Guaranteed. No matter how often you wear it. An herb cannot promise that. I have respect for herbs. They have their place, and an individual can use a vast variety of them.

Therapeutic quality gemstones are rarer than therapeutic quality herbs. Therefore, they will cost more. However, they also contain a more concentrated healing force. Unlike an herb, the value of a gemstone and its giving properties will not wane over time. Therefore, gemstones are also an investment.

Rubellite Tomorrow

My missions as I have described them will be in effect for many, many years. Perhaps Rubellite will have other missions to fulfill sometime in the future. However, I do not know what these might be. There are too many changes, possibilities, and potentials, for the future to be set at this time.

As I look at each of you sitting comfortably in this lush jungle garden, I realize that you have not caught much of what I have said. I have been given a chance to share myself; but from what I see, at this time only a small piece of my discourse actually has taken root in your hearts.

This observation only supports my own growing understanding of the law of silence. It confirms the value of using the silent method of teaching to convey information. If I had taught you in silence, each of you would have gained a knowingness of what I said. Of course, that would have been totally impractical for the purpose of this interview.

However, it suggests a way that anyone can learn more about gemstones simply by being in the company of a gemstone and contemplating it. In order to do this, you must be able to open your consciousness to that source of infinite wisdom and knowingness while you focus on the gemstone. Then, knowledge, understanding, and awareness will be able to pour into you. When you finish this exercise, you will truly know and own all that you experienced. I can think of no more effective method of learning anything.

* * *

Next you will meet the Guardian of the earthstone Sodalight.

You will find that some Earthstone Guardians are similar to the Gemstone Guardians. However, some are very different. The vibratory rate of the earthstones of which they are in charge influence the appearance of the Earthstone Guardians very greatly.

Just as gemstones work on all the inner worlds, so do their Guardians. The work of most earthstones is somewhat limited to the physical arena. Most of the Guardians of these earthstones do not have an awareness that extends far beyond the physical or the emotional areas.

Therefore, do not expect to hear much more about Soul, Spirit, or the inner bodies. Do not expect long discourses into the causes and effects of things, since their consciousness is more limited.

Thank you.

"Thank you," I heard Michael reply, as I slowly began to move out of Rubellite's aura.

For several minutes, I remained suspended halfway out of her aura. In this state I knew all that Rubellite knew; at the same time I was aware of what the listeners had experienced. I could easily see and understand that only a fraction of what she said had truly taken root in their hearts.

I only wished that my own heart could be fertile enough and my experience profound enough for her words to become my own knowledge. I hoped that most of it would take root in my heart.

Then I completely slipped away from this Gemstone Master-to-be. We watched her body fade until her vibratory rate became the mist that rose from the pool, and we could no longer distinguish them from each other.

17
SODALIGHT

I tried to move into the inner worlds where we usually met the Gemstone Guardians, but I had no success. Then I realized that I was struggling because I was looking in the wrong direction. Sodalight was an earthstone. Therefore, I should find him on the Earth.

I remembered that the Guardian of Sodalight and I had made an "appointment" to meet. Now, at the appointed time, I was feeling a magnetic pull toward the Guardian. I turned my attention toward the Earth, scanned the planet for the source of this attraction, and then let go. In the next moment I found myself in the rocky foothills of a mountain. There the Guardian of Sodalight sat waiting on a boulder.

He had short dark hair and blue-gray eyes and appeared to be in his thirties. His royal blue pants and shirt were so loose-fitting that they could have been mistaken for robes. He looked quite human. I guessed that, if he were dressed in less unusual clothing, one would probably not pick him out in a crowd.

He also appeared burdened, as though he were carrying a great inner weight. Yet I felt refreshed in his presence.

Michael soon joined us and took a seat on another large rock. No other listeners arrived.

I asked the Guardian if I should enter his aura as I had been entering the auras of the Gemstone Guardians. He told me just to sit down next to him and close my eyes. I did what I was told and began to imagine what it might be like to see what Sodalight saw, feel what his heart felt, and know what he knew. Then I felt our auras slipping into each other and the Guardian beginning to speak. . .

Greetings, my friend. Your wife is using a different technique to relay my discourse. This is necessary, because my vibratory rate is different from those of the Gemstone Guardians.

Although its importance is often overlooked by people, Sodalight is crucial to the Earth planet.

That which is hidden behind conscious awareness is often overlooked. These things are stored in the subconscious; one function of the subconscious is to collect those things that would clutter and overload the conscious mind.

Yes, I have an awareness of the mind and the subconscious levels of the individual, but my work is focused more towards the physical.

When I am in rock form and exposed to the atmosphere, I help humans by making their planet a cleaner, more enjoyable place to live. I do this by absorbing unnecessary forces and energies that collect in the atmosphere and impede life.

In a rounded form, I assist humans by making the environment of the wearers' aura a cleaner and more harmonious place to live; for, indeed, one lives within one's aura.

When worn, I will absorb all the energies in the aura that are unimportant for survival and those on which it is unnecessary to place one's attention. Without Sodalight's intervention, these energies can bog down an individual's mind and inner workings. With Sodalight, the physical body is less burdened, and the life- giving energies can flow more easily into the physical body.

The Early Years of Sodalight

You have been told over and over that the Earth is a living entity. As the Earth grew and recognized a future need for something which would balance its atmosphere, it started to formulate the chemical composition of the stone you call Sodalight. Sodalight grew in many places around the planet. It was as rock-like as rock could be, since at first the Earth only needed it for itself.

As people evolved, they began to work with their minds and emotions from a less instinctual and physical viewpoint.

This new way of thinking and feeling gave people greater freedom of expression; but they had not yet learned the sense of responsibility that must accompany such a freedom. As a result, people's thoughts and emotions became unharnessed, unruly, and negative; as they were expressed, these negative thoughts and emotions were released into the Earth's atmosphere.

The Earth noticed that its atmospheric balance was being upset by the negative energies that people were irresponsibly (though unconsciously) throwing off. It also knew that Sodalight had the potential to cleanse negative thoughts from people's auras before they were released into the atmosphere. To do this, the Sodalight would have to be fashioned into spheres and worn. The Earth realized, however, that it would be many centuries before the consciousness of the people had developed to the point where they would be ready to fashion Sodalight into spheres.

In the meantime, the Earth had to do what it could to compensate and protect itself by balancing its own atmosphere. This meant that the Sodalight itself had to change, and indeed some of it did. This Sodalight had to raise its vibratory rate to meet the vibratory rate of the humans' thought emanations. Consequently, this Sodalight became more gem-like and less rock-like. The realization of this need for a change in Sodalight occurred in the Age of Atlantis.

At the same time, the people's need for more indigo ray was increasing. As this Sodalight evolved and became more gem-like, it also gained the ability to accept greater amounts of indigo ray.

Some Sodalight is still undergoing this evolution from rock to gemstone, but not all of it. There will always be Sodalight whose vibratory rate is most compatible with the Earth; and this Sodalight will always receive the indigo ray for the planet. The vibratory rate of the Sodalight that is becoming a gemstone is moving further and further away from the vibratory rate of true Sodalight. As you know, this gemstone is named Indigo.

At this time, the Indigo gem still absorbs negativity and disharmony from the atmosphere like Sodalight does. However, its ability to absorb negativity from the Earth's atmosphere will decrease as Indigo begins to carry the indigo ray more purely. The Indigo gemstone will become more responsible for the changes that the indigo ray brings to people and for supporting them through these changes.

My evolution has already spanned many years of your time, but relatively few of my own. As far as I am concerned, I have not even reached the prime of my life. True Sodalight is undergoing its own evolution. This evolution is quite distinct from the one being experienced by the Sodalight that is being born anew in the gemstone Indigo. The vibratory rate of true Sodalight is becoming stronger and more effective for the planet. My powers for absorbing disharmony and negativity in the Earth's atmosphere are increasing, because the Earth needs this to help maintain its balance.

At this time, I am still in charge of the gemstone Indigo; the Guardian of Sapphire appears to be in charge of training the Guardian of Indigo. The Guardian of Indigo is only a boy. However, as soon as he learns responsibility and many other things as well, a split will occur. Then that Guardian will take complete charge of the Indigo gem, and I will focus my energies exclusively on Sodalight.

Sodalight Today

You might gain a better understanding of my purpose if I could somehow convey to you my love for this planet. As I look at the blue-green valley stretching below us and the bright blue sky dotted with clouds above, this love fills my heart.

I work to maintain a clear atmosphere through my absorbing abilities and through the indigo ray that I carry. By human standards and needs, the indigo ray I carry is almost insignificant. Yet, if humans gaze upon Sodalight, my indigo color might inspire them to share my dream of maintaining a clean blue sky. Then, perhaps, human intuition will open, and those with certain influences will be inspired to mine more Sodalight. Increased mining of Sodalight is important, because it is only when Sodalight touches the atmosphere that it can work on cleansing the atmosphere.

I can only hope that the growth in strength I am bound to experience will occur as rapidly as the growth of the Earth's need for me.

Are you referring to the increase in air pollution?" Michael asked.

Yes, but remember that air pollution can include disharmonious thought energies as well as disharmonious physical molecules.

I do not absorb physical air pollution directly. It must first interact with the air and be broken down by it. It is similar to the way in which your body cannot digest food easily unless the food has been chewed. I do not absorb pollution unless it has been processed by the air. The air begins to work on its pollutants immediately.

Often, the effects of forest fires or volcanic eruptions are not entirely bad. The Earth can use ingredients in the smoke or the volcanic gases to correct certain imbalances. There are even occasions when the Earth needs and uses the increased radiation that results from sunspots. The Earth also adapts as well as it can to the negative influences and stresses that people place on their planet; and it appreciates the positive influences that people provide, as well. All these things are factors in the life and health of the Earth.

Imagine all the textbooks required to explain to a medical student how the human body works. The same number of textbooks would be required to describe how the planet works and how it relates to the life that lives on it.

Sodalight spheres naturally possess a strong magnetic attraction for the disharmonious mental energies in your aura. When you wear Sodalight spheres, the Sodalight first studies your aura. During this process, the Sodalight also learns the nature and origin of your negative thought emanations. Once they are identified, you could remove the Sodalight from your aura and place it on the mantle or some other similar place in your home. The Sodalight will know which specific vibratory rates to attract. The longer you wear Sodalight, the stronger this attraction becomes.

Remember that my primary purpose is for the planet. When people wear me in my spherical form, the negative energies in their auras are absorbed before they can be released into the Earth's atmosphere. Therefore, the more that people wear me, the less pollution there will be for the Earth to have to deal with.

I would like to clarify something. The rock form of Sodalight can also absorb people's negative thought emanations. However, the air just has to "chew" them longer. Because humans carry a higher vibratory rate of the life force, human thought emanations have a higher vibratory rate than physical pollutants. The air must work on lowering the vibratory rate of human thought emanations to a point where the rock form of Sodalight can easily absorb them. Therefore, it takes the air longer to break down thought forms than it does to break down physical pollution, such as carbon monoxide.

* * *

I only work indirectly on healing the physical body. Once people's auras are a little cleaner, the light of Spirit can shine through the inner bodies to the physical body more brightly. This effect can be compared to the way the sun shines on the Earth more brightly after the clouds have dissipated.

When people's auras are cleaner, they can see themselves more clearly. It is easier to see who they are, what their strengths and shortcomings are, and in what direction of life they are headed. Once these things are known, people can choose to enhance their attributes, work on their shortcomings, or change the direction in which their lives are currently taking them. However, these are all secondary effects of Sodalight.

My work is done mostly on a subconscious level. It is only the results of my work that are felt consciously.

As you might imagine, the best place to wear Sodalight is either around the neck or around the head as a tisrati. Also, the larger the Sodalight spheres are or the more spheres worn, the more disharmonies will be absorbed.

If you cannot wear Sodalight during the day, sleep with as many strands as you wish. Wear them around your neck or keep them in the bed with you. Placing Sodalight under your pillow will only work if your pillow is made of cotton, down, feathers, or some other natural material. Likewise, if Sodalight is placed under sheets of polyester or some other synthetic fabric, it will not be able to work on your entire aura.

I have my greatest effects when I am worn and touch the atmosphere at the same time. I cannot absorb when I am covered by any man-made material, including plastic. This is also true of leather.

"Does Sodalight need to be touching soil in order to affect the home environment?"

No, it does not need to touch the soil. The atmosphere in your home is still the Earth's atmosphere; it is just bound by four walls, a roof, and a floor.

"Yes, but every home has a different 'atmosphere'."

That is right, because a family's thoughts are contained and collected within the four walls.

The rock form of Sodalight cannot effectively clear accumulated thought energies in the home. Only in rounded form will Sodalight be able to easily absorb the imbalanced, disharmonious thoughts that collect there. In rounded form, Sodalight works toward achieving greater atmospheric balance. To do this, it must be either worn or kept on a table or in some other similar place in the home.

When the rounded form is worn around the neck, it assists the individual's aura directly.

"You are called an earthstone. Does that mean you are indigenous to the Earth?"

I, as the Guardian of Sodalight, work only for the Earth planet. I have enough to do just to maintain balance on this one planet, without being concerned about other planets, too.

* * *

A balanced mind will not throw off as much mental disharmony and negativity as an imbalanced mind will. Also, it is often true that the more disharmonies the mind emanates, the more imbalanced it will become.

If the mind is relieved of the burdens it has created, it can more easily find balance. I remove the clouds of disharmony emanated by your mind and therefore free your mind to see what it has done. Hopefully, once the clouds are gone, the mind will also see the reasons that it throws off such disharmony.

However, I do not absorb or remove these reasons or the cause of the disharmony. If an individual realizes the cause of a certain mental activity and chooses not to change, and if the individual also decides to stop wearing Sodalight, eventually the aura will become just as polluted as it was before the Sodalight was worn.

I simply release the burden. Once the burden is lifted, people will more easily see their minds and themselves. They will see what they are doing to themselves as a result of their negative emanations. I can help individuals to balance their minds, but only if they are willing to make their own changes.

* * *

As soon as I am placed in the aura, it is as though a switch is turned on. I become charged. However, it may be many minutes before this charge is recognizable through kinesiological or other testing methods.

My strength and effectiveness steadily increases as I am worn. For example, if I am worn constantly for ten months, I will be much stronger for the wearer than if I were worn for only ten weeks.

At the same time, I become more saturated with the energies I have absorbed. Fortunately, my increased strength more than compensates for this greater saturation. It is similar to the way a vacuum cleaner has to work harder to clean the rug as the vacuum's bag gets fuller.

One can measure the degree of Sodalight's saturation by the degree to which its color changes after it has been mined. In general, the more whiteness that is apparent, the more saturated is the Sodalight. However, the whiteness you find in your Sodalight spheres is not necessarily an indication of how many negative thought-forms it has absorbed. The whiteness may have come from something else the rock absorbed from the atmosphere before the rock was cut into spheres. Furthermore, not all of Sodalight's white streaks are indicators of absorbed disharmony. In freshly mined Sodalight (which has never been exposed to the atmosphere and therefore to atmospheric negativity), the white streaks are just mineral contaminants.

Everyone can benefit from wearing Sodalight. However, it is a very "individual" stone. I say this for two reasons: First, each specimen of Sodalight looks slightly different, even when it has been mined from the same location; second, Sodalight works with each wearer in a very individual way. The magnetic charge of each person's thoughts is slightly different from everyone else's. Sodalight must get to know this charge, and the vibratory rate of the one who wears it, in order to be most effective for that individual. Sodalight also works best if it is worn by only one individual.

Those who may benefit most from wearing Sodalight are people who continually feel overwhelmed, often for no clearly defined reason. Because I clear "garbage" from the aura, individuals who wear me can more clearly see their own true thoughts, feelings, goals, and dreams. Therefore, I am also especially beneficial for those who have difficulty distinguishing between their own thoughts, emotions, goals, and dreams—and those projected onto them by others.

I can also protect individuals from any negative thoughts, emotions, or other energies that are directed toward them by others. This includes unwelcome prayer or black magic. When worn, I can soak up these energies as they enter the aura.

Sodalight's aura encompasses an area many hundred times the size of its physical form. Sodalight's aura acts like a sponge. In a way, it also has a slightly stronger charge than a human's aura. For this reason, negative energies easily flow from the aura of less charge into Sodalight's aura of greater charge.

I will probably not reach complete saturation within the lifetime of the wearer, unless I am continually used to protect the wearer from black magic or the unwanted intense prayer directed by a group. Under normal circumstances, Sodalight can be effective for several decades. However, if the Earth's ozone layer becomes more depleted, and if more disruptive and unneeded energies enter the Earth's aura, I could become saturated within ten years of being exposed to the atmosphere.

Sunlight will not cleanse Sodalight, nor can it unlock or release the energies I have absorbed. The only way Sodalight can be cleansed is to bury it for a few years in soil, two or three feet into the Earth. This should be done respectfully. The Sodalight must also be in direct contact with the soil and not surrounded by any container. Then the forces which naturally flow back and forth between the Earth's core and its surface will do the cleansing.

When buried in the Earth, my aura extends for only a few inches, and I am not useful to the atmosphere. This is why it is important that Sodalight be mined: when I am in contact with the atmosphere, my aura extends a great distance.

Although sunlight will not cleanse Sodalight, sunlight will erase some of its memory of an individual's vibratory rate. Therefore, in order for Sodalight to more easily accommodate its energies to another wearer, it should be placed in bright sunlight for about half an hour.

Do not be concerned that you might be affected by any energies I have previously absorbed. Nothing but the Earth's forces will be able to affect and remove these energies.

* * *

Only recently has human consciousness risen to the point where people are ready to accept the powers that gemstones unleash when they are not confined to their crystalline form, but are fashioned into spheres.

I myself am unaware of all the effects Sodalight spheres may have on the human. It is my responsibility to become aware of these effects as they become apparent and are felt and recognized. My duty as a Guardian includes collecting, recording, and cataloging data about Sodalight. This data includes the ways in which the stone's vibratory rate changes under different atmospheric, spiritual, or astrological influences.

Earthstones are more affected by the position of the sun and the planets than are the gemstones. This is because the earthstones have a greater affinity with the physical vibratory rate of the Earth. Gemstones, on the other hand, may not be at all influenced by the movement of planets and their magnetic energies, because the scope of the gemstones' effects reaches far beyond the physical.

My duties also include working in the dream state with those individuals who are either ready for Sodalight's effects or who are already wearing Sodalight.

In essence, Michael, you and I are both pioneers, exploring the effects of the spherical form. It is just that my pioneering efforts are sharply focused on Sodalight.

As far as I know, no one knows every application of the sphere. Spheres radiate their energy in an infinite number of directions. Therefore, the possible applications of a sphere are probably just as infinite.

Sodalight Tomorrow

Fortunately, time seems to expand for the busy person. I say this because I see myself only getting busier in the future. Of course, the prospect of doing more work implies that more people will be touched by Sodalight's effects. This also means that my role for the planet will be increasingly fulfilled. As I have said, my strength will be growing to meet the needs of the planet if and when it requires more atmospheric cleansing.

It is not possible to mine too much Sodalight. In fact, it would be wise to prepare for protection against possible surges of disharmonious and unnecessary thoughts, vibratory rates, energies, or conditions that could one day enter the atmosphere. It would also serve my mission to be distributed among the people of Earth, because when I am evenly distributed around the planet, I can serve the planet most effectively.

Sodalight is often overlooked because of the brilliance of the gemstones. However, Sodalight is too important to continue to be overlooked. This will be especially true if the atmosphere continues to be depleted and if scattered mental energies remain largely negative. Without the help of Sodalight, the planet could be assaulted by many other forces that would impede human life and, subsequently, the life of the Earth.

"What is your opinion about gemstones and earthstones being worn in their natural form?" Michael asked.

I know you are referring to the shape of gemstones and earthstones as they are found in the ground. Be careful with the word "natural." It is very natural for human beings today to wear spheres. Their state of consciousness is ready for spheres.

Once a gemstone or an earthstone is shaped into a sphere, its energies can be unleashed on its wearer in a way that would not be possible if it were in its crystalline or rock form.

"Many people seem to think that it is wrong to change the shape of gemstones or earthstones."

The information the Guardians are giving you is on the crest of the wave. This means that not everyone on the planet is ready to accept the powers of gemstones in spherical form. Still, enough people are ready to accept this information, work and experiment with it, learn from it, and grow from it.

People often hold on dearly to what they know, and they cling to things that have worked in the past. Give them time. As the wave moves closer to the shore, their consciousness will unfold. People only limit themselves by clinging to the crystalline form. However, if individuals who cling to crystals were to let go of their concepts and experience the power of the spherical form, they might grow faster than they are ready to grow. So, be compassionate and be patient. Let people have the space and time to grow at their own rates.

The Earth uses the crystalline form, because it is particularly effective for the Earth. However, when crystals are used in certain special ways, they can also be very effective tools for humans.

Follow me further up into these rocky foothills, and I will lead you to the Guardian of Leopardskin Jasper. We will enter a cave, and somewhere within the mountain you will meet the Guardian. Do not be surprised if you are not met by a physical form. You might only meet an energy.

We will rest before we begin our journey.

18

LEOPARDSKIN JASPER

The path was rocky and steep. I was glad that we did not have to walk far before the Guardian of Sodalight pointed out the narrow opening of a cave.

As soon as we squeezed through the entrance, the passage widened and the sunlight dimmed. I wondered what, if anything, would light up the path, since we carried no lamp of any kind. My answer came when, in the darkness, the soft blue glow surrounding Sodalight's body became more evident. It gave us just enough light to see by if we kept close behind him.

We followed the path downhill for about fifty yards until we entered a large, bone-dry cavern. Sodalight's voice echoed as he spoke: "We have entered one of the Earth's major deposits of Leopardskin Jasper. Feel its energy. You have probably not experienced anything like this before."

I opened all my senses to Leopardskin Jasper's energy. I can only describe it as a grounding, earthy, solid, and practical kind of energy. Then I felt a swirling cloud of this energy collect in an area about three feet in front of me. The cloud was several yards in diameter. I knew that if I walked into this swirl of energy, I would be able to speak the words that flowed from the heart of the Guardian of Leopardskin Jasper.

I stepped into the swirl and entered the most unusual state of consciousness I had ever experienced. I felt like I had become the Earth itself. It was as though I knew the entire Earth planet. If I placed my attention on a specific geographic location, I knew everything the Earth knew about that location. I could feel the Earth's nervous system sending messages to each part of the planet. Then I felt these messages returning into my heart. They carried information, feedback, and reports on the energy changes that had recently occurred in these places.

As I wondered whether this network of Leopardskin Jasper tunnels spanned the entire planet, the swirling energy began forming into words, and I felt compelled to begin speaking.

I am like the planet's nervous system. I collect information from the surface and from beneath the surface. Then I act on the information I have gathered. My reactions are mostly in the form of magnetic impulses. I also have a direct line of communication with the Guardian of the Earth.

I learn what is needed by the planet and then work to fulfill those needs. Once I receive information that some part of the Earth requires a change in order to maintain planetary balance, I send magnetic impulses to other gemstones or earthstones. It is these stones which need to take action in order to initiate the change. I tell the gemstones and earthstones what needs to be done; then they initiate and direct whatever changes are required.

Although I can be enjoyed by humans in any form, I only have effects on humans when I am in spherical form. Any other rounded form will not work as strongly.

I do not need to cover the Earth entirely in order to know what is happening within every part of it. I only need to be in certain strategic locations.

The strategic location on the human is the neck. When I encircle the neck, I can touch the whole aura and get to know the entire human. This is similar to the way I get to know the entire Earth even when I am located in only a few strategic places.

The energy contained in the spheres flows into the aura, where it captures information. Then the energy bounces back to the Leopardskin Jasper spheres. In this way I get to know what is needed for the human. Just as my magnetic impulses draw what is needed to balance certain areas of the Earth, they draw toward my wearers whatever they need to achieve greater balance.

The aura reflects a person's needs, and the mind focuses and defines them. This action is similar to what occurs when I express one of the planet's needs to another earthstone; this earthstone then works to focus and define the need more clearly. It also determines the possible solution to that need. I do not understand the human's mind, so I cannot tell you how this mechanism works in the human. However, I have noticed that there is a parallel between a human and the planet in this respect.

The Early Years of Leopardskin Jasper

I was formed when the Earth formed, just as the human nervous system forms along with the fetus. I am necessary for the life of the planet, and I will be here for as long as the planet is alive or is capable of supporting life.

Leopardskin Jasper Today

When Leopardskin Jasper is cut into spherical form, circular patterns appear on the spheres. My magnetic rays emanate from these circles. The more circles there are, the stronger and more effective the spheres will be in drawing what is needed to an individual. Therefore, the more spheres of Leopardskin Jasper that an individual wears, the more powerful will be my effects (as long as the spheres worn contain circles).

These circles are also like control knobs. When they read an aura and identify its needs, they are able to judge what is a true need and what is an artificial one. An example of an artificial need is a child's "need" to have ice cream for dessert. The child's true need might really be for an apple. Likewise, when a certain imbalance occurs in the planet, the immediate surrounding area might think that it needs what we shall arbitrarily call "ten points" of compensation to restore its balance. However, from a global viewpoint, the true need might be only three points of compensation.

The more circles that are apparent, the greater will be my ability to discriminate between true and artificial needs. A greater number of circles will also create an increase in my ability to draw compensation to the area of true need.

The overall color of Leopardskin Jasper might vary somewhat among individual specimens. This variation in overall color is simply a result of the vibratory rate of the location in which a specimen formed.

Also, within any Leopardskin Jasper specimen is contained

many different colors. Since colors are vibratory rates, this phenomenon reflects my ability to know, recognize, and understand many different vibratory rates. Having several colors gives me the ability to have more options, be more flexible, and be as helpful as possible both for the Earth and the human. The variety of colors reflects my ability to work with different frequencies on many different levels.

I can be even more effective for the human when spheres of different sizes are worn at the same time. Then I can penetrate the aura more deeply and access more frequencies on different levels of the aura. In this way, the needs of the wearer can be fulfilled more effectively.

If you are attracted to Leopardskin Jasper, it will be most effective if you wear it continually, instead of just every now and then. This will be true, regardless of the length of time you wear it. For example, it would be better to wear it for seven days in a row during a given month, than to wear it on seven different days throughout that month.

Leopardskin Jasper Therapy

The one word that characterizes my effects is "regulation." In essence, I am a regulator of energies.

If an Earthquake occurs and creates an imbalance, I must regulate the planet's energies in order to compensate. I must reestablish balance on a global scale.

When I am worn around a person's neck, I work to establish balance for the entire person. I can also help if one part of a person is out of balance or does not work in harmony with the rest of that person. If Leopardskin Jasper spheres are placed over the imbalanced area, I will regulate that area.

Since my vibratory rate passes through solid rock, it also easily penetrates skin and bone.

Leopardskin Jasper can be placed over any organ that is not regulating itself properly or is not functioning in harmony with the rest of the body. This includes organs with a metabolic dysfunction, those that are not synchronized within themselves or with the rest of the body, and those that are not responding properly to messages from other body parts. I will satisfy the organ's needs. I will call to it physical life forces or vibratory rates, such as minerals or ions, that the organ's cells need in order to function in harmony with the rest of the body.

My work will be most effective on those organs with regulatory functions—such as the brain, heart, and glands.

To help regulate brain function, Leopardskin Jasper should not just encircle the head, but should cover every square inch of the skull like a skullcap. To help the heart regulate its beat, Leopardskin Jasper should be placed in a clump over the heart. The thicker the pile of Jasper is, the more deeply into the organ I can penetrate.

My vibratory rate will still penetrate the organ if the Leopardskin Jasper is only placed in one layer. However, if you have an organ that is not functioning properly, it is best to place many layers of Leopardskin Jasper over the area. This will allow my vibratory rate to penetrate more deeply into the cells. This is true for humans, because they are not just physical beings. They consist of many more levels than does the Earth.

The Leopardskin Jasper should be kept over the area you wish to reeducate for as long as possible. If you cannot keep it there constantly, apply it to the area for a minimum of one or two hours at least once or twice a day. When the Jasper cannot be over the affected area, wear it around your neck. This will help your body remember how it and the organ in question should be working.

You can make changes happen within weeks, even if you cannot keep the Jasper over the area constantly, but can only apply it there for short periods every day.

I believe that I can work very effectively on a human—especially since, from my point of view, humans are so changeable and frail. Yet there are many influences affecting the life of a human body. Therefore, when treating a physical problem, there will probably be other, non-physical factors to be addressed. The focus of the Leopardskin Jasper will be on the physical reconditioning of an organ that is not regulating properly.

I know how strong I am for the Earth planet. However, I do not know exactly how strong I can be for a human when my spheres are applied directly over an area. Therefore, be careful. Use your intuition when you work with Leopardskin Jasper.

Let me give you an example. Often, after an earthquake, the area surrounding the earthquake feels that it needs ten points worth of compensation. I know it only needs five points of compensation, and I will supply only five. Similarly, there is no way I can convince you that your body only needs only one strand of Leopardskin Jasper over an organ, when you think that it needs ten strands.

If too much Leopardskin Jasper is applied, the organ might overcompensate. Then it may seem that the Jasper is making the condition worse, when in fact you are either wearing too much at one time, or your treatments are too frequent. Cut back. Find a balance.

I work for the benefit of both Earth and humans, simply because my nature is to regulate. I know that living things need to be very well-regulated in order to sustain life. They must be regulated with extreme definition and impeccable synchrony. They must work like clockwork. All parts must be reliable, because every part depends on the reliability of every other part in order for life to continue.

An organ which is out of synchrony would not be out if there were not another imbalance somewhere in the body. The human body is similar to the Earth in this way. Earthquakes, certain weather patterns, and other events in nature occur because something else has happened to upset the balance. These events are manifestations of the Earth's striving for balance. Wearing Leopardskin Jasper around the neck, especially if it touches the skin, will bring greater balance and regulation throughout the physical body as a whole.

I do not remove disease from the Earth or from humans. I just help the body become more balanced. Of course, disease is an imbalance.

I do not take responsibility for what occurs when an individual becomes more balanced as a result of my influence. Again, my responsibility is only to bring the physical body and that which the body needs closer to each other. Do not be surprised at what I might draw to the body. It might be a book on a new healing method; it might be a physician; or it might be certain foods or medicines. All these things are just vibratory rates. A physician with certain knowledge is a vibratory rate. So is a book. Medicines, herbs, fresh mountain air and a trip to the beach are also distinct vibratory rates. I do not distinguish between vibratory rates and the physical forms they take on.

I recognize what vibratory rate is needed to help maintain a balance. With my magnetic quality, I bring the person who has a need toward the vibratory rate that is needed, and vice versa. They are drawn to each other, just like the north and south poles of two magnets.

Ideally, I should be given to a child and allowed to live with that child throughout its life. The more I am worn by one individual, the more I can get to know that individual and what his or her needs are.

* * *

If Leopardskin Jasper is placed in the sun for about one hour, the sun will help wipe away any patterns or other information I have stored about my wearer. It is as though the sun erases what is on the "chalkboard" of the Leopardskin Jasper.

If a gemstone therapist uses the same Leopardskin Jasper on only one individual without cleansing it between treatments, less ground will be lost between treatments. Each time the individual receives a treatment, I will take the next step needed. If the Jasper were de-programmed in the sun, I would have to relearn the individual's needs each time the therapy was applied.

* * *

The way I regulate is specific to the Earth and to Earth humans, just like the manner in which a cow's brain regulates a cow's body in a way that is specific to cows; a cow's brain would not work in a human's body, and vice versa.

Yet, despite their similarities, each Earth human is a unique individual. This is why a human body will sometimes reject an organ transplant from another human. When a body rejects an organ transplant, it is because the vibratory rate of the organ donor is too different from that of the organ recipient; or, more specifically, the regulatory mechanism of the donor organ is too different from that of the recipient. When this is the case, the organ will not be able to live in the recipient's body, and the recipient's body will reject it.

If a human wears Leopardskin Jasper spheres long enough, that person's overall regulatory mechanism will become more defined and specific. It will also become very strong. As a result, the individual's personal magnetism and individuality will increase; the definition of who that individual is will become more specific. Therefore, those who wear Leopardskin Jasper almost continually are not good organ-donor candidates: their organs will become less adaptable to the regulatory mechanisms of other people's bodies.

As the person wearing Leopardskin Jasper becomes more self-defined, individuals from this planet or other planets who may have dishonorable intentions will be magnetically repelled by the person. Just as I can attract that which is harmonious, I can also repel that which is disharmonious. The more Leopardskin Jasper worn, the stronger the repelling force will be. Still, it may take many months of wearing Leopardskin Jasper before this force becomes strong enough to actually repel other people.

By wearing Leopardskin Jasper, those who feel that they are constantly bringing disharmony into their lives will begin to attract things that bring greater harmony. At the same time, they will begin to repel things that feed disharmony.

Those who think that they only attract disharmony are perhaps looking at their lives from a viewpoint that does not encompass the whole picture. With or without Leopardskin Jasper, whatever you bring into your life represents the force which continually strives to create balance. This is the nature of life; in order for life to exist, there must be balance, and give and take.

Often people who are caught in a situation in which they feel like disharmony is constantly entering their lives are convinced that they need more compensation then they actually do. This is similar to the way in which a child might think he needs five scoops of ice cream, when in reality he only needs one. Leopardskin Jasper can help convince the child that he only needs one scoop by drawing only that one scoop into his life. If people have set up the circumstances which continually draw the other four scoops into their lives, I can help repel these other four scoops.

However, one must remember that mental energy is much stronger than physical energy. My work is focused on the physical. On the other hand—and this is not meant to be confusing or paradoxical—when I touch the aura, I can work to attract or repel what is needed or not needed by the mind and the emotions. This is because the aura reflects the needs of the mind and the emotions. However, I attract or repel only as these mental and emotional needs relate to the physical body.

Leopardskin Jasper can help repel negative influences from the individual who wears it. However, if the individual resists the changes I initiate and insists on opening the door to these influences and inviting them in, there is nothing I can do to repel them. This will be true even if the individual's resistance occurs on an unconscious level.

I work powerfully for the Earth, because the Earth is 100 percent willing to work with me. Likewise, I can be powerful for humans if they are 100 percent willing to make the changes or accept whatever influences I can attract.

Humans are given many gifts that they leave unopened and unaccepted. If people wear Leopardskin Jasper, I will bring the vibratory rates they need into their lives. These vibratory rates are like gifts; I cannot tell people to accept them. They will only receive them if they are 100 percent willing to accept any changes that may occur in their lives as a result of accepting the gifts.

As I get to know people's auras, I can sometimes get to know people better than they think they know themselves. I know their needs better than they do. I know what influences are most harmful to them. Sometimes people enjoy the influences that harm them, and they are not willing to put up the mirror that would reflect these influences away from them. In other words, they are not ready or willing to accept the gifts of Leopardskin Jasper.

I can do nothing if a child is not willing to accept an apple for dessert instead of ice cream—even if I know that the child needs the apple's nutrients. I have no power to change people's minds. I am a tool, and I can only be as effective as the individual is willing to work with me.

Leopardskin Jasper Tomorrow

My mission for the planet has been and always will be as I have described. People may find other applications, as they begin to understand Leopardskin Jasper and the effects it has on them when it is fashioned into spheres. That is the nature of humans: to experiment, explore, and expand their awareness. It is for this reason that they have earned the right to become aware of the effects of the spherical form.

You are alive because of two spheres: the sun and the Earth.

Doesn't it make sense that if you fashion life-giving substances—what you call earthstones and gemstones—into spheres, that you will gain additional life from them? Isn't that obvious? Perhaps it is not so obvious to everyone—yet. Of course, it took many centuries before people all over the planet came to understand that the Earth revolved around the sun. These days people think, "Of course, the Earth revolves around the sun. How obvious."

At the far side of this cavern, you will find a passageway that leads to a different network of caverns. There you will meet the Guardian of the earthstone you call Poppy Jasper.

Before you leave, I want you to know that this discourse was an important part of my work. Now you have the opportunity to understand more clearly the effects of Leopardskin Jasper without having to endure many years of trial and error and experiments. Now you have a direction in which to look for an even greater understanding of the possible effects of Leopardskin Jasper on the physical body of a human or an animal.

Indeed, animals may experience greater effects than humans when they wear Leopardskin Jasper, because their minds do not get in their way. Their minds do not constantly tell them that they need ice cream instead of apples.

"Thank you for sharing this information," said Michael.

It is my duty.

I was suddenly ejected from the swirling energy. It did not surprise me, since it is apparently Leopardskin Jasper's nature to repel that which is no longer needed.

To my right I saw the blue glow of the individual who I assumed was the Guardian of Sodalight. Silently, he started to move toward the other end of the cavern. There he entered another passageway and we followed.

This time the path was relatively level, but the passageway was small and narrow and required some crawling to get through. Luckily, the spirit of adventure squelched any feelings of claustrophobia I may have had.

Finally, the tunnel opened up into a large room. This room had many stalactites and stalagmites through which we had to wind our way. The atmosphere was very damp. The walls and ceiling were like sponges that were so saturated with water, that it dripped from the walls and ceilings uncontrollably.

Somewhere in this cavern, I knew we would meet the Guardian of Poppy Jasper.

19
POPPY JASPER

Suddenly, in the very center of the wet cavern, a campfire appeared. It was an unusual fire in other ways too, for it did not produce smoke, and its light did not dance on the cavern walls. It simply radiated a constant glow which allowed us to see the entire cavern more clearly.

The Guardian of Sodalight showed no concern about the fire. It merely seemed to be his cue to request the presence of the Guardian of Poppy Jasper.

Again a formless swirl of energy collected a few feet in front of me. I noticed that its vortex was turning in the direction opposite to that of Leopardskin Jasper's vortex. I walked into the swirl and caught my breath. The energy was like a physical pressure on my body. Even more striking was the change in my perception. I no longer saw the cave walls as rock. Now they were alive—a living part of my own body.

Michael and the Guardian of Sodalight also looked different. I could only see a dim outline of their physical forms, for now I perceived their bodies as masses of water and minerals. Within each of them vibrated a coil of concentrated, brilliant light that gave the collections of water and chemicals life. I knew that this light must be Soul.

Then I felt an urge to rest my mind, listen, and serve as the vehicle for what the Guardian of Poppy Jasper wished to say.

I am like a cousin to Leopardskin Jasper. My work follows his; and when I am fashioned into spheres, my effects on the human parallel my effects on the planet.

My mission for the planet is to provide it with the equivalent of adrenalin. When your adrenalin flows, you work harder and faster. Often your adrenalin flows because you are excited, and it generates a feeling of joy that keeps you going. Adrenalin can also give you the extra energy you sometimes need to get through negative situations. This extra energy is what I give to the Earth. I do this whenever Leopardskin Jasper determines that there is a need for it.

The Early Years of Poppy Jasper

Just as your organs formed as the rest of you was forming, I was formed as the planet formed. You will find that all the earthstones are similar in this regard. Earthstones function for the planet in the same ways that your organs function for you. Your organs will perform the same functions no matter how old you are; and they will die when your physical body dies.

Poppy Jasper Today

I am not as widely distributed within the Earth as Leopardskin Jasper, and the pockets in which I am found are smaller. It is not necessary for me to be distributed equally around the planet, just as it is not necessary for you to have a heart in every organ of your body; you only need one.

The Earth only needs a few deposits of Poppy Jasper; the Earth's circulatory system distributes my vibratory rate wherever it is needed. This circulatory system consists of lines of magnetic flow. Communication throughout the planet is very swift along these magnetic pathways. It is similar to the human body in this way; a painful stimulus in any part of your body is quickly registered by your brain.

The Earth's form is as complex as your human body. However, we are not here today to learn about Earth physiology.

Many earthstones and gemstones are involved in the process of fulfilling the Earth's needs. Our relationship is like your digestive system, in that it consists of many components, all with a single purpose. Your teeth, stomach, intestines, and many other organs are required for the job of digestion and to keep your body nourished.

Now, I am not saying that there is a parallel between the organs involved in the human's digestive system and the functions of Leopardskin and Poppy Jasper. I am using this comparison only to help illustrate how Leopardskin and Poppy Jasper are just components of the whole picture, and how they are both required to keep the Earth functioning.

Leopardskin Jasper recognizes the Earth's needs; it gathers the information that something must be done. Poppy Jasper provides the energy and push to get it done.

When Poppy Jasper receives information from Leopardskin Jasper, its reaction can be described as that of a positive attitude. A positive attitude is the key to getting work done most efficiently and to everyone's benefit. You have probably experienced this for yourself. When you do something with positive energy, more gets done, you feel better for doing it, and others are positively affected by your good humor.

You noticed that my vortex swirls in a downward direction. This is because I get my energy from the atmosphere. The vortex of my vibratory rate pulls this atmospheric energy down through the soil to where the Poppy Jasper is located.

When there is a certain job to be done in a certain place, I spin a "baby" vortex off from the main vortex of the Poppy Jasper deposit. Sometimes the baby vortex is thrown toward the area in need; other times it is thrown toward the gemstone or earthstone that can affect the area more directly than I can.

The baby vortex spins in the direction opposite to that of the main vortex. If it spun in the same direction, the main vortex would not be able to propel it with any degree of force.

As the baby vortex spins in an upward direction, it brings uplifting energy to its target. This uplifting energy can be described as positive, happy, and joyful. It gives a good attitude and good humor. It is acts like adrenalin, giving inspiration and energy to the next earthstone or gemstone in line to carry out the mission identified by Leopardskin Jasper. Wouldn't you agree that you would react more positively to a stimulus if it were uplifting and positive?

* * *

When I am in spherical form, my energy swirls neither upward nor downward, but randomly around the sphere in all directions. This helps to break up crusty patterns, physical impediments, and blockages that prevent energy from entering certain areas of the physical body.

When your physical body is opened up by the effects of Poppy Jasper, it becomes free to accept more energy. This makes you feel good. When you are given a little more adrenalin, your outlook is brightened and becomes more cheerful. You feel joyful and happy to be alive. By wearing Poppy Jasper, you may also feel invigorated as you come to recognize your connection with the life of the Earth. Also, once your physical body is relieved of the blockages that prevent some of its parts from accepting energy, your physical body will be able to do things it was previously unable to do.

I work only on the physical level. I know that your physical body is connected with other levels and is influenced by their energies, but I know nothing about them. I do know that these inner energies affect the body differently when physical blocks are removed; however, I do not know how.

When I propel a baby vortex toward another earthstone, that earthstone is invigorated and enlivened. It acts as though it received a shot of adrenalin. Sometimes that earthstone is aware of its mission as soon as my energy awakens it; sometimes others help to define its job.

I have a similar effect when I am worn on the human body: I can enliven those areas that appear to be dead or sleeping but that should be woken up, because the rest of the organism is awake and alive.

"What do you mean when you say that you 'wake up' an area?" asked Michael.

When your stomach is empty, you might say that it is asleep, because it is not secreting any digestive juices. When you eat food, the stomach wakes up. It becomes enlivened and starts to secrete its juices. I am like that food.

When I work for the Earth, I focus on accomplishing certain missions. When worn around the neck of a human, I do not have a specific focus. However, if Poppy Jasper is placed over a part of you that you know is asleep and that you want to wake up, I can do this. I can also be placed over an area into which you want energy to start flowing more freely. In other words, when I am placed over specific areas, there will be a focus to my work on the human.

This enlivening effect will occur as I work to release certain blockages. The release of these blockages allows the body to accept the force which keeps it alive. Remember, my energy is uplifting. It initiates movement in places where my wearer's energy is stuck or blocked. When I am worn, my vibratory rate flows throughout the entire body. However, I concentrate my energy on areas that are blocked.

I do not see your body as a limitation. As my energy spins around the sphere, it is not impeded by physical matter. My energy will project into a certain area or circumference around the sphere, depending on the size of the sphere. When Poppy Jasper spheres are worn around the neck, the physical body does not interfere with that circumference. Although my energy gradually expands to fill the aura, my greatest strength will always lie within the original circumference. When I am worn around the neck, this area includes the head and most of the torso.

* * *

Blockages do not always manifest as pockets in specific places in the body. Cells throughout the body often have a blocked quality; they are tight, and energy cannot flow through them like it should. When worn, I cause these blockages to be released. Sometimes these releases manifest as spontaneous muscle twitches and stretches. I believe you call them "unwinding" movements. Again, if you want to focus on specific areas of tightness or blockage, it would be best to place Poppy Jasper directly over those areas.

As I mentioned earlier, when an individual wears Poppy Jasper and these blockages open up, he or she will feel good. The earthstones that I enliven are also grateful to be alive, to have a purpose, and to be doing something for the planet which, in turn, is giving them life. Similarly, the more that Poppy Jasper is worn, the more that its wearer will feel happy to be alive.

* * *

In the past year, a change occurred that allowed me and several other earthstones to gain conscious awareness of our own functions and how we work together. Before this change, many earthstones worked by instinct alone and performed their jobs as if in a dream.

With this increase in awareness has come greater harmony or the potential for greater harmony among all parts of the Earth. It has also brought greater responsibility and the potential to work with more difficult situations. If one functions only by instinct or "on automatic," one may not be able to function accurately when any unusual circumstances or variables arise. With conscious awareness, I can cooperate more effectively with the other conscious earthstones to resolve these unusual circumstances.

As your technology is changing, you are growing. However, as a race of beings, you are still basically unaware of the nature of your planet. As a result, you do things to the planet that hurt it. We earthstones must find creative solutions to keep what you do to the planet in balance. We must find ways to keep the Earth alive and, consequently, to keep you alive.

Some unknown force—Spirit, perhaps—has inspired people to fashion earthstones into spheres so that they can be worn. This inspiration is truly a gift to the planet. When people wear earthstones, they become more in tune with their planet. They become aware that their planet is indeed alive, and their understanding of the planet increases. The Earth is such a perfect reflection of the human body in so many ways. Therefore, as people begin to wear earthstones, they will also begin to know themselves better.

In spherical form, I will give a person the same kind of motivation, inspiration, and energy to move and act that I give to other earthstones. One who sits still should not expect to wear Poppy Jasper and remain still. Perhaps the worst thing you could do would be to give Poppy Jasper to someone who must stay in prison. The person will want to move, do something, and change. This person might become very frustrated if he or she were physically prevented from doing so.

* * *

You have caught me within a moment of time. When you leave I will continue my work.

There is much more we could talk about. However, before

we do, you must grasp the information I have already given you. You must take it a step or two further. You must understand enough to be able to ask focused questions, and then we will have much more to talk about. You will know where to find me when you are ready.

I provided the fire only to help you see this cavern more clearly, for I know that darkness often makes humans feel uncomfortable. It makes them reluctant to move. Actually, it is not really a fire at all; it just looks like one. I did not know what other kind of light to manifest.

Perhaps this light will have a symbolic meaning for you. Perhaps the symbol may help you understand how I work on the human. But be careful not to take symbols too far.

"Thank you," said Michael.

Even as the vortex moved away from me, my body continued to feel Poppy Jasper's energy. All my muscles took turns stretching as they released stresses and blockages. These releases were not uncomfortable. Indeed, they were as refreshing as one's first stretch in the morning.

20
BLOODSTONE

We did not have to wait long before another whirlpool of energy emerged from the cavern walls. Its vortex swirled in an upward direction, like that of Leopardskin Jasper's.

"This is the Guardian of Bloodstone," said Sodalight. "As you enter into the aura of each earthstone and gemstone, you experience their characteristic energies firsthand. At the same time, the Guardians get to know you. In knowing you, they learn more about all humans and, therefore, how to work more effectively for those who wear them.

"As you enter this vortex, you may feel like you are entering a tornado. But the wind you will feel is only Bloodstone's energy moving through the molecules of your body. When you reach the calm center of the whirling vortex, you will feel the greatest 'at-one-ness' with Bloodstone."

I walked into Bloodstone's vortex and felt the tornado exactly as Sodalight had described. When I entered its tranquil middle, a line of communication seemed to open, and I felt the urge to speak.

I have a relationship with the Earth and with all the earthstones. I can see specifically where on the planet there is an imbalance or disharmony. Sometimes another earthstone calls my attention to these areas. Leopardskin Jasper is one who does this, but there are others as well.

I know exactly what is needed to correct these imbalances and disharmonies. I help to collect the energies that the planet needs to re-balance itself. These are the energies of different earthstones and gemstones.

"How do earthstones work to balance the disharmony created, for example, by toxic waste dumps?" Michael asked.

This would be a serious situation. All the components of the Earth would have to work as a team, as we always do, to keep the Earth alive. We would all work together, just like all the organs of your body work together to keep you alive.

My role in the team is to gather information about the disharmonious situation and present a proposal to the Guardian of the Earth. The proposal would include a description of the problem and its magnitude. I would also suggest a level of priority I think the Guardian should assign to the problem. I would provide a list of available resources—that is, earthstones and gemstones—that are closest to the area. Finally, I would tell the Guardian how much energy those resources could contribute and how the earthstones plan to solve the problem.

A toxic waste dump would be top-priority. If we got permission to act from the Guardian of the planet, the first thing we would do in this situation would be to shield the toxic area from the rest of the planet. If you do not remove a splinter from your skin, your skin will eventually form a callus around the splinter. In the case of a toxic waste dump, the earthstones would work to form a similar, callus-like shield around the toxic area.

There is a black earthstone, whose Guardian you have not yet met, and whose vibratory rate acts like a shield. This earthstone would encase the toxic deposit. First, it would have to calculate how quickly it could get its energy to the area, how quickly it could start to manifest itself and begin to form a callus, and how quickly the toxic vibratory rate was penetrating the Earth. Once these factors were considered, this earthstone would decide how far away from the borders of the toxicity it would have to start concentrating its energy.

Within days after the toxicity was deposited, the earthstones would analyze the situation, and the proposal would be submitted to the planet's Guardian. If the situation had, for example, a priority level of thirty, we might not get an answer for weeks. If the situation had a priority level of one, we would receive an answer as soon as the Earth completed a day's cycle.

Even if the Guardian of the Earth approved our proposal immediately, we would not be given immediate permission to act. The Guardian would first have to examine the possible effects of the proposal. This would be done by assuming that the proposal had already been put into effect. The Guardian would wait until the Earth had made a complete rotation. This would allow the sun to shine on the entire planet and give the Guardian the chance to see what ramifications the proposal would have on the entire planet.

By the way, the sun affects the earthstones and the Earth's magnetic energies more than you might think. The lines of communication between earthstones are magnetic; so are the lines of investigation that every earthstone uses to scout the planet. The Earth's magnetism gives us our energy and enlivens us.

The sun's energy creates this magnetism. It does not recognize the limitations of physical matter. This magnetic energy flows right through the planet and is picked up by the earthstones, even when they are several miles beneath the surface. The earthstones will store this energy to some degree; however, if the sun dies, we will also die. Ultimately, we are nourished by the sun's energy.

Now let's return to our hypothetical toxic waste situation. Depending on its priority level—and whether or not our proposal to balance one part of the planet is found to imbalance another part—our plan would be accepted, rejected, or redefined.

As soon as the Guardian of the Earth accepted our plan for isolating the toxic waste dump, the vibratory rate of the black earthstone would begin to collect in the area at the distance selected.

It might take several months or years before the earthstone's physical molecules actually started to manifest. However, earthstones and gemstones will grow at a faster rate if there is a special need for their presence. Toxic waste deposits are an example of such a need, since it is crucial that the Earth protect itself from them. In this case, certain earthstones would direct the sun's magnetic energy toward the black earthstone. This would give the earthstone so much extra life and vitality, that its molecules would begin to form a callus around the toxicity at a much faster rate than they would normally form.

Still, it would probably take several years before a shield with a thickness of one or two molecules was created. And it might be several decades before the shield would be big enough to be obvious. Then it would continue to grow until it created a callus thick enough to protect the rest of the Earth from the toxic waste.

I am the one who draws up a plan, because I know the other earthstones and what they can do.

When the Earth's Guardian approves a plan, I use my own energies to help resolve the disharmonious situation in two ways. First, I am like a lighthouse that spotlights the target area and directs the energies of the other earthstones toward it. Second, I draw to the area a physical form of the rainbow's colors. The vibratory rate of these colors is easily recognized and accepted by the Earth.

The colors of Bloodstone contain little blue, indigo, or violet. This is not surprising. Although these colors are necessary for life, the Earth is more nourished by the colors red, orange, yellow, and green.

"When Bloodstone is worn in spherical form, what are your effects on humans?"

My work for the human parallels my work for the Earth. When worn around the neck, I am able to sense those areas that are particularly out of balance or disharmonious. I see where the disharmonies are and what is needed to correct them. I then bring these areas to the awareness of the wearer, just as I bring disharmonious areas to the awareness of the Earth's Guardian.

Then, if I am given the permission, I act like a lighthouse and encourage certain healing energies to come to these areas.

Instead of the Guardian of the Planet, the wearers themselves must give the permission. This permission might simply be the person's sincere willingness for changes to be made in the disharmonious areas I have highlighted.

As soon as the permission is given, I can strongly direct the flow of the body's own energies toward these areas to assist in their change and re-balancing. The energies I call are physical (such as white blood cells) as well as super-physical. The super-physical energies I draw are mostly in the form of light rays.

If the individual is not in tune with the messages I am giving, the individual may feel increased pain, soreness, or redness in the area. I do not cause this discomfort. These effects simply occur if the individual is resisting, not paying attention to, or not accepting the awareness I am trying to bring.

When worn around the neck, I will select and focus on the area of greatest disharmony first. When placed over a specific area chosen by the individual, the physical and super-physical forces will be brought to that area, even if it is not the area of greatest disharmony. In both cases, physical changes will result.

I take no responsibility for healing, and I take no responsibility for altering the cause of a situation. Therefore, once the individual acknowledges the disharmony and is willing to accept a change, the individual would be most wise to take further action, just like the Earth does.

When the Earth acknowledges a situation, and gives me permission to collect energy at a certain place, it then takes further action by initiating a change somewhere within itself. An obvious example is a volcanic eruption. One interpretation of such an event is that the Earth erupts the medicine it needs to heal or re-balance a particular area.

Similarly, a human could go to a physician, take the proper medicine, accept a particular therapy, or take some other form of action in order to take total responsibility for the area in question.

All I do is to draw physical and super-physical energies to the area. This does not mean that these energies will cause the area to heal. It just means that I provide the individual with additional tools to allow a positive change to occur in the area.

My primary mission is for the Earth. Yet, the way I function for the Earth almost perfectly parallels the way I function for humans when they wear me in spherical form.

"Can you explain the difference between the way earthstones and gemstone crystals work for the planet?"

Earthstones and gemstones work on two different levels of vibratory rate. In general, the earthstones only work with physical and super-physical energies. Gemstones work in a different arena: their work includes energies that possess a much higher vibratory rate than the physical.

However, if the physical body's doors are closed to healing energies from the inner levels, Earthstones can sometimes help to open these doors.

* * *

I was born when the planet was born. You will find that this is true of most earthstones. It is also true that my mission as I have described it will continue for as long as the planet is alive.

My work is simple, basic, and straightforward. I think you now have a good idea of who I am. For your purposes, I have given you enough information.

"Thank you for sharing this information," said Michael.

Thank you for the opportunity.

As I and the vortex of Bloodstone separated from each other, I felt an unmistakable flow of gratitude and a mutual understanding develop between us. Yet I sensed that this understanding was not forming just between Bloodstone and me, but between Bloodstone and the entire human race.

21
IVORITE

"Now we will stretch your imagination," said the Guardian of Sodalight. "Keep the focus of your mission pure and your attention on the core of your being—the part of you that you know is truly you. Then walk with me."

Together, Sodalight, Michael, and I walked right through the wall of the cavern. My mind complained that this was not possible, so I did what I could to keep my mind separated from the rest of my body. I let it look at the situation with all of its doubts and objections, until it began to laugh for not believing what it was seeing.

Indeed, we were inside the rock. I believe the molecules of my body occupied the spaces between the molecules of rock. Of course, at the atomic level, matter is not solid; there is a vast amount of space between each atom. Michael and I smiled at each other. We were aware of what we were doing and of how impossible it was from a certain point of view.

"You will not find Ivorite in large deposits, but in veins such as these," explained the Guardian of Sodalight. "Position yourself inside one of these veins as best you can."

It was easy to distinguish exactly which rock was Ivorite. Since we were destined to meet the Guardian of Ivorite, his vibratory rate stood out from the energies of all the surrounding rocks.

Once I had entered the Ivorite vein, I realized that my body was positioned somewhat horizontally. I had the thought that this must be what it feels like to be in outer space. Within the rock I had no sense of up or down, and the law of gravity seemed to be suspended.

Then I sensed the familiar feeling that the Guardian's vibratory rate was forming into words. I allowed the words to flow through me.

I am Ivorite. My importance for the Earth is often overlooked by humans, but it is not underestimated by my fellow earthstones. The earthstones respect one another greatly, for we know that each one of us has been formed on the planet for a purpose. There is not one of us that is unnecessary or that the Earth could do without. We are all important pieces of the puzzle.

So far, you have learned that many earthstones play a role in detecting imbalances and then focusing their energies to correct them. This is done on both a local and global scale.

My purpose is to make sure that the sum of these energies is kept in balance. I provide the anchor for these energies. I make sure that the changes initiated by the other stones do not occur so rapidly that the balance of the whole planet is upset.

My function is to hold the reigns and prevent changes from occurring too swiftly. I remind the Earth that its changes must occur slowly. Slow changes are best for the Earth's overall balance and benefit, and especially for the life that lives on its surface.

This is why you will find capillaries of Ivorite all over the planet, but only a few deposits large enough to be mined for the purpose of being worn by humans.

Once I am exposed to the air, my connection to the planet is broken; it is as though the umbilical cord is cut. Then all I can do is to work for humans.

To do my work for humans, I must be fashioned into spheres and worn. Of course, I can be fashioned into many different shapes. However, for my effects on the human to reflect my effects on the Earth, I must be fashioned into the shape of the planet. This is the shape that reminds my energy of what its function was when it was still in the Earth. Also, this is the only shape that allows my energy to be expressed in a way that can fill a person's aura.

When worn in spherical form around the neck, I provide an anchor for the human, just as I provide an anchor for changes that occur in the planet. I allow the changes that the human experiences to be put in perspective.

Of course, a human consists of so many levels, that I could

not possibly stop every change on every level from occurring. However, individuals' changes usually have some focal point, and this is where I do my work. My focus is on the area of an individual's life that is experiencing the most change, activity, and growth. This area is usually the most highly-charged area in the aura.

The aura reflects all aspects of the human. When I am worn, my vibratory rate fills the aura. Then I find the area that is most charged, regardless of what level of the aura it has manifested on. Then I throw the anchor on this area.

It is the same with the Earth. The earthstones place most of their attention on the areas of the Earth that are undergoing the greatest amount of changes. I, too, am naturally drawn to these areas, because that is where my energy is needed most.

When people experience rapid changes, they often lose their perspective. They lose sight of where they have come from and where they are going. Ivorite helps people to regain perspective and gives them the opportunity to readjust their lives accordingly. As soon as I am removed from the aura, the anchor is also removed. Then people are able resume their changes at their previous rate. Hopefully, however, they will have made some adjustments and will continue in a new, more harmonious direction.

Ivorite Therapy

The individual can control my focus by placing me over a specific area. If I am placed over a knee where physical therapy has just been applied, I will help the effects of that therapy to remain with the knee. Then, the other forces in the body will have more time to accept the change that the therapy has provided. The effects of the knee's therapy will essentially be frozen, while the rest of the body continues to be capable of making changes.

In other words, the rest of the body is given a chance to exercise its natural ability to readjust and adapt itself to the knee's new orientation. Then, when the Ivorite is removed, the body will be in a better position to accept the effects of the therapy for a longer period of time.

Too much Ivorite placed on the knee would not only stop the knee from changing, it would also inhibit the rest of the body from adapting itself to the changes that the therapy initiated. The largest amount of Ivorite that one should ever apply to the body is a double strand long enough to reach from the top of the spine to the bottom of the spine.

In fact, this amount would be ideal to place over the length of your spine after you have received a chiropractic adjustment. I will help the spine to maintain the changes brought about by the adjustment, by giving the rest of the body time to strengthen itself and adapt to the spine's new situation.

A relatively healthy individual should keep the Ivorite on the spine for five to fifteen minutes after the adjustment. If the change made was very great, or your if condition is very weak, keep the Ivorite in place longer. Then wear it around your neck at least until you arrive home.

* * *

"Can you speak of other specific therapies or ways that humans could use Ivorite?" inquired Michael.

I suggest that pregnant women only use Ivorite on their extremities, such as the knees, feet, elbows, or hands in order to maintain adjustments or treatments. Until the child is born, they should not wear Ivorite around the neck or on the spine. Otherwise, the Ivorite might obstruct the vortex of life force centered on the fetus; and this it would not be at all wise.

* * *

Often when a great deal of attention is placed on one area of an individual's life, other areas are neglected. When Ivorite is worn, the area that has been given the most attention is put "on hold." Then the other, neglected areas can be nourished or given the attention they need. If these areas need to release something, they will be able to release it. If they need to change, they will be able to change. If they need to relax, they will be able to relax. Or, if in the name of overall balance, they simply need more attention, they will receive it.

Attention is life. If your attention is withdrawn from every area except the one area of your life where most of the changes are occurring, all your other aspects will suffer from a lack of life force. Ivorite can give you the chance to put the focus of your changes in a holding pattern, so that these other areas can become more enlivened and nourished. Then, once the Ivorite is removed, you will be in a better position to handle your changes.

Therefore, Ivorite can be an important part of any therapy, whether the therapy is for specific parts of the physical body or for the physical body as a whole. Ivorite will also be an effective addition to emotional, mental, and spiritual therapies. It is especially beneficial in cases where the therapist finds that the patient tends to slip back between treatments, or where the body forgets and loses the changes made by the therapy too quickly after the therapy is given.

If the therapy has a physical focus, the Ivorite can be placed over a specific physical area. If the therapy has an inner focus, the Ivorite can be worn around the neck.

When an individual has experienced a healing, a change, or some degree of progress, my presence will help to stabilize that progress. It will help the body to re-establish a balance that includes this new change. Then, when the Ivorite is removed, the body will be more inclined to take the next step forward than to slip back to its old state of affairs.

If I am used with another earthstone or gemstone, my effects will be canceled. This will happen if other stones are included with me in the same necklace, or if a strand of another earthstone or gemstone is worn around the neck at the same time I am being worn. The Earth is different in this regard. It knows how and when to place its attention on me in order to experience my effects. To work for a human, my vibratory rate must be singled out, and I must be worn alone.

"Among all the gemstones and earthstones we have met so far, this property seems to be unique to Ivorite," Michael commented.

Yes, I believe it is.

As soon as the earthstone you call Ivorite is exposed to the air, it becomes lifeless. I, as its Guardian, lose my influence on it. The only way that Ivorite can be re-enlivened, and that I can influence it once again, is for the Ivorite to be fashioned into spheres and placed in an individual's aura. Then it will take at least several minutes before the re-enlivenment occurs.

In the Earth you will find that my color is a variegated, light gray. You may consider the specks of different colors you find in me to be "impurities." But, the fact is, you could paint me pink—or any other color—and I would still do my job. This is because it is not the vibratory rate of my color that produces my effects. It is the vibratory rate of the earthstone Ivorite itself.

"So the fact that Ivorite is often dyed a cream color in order to make it more attractive, makes no difference to the way you affect people?"

Correct.

There is nothing scientific about using Ivorite. One can wear it around the neck, place it in a pile over a specific area, or place it down the length of the spine. However, if Ivorite is worn around the neck, the strand should never be long enough to touch the stomach chakra; it should always fall to a point somewhere above the stomach.

It is not necessary to wear Ivorite for long periods. If you are wearing it around the neck, wear it constantly for no more than one week at a time; then give yourself several weeks before considering whether you need it again.

In most cases, it will be adequate to place Ivorite over a specific area for fifteen minutes when using it as a follow-up to therapy.

Ivorite is a tool, and it can be a very effective one. It can be worn from one wearer to the next and the next without cleansing. Although I do not tend to pick up the information contained in people's auras, Ivorite should be wiped with a cloth before it is given to the next wearer, simply out of consideration.

Ivorite Tomorrow

It would not fulfill my purpose to be widely used by humans, because the more Ivorite that is mined, the less there will be for the planet to use. Because things are changing so rapidly for the planet, the planet needs most of its Ivorite.

People often look forward to changes. Because they are a barometer of growth, changes are often perceived as good things; the more changes that are occurring in your life, the faster you are growing. Changes will occur in that area of your life where you need to grow the most. Since life constantly strives for balance, you will probably grow the most in those areas where you are the most immature or inexperienced.

When changes seem overwhelming, it is probably just that they are happening too rapidly, and your other aspects are trying to tell you that they also need attention and nourishment. This is the time when it would be wise to wear Ivorite. Then the focus of change would be put "on hold," and the other aspects would be nourished and given what they need.

Once the Ivorite is taken off, your original focus of change will again have all your attention. This is why it is best not to wear Ivorite constantly for more than one week at a time. Then, when you remove the Ivorite, your body will not be shocked by the effects of change returning to your life.

"Thank you for sharing this information," said Michael.

As you would say, may the blessings be.

"May the blessings be," Michael replied.

I was anxious to step out of the Ivorite vein and completely remove myself from its vibratory rate. Its energy just wasn't right for me at that time in my life, since I was greatly enjoying the growth and changes I was experiencing.

The Guardian of Sodalight noticed my discomfort. So he led us up through the rock, as though we were on an elevator, to the Earth's surface. Then we rested under a cloudy sky in a field of waist-high, wild grasses. Sodalight encouraged me to take many deep breaths and to completely relax my body in order to prepare for our meeting with the Guardian of Opalight.

22
OPALIGHT

After we had rested a while, the Guardian of Sodalight led us into another group of mountain foothills. There we entered a cave in which a cold wind blew. We walked against this wind, deeper and deeper into the darkness, with only the faint glow of Sodalight's body to light our way.

We stopped when the wind stopped, and I realized that we had reached its source. Just ahead was the entrance to a long and wide tunnel. Through the opening I could see that the tunnel was illuminated by a bright white light. I peeked inside and saw that the tunnel was made entirely of Opalight, and that the source of the light was the earthstone itself.

Sodalight said that he and Michael were to wait at the entrance, and that I was to enter the cavern alone. I stepped inside. The light that emanated from the walls of the cavern began to bounce back and forth between my aura and the walls. This continued until the Opalight seemed to know all that it needed to know about me.

Then I noticed that the light was growing dimmer over certain parts of my body. With this observation came the knowledge that the darkest of these areas were associated with situations from my most distant past. Lighter areas, or those that were merely gray, were related to events of the more recent past. Soon every part of my body reflected a different degree of light or shade. I also realized that every part of me had been formed as a result of past conditions. It struck me that, with these variations of light and darkness covering me, I probably looked much like Opalight itself.

Then I heard Michael begin to ask a question, and I felt the answers forming in my heart.

"How does your appearance affect your purpose and mission?" he inquired.

The light that I reflect is the light of Soul shining on the physical body. It is not the light of the sun. As you observe, this light of Soul becomes gradated in my presence.

When I am worn in spherical form, the light bounces back and forth between the wearer's aura and the Opalight spheres. In this way, I learn all about the wearer.

All of your conditions and every cell in your body were formed in a way that was dictated by the past. Therefore, what you do in the present has the power to change the way your conditions and your cells will be in the future.

My work is inhibited by individuals who have strong mental energies, because the mind often wishes to negate or deny what I highlight in the physical body. The reason that I highlight certain areas of the body and darken others is to let Soul know of the present condition of the physical body.

"Why wouldn't Soul already be aware of the physical body's conditions?"

As long as Soul wears a physical body, it has the responsibility to care for that physical body. Yet it also has a mind. The mind exists between the physical body and Soul. Often the mind clouds the truth, because it is the mind's duty to play tricks with the individual in order to prevent communication between the physical body and Soul. The mind is usually successful at this until the individual becomes enlightened.

I can be used as a tool to pinpoint and let people know about those areas of the body that have the deepest roots or causes in the past. The conditions associated with these areas are often the most difficult to change and resolve, and they are usually the most serious. When one is wearing Opalight, these areas manifest as the darkest areas in the aura.

It is natural for people to place attention on the conditions that they know are the most serious. Attention holds the hand of light, and light holds the hand of love.

Therefore, when attention is placed on these deeply rooted conditions, light enters the area. Light is the healing force; and when light enters, so does love. Love is like a liquid catalyst that helps changes happen. It is the magic element that allows miracles to occur.

Before people are ready to make changes, they must usually resolve many past entanglements. That is why I help people to sleep. Much of this resolution of the past is done in the dream state. Therefore, it only helps my mission when my wearers are able to sleep. When the body is asleep, it is much easier to focus that light—which is holding the hand of love—on the darkest areas of the aura.

As the days pass, these individuals will start waking up with an almost uncanny knowingness that they must see a doctor for a particular condition or that something has been resolved during the night. Often the individual wakes up knowing about a past situation that directly relates to a present condition.

This knowingness is so natural, that the person may not even be consciously aware that something from the past has been resolved or that something new has been learned. This knowingness will simply be a part of the individual. Therefore, one should at least wear Opalight to sleep.

By the way, not all the dark areas that I highlight in the aura reflect physical ailments. Some will reflect mental or emotional situations or conditions that affect the physical body. To help individuals to get to know themselves better, I must get to know them well. I learn about an individual from his or her aura. What better friend can you have than someone who knows you perhaps even better than you do?

Even though I allow individuals to become aware of certain things that might make them uncomfortable, I can also assure them that things are not as bad as they seem. I can do this, because I also highlight the positive qualities and conditions that have resulted from the past.

* * *

As I mentioned, the mind's ideas, attitudes, and concepts about the individual's condition often get in the way of Opalight's work.

If these mental concepts are incorrect, the Opalight will work to quiet the mind. For example, the Opalight might learn from an individual's aura that he or she has a hip ailment because of a certain situation in the past; the individual's mind might think there is a different reason for this hip ailment. The Opalight will work on bringing the truth to the individual's awareness by quieting the part of the mind that harbors the incorrect concept.

When part of the mind has false ideas and concepts about the physical body, it will inhibit the body from making positive changes and from healing. I will work on preventing this part of the mind from affecting the physical body.

The mind is a vast, vast area. Most people have not yet even imagined its true potential. Therefore, even though I block part of the mind, there is still a vast amount of the mind still available. Individuals who wear Opalight and begin to feel their mental energies becoming dulled should try to place more attention on using another part of the mind. Remember, the part of the mind that is being dulled is the part that is working with false concepts.

False concepts will limit and prevent the physical body from making changes. This is because the mind can easily lock a physical body into a state of non-growth and non-change. Change is necessary for healing. It is only hoped that, once Opalight blocks the part of the mind that is inhibiting the body's changes, the individual will start to use other parts of the mind that possess more clarity. Hopefully, the individual will start to use parts that are not limited by false concepts, and that are more receptive to the truth and to allowing the body to make changes.

The Early Years of Opalight

During the Age of Lemuria, I did not have a great need to be worn by humans. My mission and effects were for the Earth. However, during this era I was undergoing a change. The emphasis of my effects was gradually moving away from the Earth, and I was becoming a more appropriate tool for humans.

By the end of the Age of Atlantis, this shift had been completed.

Opalight Today

Today my mission, effects, and focus are on people. One might think that I could do much good for the Earth by allowing it to realize its own limitations and helping it to move away from them; but this is not so anymore.

My vibratory rate is still an essential piece of the Earth's living puzzle. In that way I am still valuable to the planet. However, the work I could do for the planet is done more effectively by other gemstones now.

"Is the Opalight with the greatest variation of color from cream to brown the most effective?" Michael asked.

Gradations in color are only for the sake of beauty. They do not signify the amount of light and dark that will appear in the aura. Depending on how the Opalight is cut, spheres may be formed that are almost completely brown or almost completely white. As long as the Opalight has some degree of color gradation, it will have the effects I have described.

Opalight Therapy

When I am worn around the neck, my vibratory rate will touch as much of the aura as possible. Once my energy fills the aura, I will act like a filter that diffuses, calms, and soothes any harsh or rough vibratory rates contained in the aura.

This effect can often help people to become more calm and then help them to sleep. Sleep benefits the body, and it benefits my work.

If insomnia is caused by anything physical—such as drugs, caffeine, certain foods, or chemicals—I can do little to assist. However, I can be very helpful if the individual cannot sleep because of natural causes. Then my calming effect will often be just powerful enough to allow the individual's own natural sleep abilities to take over. In contrast, artificial stimulants will inhibit natural sleep abilities; it will also supersede the calming and soothing qualities I offer.

When I am placed over a certain area of the body, I can help the individual remember the past experiences that created the area's current condition. However, this will only work if the individual has already been wearing Opalight for quite some time.

It would be best to place the Opalight over the area during sleep and then to record one's dreams. Often the truth about a certain condition is hard to accept consciously. During sleep, the individual is most receptive and open to truth.

If people wear Opalight to help them sleep, they should wear it to bed—or let it lie next to them—for as long as the Opalight continues to be effective for this purpose. If they wear it to help resolve certain effects of past situations, they should wear it until the situation resolves. This could take a month or several years; each circumstance is unique.

My main purpose and function is to highlight areas in the aura that relate to past conditions, and to inhibit false mental concepts from affecting the physical body. Any other effects that an individual may experience should be considered side effects; they might not be experienced by all who wear Opalight.

Opalight Tomorrow

It is difficult for me to see the future, since my attention is so involved with the past and present. However, I will say that I don't believe Opalight will ever be mined to any great extent, because I am a specialized tool. Obviously, I will work best for those who are attracted to me. They will be ready and in tune with the kind of therapy I provide.

Do not underestimate the power of the earthstones just because we are often thought of rocks and not true crystals. We are particularly powerful when fashioned into spheres and worn by humans. We become enlivened by their auras.

My work is simple and basic. I work for everyone in the same way, because my mission is the same for everyone. Different individuals may feel different effects. However, my mission is always the same.

This is true of any gemstone, earthstone, or oceanstone. Our missions and purposes reflect who we are. How we are perceived may be as varied as the individuals who perceive us. It is the same with you: you are who you are, but everyone you meet has a different perception of who you are and what you do.

You shall meet the Guardian of Riverstone next.

Good night, and farewell.

Opalight withdrew from my aura, and I ambled out of the cavern feeling as though I had just awakened from a good night's sleep. Then I joined Michael and the Guardian of Sodalight in the adjacent passageway.

23
RIVERSTONE

"Are you ready to meet the Guardian of Riverstone?" asked Sodalight.

"Yes," replied Michael and I, both eager for another adventure. We were not disappointed, for moments later the cave floor lost its solidity and we began to sink into the Earth. We had moved through the Earth this way after our visit to the Guardian of Ivorite, so the experience was not alarming.

I do not know how deep we sank. It felt like we were traveling several miles beneath the surface. I noticed that the pressure increased, and the space between the Earth's atoms decreased, as we moved. We stopped when our feet reached a layer of rock that was saturated with flowing water.

"We will meet the Guardian of Riverstone within this watery rock," said Sodalight. Again, we started to sink—this time into the wet rock. As we entered the rock, I sensed a quickening throughout my body; it felt as though the energy flows in every cell had sped up. I also noticed that the life force in each of my cells was excited, and that my cells had become highly impressionable.

Then I placed aside any additional thoughts and opened my heart for the words of Riverstone's Guardian.

I will not have much time to be with you. My attention must keep up with the changes I initiate. As the Guardian of Riverstone, it is my responsibility to be constantly aware of the wild energy and the force of change I bring.

My purpose is for the Earth, and it is for the Earth that I have my life. It is only when my rock is shaped into spheres and worn by man or woman that I can affect the human in the same way that I affect the Earth.

The use of Riverstone in spherical form is just an example of humans' ingenuity and resourcefulness. It is wise to look to the Earth, which gives you life, for the tools to master life or take greater control of it. That is what you do when you take anything from the Earth and use it as a tool: you promote life—your own.

I exist deep beneath the surface, although the movement and upheavals experienced by the Earth also allow some Riverstone to come to the surface. As a Guardian, I do my greatest work at various depths under the ground. I am not as abundant as I might seem, although I am scattered throughout the planet. It is not necessary that I be plentiful, because I am powerful.

There is a charge which runs through Riverstone; this charge attracts energy and causes it to flow and move. Like wild, unbridled horses, the energy of Riverstone races in every direction.

One could also compare the energy I generate to an airplane that gains speed and momentum on the runway and then takes off into the air. My energy gains momentum as it flows from one molecule of Riverstone to the next, until it is launched into the planet. As my energy launches itself into other rocks, crystals, or elements in the soil, these elements and particles focus my unbridled energy. In this way, I help to keep the Earth from becoming stagnant.

You know that change is necessary for growth, and growth is necessary for life. It would be easy for the life energy of a planet to become stagnant and unchanging. I prevent this from happening. For example, my energy assists in the movement of the plates of the Earth's crust. Surely you know that the energy that causes the continents to move against each other must come from somewhere. It comes from the living rock that lies beneath the planet's surface. Riverstone would not work if the planet were not alive. It would not work if the Earth were just a hunk of rock floating in space with no life energy. It is similar to the way your heart would not pump blood if Soul were not housed in the physical body; your body would be considered dead.

I do not generate energy from within myself; I absorb it from moving water. A type of energy is released when water moves; some call this the release of ions. When I absorb this energy, it passes from one Riverstone molecule to the next. As it does, it becomes transformed: it increases in velocity, strength, and power.

The longer the runway is, the more speed the plane can gather before it takes off. For a similar reason, you will find that Riverstone exists in long veins. My energy is either released when it reaches the end of the vein; or it is released somewhere along the vein whenever a rock, crystal, or element of the soil needs that energy. Whenever another rock needs my energy, it creates a magnetic attraction. I respond by releasing energy to it. My energy enlivens the rock, crystal, or element, and gives it the ability to carry out its mission.

I can be particularly powerful for the human, since humans are made mostly of water. In the human I have a vast source of potential energy to tap into and transform. Once I've tapped into this energy, it manifests in the aura. Since the body is encased in an aura rather than in a rock, it is to the aura that I give my energy.

When Riverstone is worn around the neck, my energy becomes focused on exciting the entire aura. When I energize the aura this way, the result is that everything—including what you call karma—is sped up. The movement of the body, no matter what its direction, is sped up. If the body is in a cleansing mode, the cleansing is sped up. If the body is in a specific, focused healing mode, the healing is sped up. However, one must be careful when using Riverstone, because I can also speed up the vibratory rate of a disease. That is why the healing mode must be very focused.

When I am worn by a human, the vibratory rate of each of my wearer's cells is sped up. As a result, overall changes in the body occur. This speeding up does not change the direction of the vortexes of your energy; nor does it increase your metabolism. It is a speeding up of your vibratory rate, and this is what compels changes to happen.

Michael needed clarification. "Are you saying that one's movement in a certain direction will be sped up, so that the need for a change in direction will occur sooner? Do you also mean that one will resolve a situation or move through an experience more quickly and, therefore, have an abundance of energy with which to start the next experience?"

The answers to both of these questions will depend on how long the Riverstone is worn and how disciplined the wearer is in focusing his or her life. The results of wearing Riverstone with a focus will be different from the results of wearing it without one.

When I say "wearing Riverstone without a focus," I mean wearing it with no direction, goal, or dream for your life in mind. It could also mean wearing it with no other influence of the Earth—that is, no other metal, gemstone, or earthstone. No focus to your changes means that your life is continuing as usual: you go to work during the day, come home in the evening, and fall sleep at night; you do not expect anything unusual and have nothing realistic to look forward to.

If you wore Riverstone without a focus, confusion could result. This is because undirected changes would start to happen. These might be changes in one's outlook, attitudes, feelings, physical circumstances, or in the way you react to certain stimuli.

The changes would occur, because Riverstone would be throwing its energy into the aura; and my energy speeds up changes. I do not know how deeply into the aura Riverstone's energy goes, nor do I know whether it stops at the emotional or mental level. As soon as the Riverstone was removed, the force behind these changes would stop, because its source would be gone.

The results of wearing Riverstone without a focus might be helpful if a tool is needed to help get the individual out of a rut or a situation that is preventing him or her from achieving a goal. Actually, this intention would itself be a focus.

Now, when Riverstone is worn with a focus or a direction, I can be an especially helpful tool.

Wearing Riverstone with a focus might mean wearing it with another element, earthstone, or gemstone somewhere on the body. Let's use gold as an example, because gold is commonly worn as rings or earrings. If you wore Riverstone at the same time you wore gold, I would begin to stir up your gold consciousness. The effects that gold has on your body might become more acute and therefore more obvious to you. In this way, I would help you to move through the experiences that the vibratory rate of gold offers.

This type of effect would also occur if you wore me with any other gemstone. I would help you to move more swiftly through the experiences or changes characteristic of that particular gemstone. If the gemstone has a specific healing effect, this effect would be hastened. If the gemstone has a balancing effect, I would hasten the movement toward balance. However, as your life was sped up, it might seem to go further out of balance. This result would appear to contradict what I have described as my effects, but it really doesn't. Actually, you would be sloughing off those things that were creating the imbalance at a much faster rate than before.

* * *

There is no more focused activity in human experience than the birth and delivery of a child. During labor, every cell in the mother's body is geared up for this one goal. Wearing Riverstone around the neck during labor will help to speed up the process.

"Should it be worn only during labor or prior to labor as well?"

Prior to labor there is no particular focus in the body. Therefore, it is best to put on Riverstone as soon as the hormones are activated, and the body begins the process of labor. I also suggest that immediately after the birth, the mother replace the Riverstone with a necklace that has a very soothing effect, such as a combination of Emerald and Light Green Aventurine.

* * *

The procedures and effects I have described so far call for wearing Riverstone around the neck. Riverstone is most powerful when there are no knots tied between the spheres. However, even if there are knots, the magnetic attraction from one sphere to the next will be strong enough for the energy to pass through the air that separates them. Although the effect of a knotted strand is not as strong, it might be more balanced for most individuals.

I can also be placed over a specific part of the body prior to the start of another gemstone therapy—or perhaps any other therapy. Whenever Riverstone is placed over a specific organ or area of the body, its energy concentrates on that area. This brings more energy to the area, loosens the energies that already exist there, and prepares the area for the therapy.

However, my energy will be undirected until the other therapy is applied. Therefore, the other therapy should be started as soon as the Riverstone has prepared the area. Then the readiness and receptivity for change that I infused there will become directed. This readiness is the excitation of the cells' vitality, and it occurs within fifteen minutes after the Riverstone is applied.

If Riverstone is placed directly on the skin, the Riverstone will begin to feel warm within minutes. This warmth is the awakening that your aura and your body's life force produce in the Riverstone. The onset of this warmth indicates that the Riverstone's excitation of cells has begun.

This excitation might begin in less than fifteen minutes. Adapt the length of the application according to the density of the organ or area involved. For example, the cells in a bone will take longer to reach a state of ideal readiness than will the soft tissue of an organ or muscle.

* * *

Those who enjoy meditation or spiritual contemplation can wear Riverstone around the neck either during their quiet time or beforehand. Again, they should wear it for about fifteen minutes or at least until the Riverstone warms. During contemplation, they will be focusing on the spirituality within themselves, and this is indeed a strong focus. Remember, I am an effective tool whenever an individual has a strong focus.

When I am used in this way, my wearer will find that his or her whole being becomes energized. Then, I will help the individual make the changes that will lead to greater spiritual experiences. Often it is physical blockages that prevent people from placing their attention more fully on their inner goals—yes, physical blockages.

My action plus the wearer's inward focus of attention will help to break up, change, and resolve anything that is in the way of the individual's focus. Then this will make it possible for that focus to be achieved more fully.

* * *

You and your fellow humans are intelligent. I am sure that you will discover many ways to use a tool such as Riverstone. There are many ways to use a screwdriver other than just to screw in screws. You are limited only by your degree of resourcefulness.

You now know my basic nature, and you have been given some examples of how I work. Now go ahead and use me for the tool that I am. I am very powerful when I am in spherical form and awakened and enlivened by a human's or an animal's aura. By the way, when in spherical form, I no longer work with the Earth.

Now that you know me, use me with respect and responsibility. That is all.

"Thank you," said Michael.

We were lifted out of the watery rock and slowly rose to the surface. Then the Guardian of Sodalight suggested that we rest in the bright sunshine. We felt revitalized and refreshed by its warm, life-giving rays. Yet we did not relax altogether. We were aware that our mission was not yet complete. Our attention had turned to Rhodonite and the lessons we would learn from its Guardian.

24
RHODONITE

After we had rested and refreshed ourselves, we walked to the base of a low cliff. There Sodalight pointed out the veins of a pink and black rock within the cliff walls. He called this rock Rhodonite. As we studied the veins, wondering how they had been formed, I sensed that someone was approaching us.

Greetings, *said the Guardian of Rhodonite.*

The individual who stood before us was no more than five feet tall. The energy that surrounded the Guardian vibrated so intensely that I could not discern any features or determine whether this individual was male or female.

The Guardian looked at me and sat down on the ground. I sensed that I should sit nearby, so I moved closer. Then, without really knowing how I had gotten there, I suddenly found myself sitting within the Guardian of Rhodonite's aura.

Shall we begin?

"Yes. Will you tell us of your mission for the Earth and for the human?" Michael asked.

My mission for the Earth is to draw the pink ray to the rock of the planet. The pink ray is the color ray that comes from the world of emotions. This is the color that represents and draws to itself higher vibratory rates than those of the physical level. As this greater vibratory rate is called to the physical, an upliftment occurs. The upliftment of rock occurs over thousands of years; therefore, my effect is slow, steady, and gradual.

This is evolution. This is life, and life must evolve and grow. I help the Earth to grow by drawing the physical vibratory rate of the Earth toward the higher vibratory rate represented by the pink color ray. This causes the Earth's patterns to change. These changes then allow the Earth to create new patterns that reflect a higher state of consciousness.

When humans wear Rhodonite in spherical form, I have the same effects for my wearers that I have for the Earth: I give gradual, steady upliftment. I give humans a foundation. Because I am of the Earth, I also give them solidity and security, which are qualities of the planet. However, because the human vibratory rate moves much more quickly toward higher states of consciousness, I work more rapidly for the human than I do for the Earth.

I very quickly draw people away from a physical point of view to an emotional point of view. I raise the individual's vibratory rate to that of the emotional level. When the individual has gained the perspective of the emotional level, the result will be a rearrangement of the emotions: any emotions that are scattered, out of balance or undefined will become more grounded. In the process, a greater emotional foundation, solidity, and security will be created.

This will happen because unbalanced emotions are not in harmony with Rhodonite. One cannot wear Rhodonite and continue to have emotional imbalances. The Rhodonite calls order to the emotions.

When any gemstone in spherical form is placed in an individual's aura, the gemstone becomes enlivened, and its vibratory rate begins to radiate throughout the wearer's aura. Gemstones are tools. They will produce their effects whether or not the wearer realizes what those effects are. However, if the wearer recognizes the gemstone's abilities and is aware of what it can be used for, that tool will be able to work with more focus, depth, and energy.

My uplifting effect on the physical aspect (which parallels my effect on the Earth) will occur regardless of whether the individual is aware of it. However, my effect of soothing the emotions in order to create a strong emotional foundation will occur only to the degree that the person is aware of and understands this effect.

The speed at which this second effect occurs will depend on how willing the wearer is to allow me to do my work and to accept the changes I bring. You see, I will make fundamental changes.

Each emotional experience you have is like a brick in your emotional foundation. For each brick, there is an optimal place for it to be laid in that foundation. When a brick is in its optimal place, it contributes most to the foundation's stability. Emotional imbalances occur when bricks are not laid in their proper places.

Therefore, if you have emotional imbalances, and you wish to create a more solid emotional foundation, some of your out-of-place bricks may have to be moved. You may also have to fill some holes or make some bricks fit more tightly; and, of course, before you move the bricks to their optimal places, you will have to learn which of them are out of place. This is what I meant when I said that I make fundamental changes.

The rebuilding of an emotional foundation is an ongoing process, because people are constantly growing—physically, emotionally, mentally, and spiritually. As long as Rhodonite is worn, the wearer will be able to place any new emotional experiences in the optimal space in his or her emotional foundation.

It takes several minutes for Rhodonite to become charged by an individual's aura. After that, my effects will continue to build for as long as I am worn.

Wearing a strand of eight- or ten-millimeter Rhodonite spheres for a minimum of three weeks will probably allow enough time for some emotional rearranging to occur. It will at least provide the wearer with enough time to get to know his or her emotions well enough to remain more balanced during any emotional trauma that might occur. In order to do this, the Rhodonite must also be worn during the traumatic experience.

"Do the black markings found in Rhodonite affect your purpose?"

Rhodonite is available in many varieties: it occurs in many shades of pink—from light to dark—and with many degrees of black markings. Yet there are even more varieties of people, since every individual's emotional foundation is arranged in a different way.

If given a choice of several different varieties of Rhodonite, an individual will be attracted to the one that is most in harmony with his or her emotional condition. This will be the variety that will provide the most help in rebuilding the individual's emotional foundation. However, it will only be able to do so to the limits of that variety's capacity.

When that limit is reached, the individual should start to wear the Rhodonite that has either a stronger pink color or fewer black markings. This will allow the individual to achieve an even greater emotional understanding and a stronger emotional foundation.

Black and gray markings reflect impurities or imbalances in the emotions. A light pink color reflects emotional immaturity or weakness. As an individual wears increasingly finer qualities of Rhodonite, that person's emotional condition will also reflect this finer quality: the emotional condition will become more balanced, mature, and strong.

The highest quality Rhodonite has a rich, dark pink color and little or no black markings. It may be difficult to start out wearing this variety if the individual has not yet taken the steps required to be in harmony with this variety. Sometimes it is easy to skip a step or two when we walk up a stairway; and some of us have long enough legs to skip even four or five steps. For most people, beginning with the finest quality Rhodonite would be like skipping more steps than their legs can reach.

Whether or not you are ready for the finest quality Rhodonite, wearing it will still uplift you and begin providing you with a greater emotional foundation. However, if you are not truly ready for this quality, the resulting renovation of your emotional foundation may not be complete. This is because some of the necessary interim steps may be skipped during the process of rebuilding. In that case, other influences may be needed to help work through certain emotional blockages.

Rhodonite Therapy

A therapist can use Rhodonite to determine the status of an individual's emotional state and whether the individual is making progress. To do this, the therapist should present the patient with several strands of Rhodonite spheres. Each strand should be the same length and contain spheres of the same size. However, each strand should be a different shade of pink with a different degree of black markings. As the therapist presents the strands, he or she should ask the patient: "If I were to give you a gift, which strand would you most prefer, and which would be your second choice?"

The patient's first choice will indicate the emotional state toward which he or she is moving. The second choice will reflect the patient's current emotional condition. Remember that the darker and richer the pink, and the less black that is apparent in the Rhodonite, the finer is the quality. If the patient chooses a lighter pink Rhodonite with some black in it as the first choice, and a darker pink Rhodonite with little black in it as the second choice, the therapist would know that the patient's emotional condition was probably on a downward spiral.

In this case, the therapist should suggest that the patient wear a quality that falls between the two strands chosen. This will be the best choice, because the patient may not be ready to accept his or her current emotional state; nor may the patient be ready to let go of whatever is having a negative impact on his or her emotional health.

Each time the patient visits the therapist, the therapist should ask the same question. The therapist will know that the downward emotional spiral has ended when the patient's first choice becomes either the strand that was originally the second choice or a strand with a higher quality than the original second choice. Then the therapist will know that the emotional foundation has become more stable. At that point, the therapist should suggest that the patient start wearing a higher quality of Rhodonite than he or she is currently wearing.

* * *

When worn around the neck, I bring the changes I initiate on the emotional level to the physical level. I do this by drawing emotional energy into the physical body.

When certain emotions are expressed over and over again, they form patterns. These patterns often manifest on the physical form as certain postures, facial lines, or features. By using Rhodonite in the way I have described (that is, by gradually upgrading the quality of Rhodonite worn), the emotional patterns and the blueprints for emotional reactions will change. Then a total restructuring of the origin of one's emotions and the way they are expressed will be able to take place. Of course, this restructuring will also result in the creation of an essentially different person.

The physical manifestations of emotional patterns may not change or disappear, because they will have been set in the "stone" of the physical form. However, the patterns that caused these physical manifestations can be changed.

"Are there any specific therapies that you can offer?"

When worn around the neck, Rhodonite touches the core of the individual and is in the best position to access the individual's emotional aura. This is also the best place to wear Rhodonite to fulfill its tendency to call a higher vibratory rate to the physical body.

My mission does not include working on specific parts of the physical body. However, because I have a specific vibratory rate, I am sure that Rhodonite will have an effect if placed anywhere on the body. That effect will probably vary from one individual to the next. I believe you call these individualized effects the "side effects" of earthstones and gemstones.

For those who are emotionally unstable, I work on the scrambled pieces of the emotional puzzle that are causing the emotional imbalance and instability. I readjust these pieces so that each one fits better in the emotional puzzle. Once greater emotional stability is gained, the individual can wear Roselle, Ruby, or Rhodocrosite, depending on the wearer's needs. This will help the individual to take further steps toward achieving even greater emotional well-being. Of course, in some cases, a separate strand of Rhodonite could be worn along with these other gemstones. This would allow the changes these gemstones initiate to occur more slowly and in greater balance.

Rhodonite Tomorrow

"Do you see your mission evolving in the future?" Michael asked.

The Earth moves very slowly in the upliftment of its physical matter. I shall be here a long time, supplying the planet's physical matter with a magnetic pull toward a state of consciousness greater than the physical. I work on the physical molecules themselves. I teach or remind them that something greater than the physical exists.

The more that Rhodonite is worn by people, the more that I, as the Guardian of Rhodonite, will know people and understand how I can assist them. My primary mission is for the

Earth. It is only when I am fashioned into a rounded form that I can affect people.

* * *

Now you may enjoy meeting an earthstone with properties very different from mine or from any of the others you have met so far. May I suggest that you interview the one you know as Malachite. Spirit itself will lead you to the Guardian of Malachite, because the Guardian of Sodalight has completed his mission with you.

"Thank you for taking the time to share of yourself. You honor us by your presence," said Michael.

The honor is mine.

Then the Guardian of Rhodonite simply vanished. One moment I was inside the Guardian's aura, and the next I was alone with Michael, the Guardian of Sodalight, and the rock with the Rhodonite veins.

Michael and I each embraced the Guardian of Sodalight. Then we thanked him for guiding us into the Earth and for introducing us to many of the Earthstone Guardians.

Now we would again look to Spirit as our only guide. My intuition told me that even more profound information about our planet was about to be shared.

25
MALACHITE

As I turned my attention to the Guardian of Malachite, I became caught up in a wave-like, rhythmic motion which flowed down and then up my body. Then, after several repetitions of this movement, the upward wave did not stop at the top of my head, but kept going. I rode with it further and further upward until I found myself hovering in space and looking down upon the Earth. There I met Michael and the formless Guardian of Malachite. The Guardian had manifested as nothing more than a vortex of energy. It was easy for me simply to move into this vortex.

You have met me high above the Earth so that we may have a greater view of the planet and of my function for the Earth. When a greater picture of the whole is seen, a more complete understanding can be gained.

Briefly, my purpose is to keep records of information about the planet.

I was not brought to Earth, nor did I form as the planet formed. A certain race of beings—and I believe you have heard about them from other Gemstone Guardians—took materials that were already on the planet and used their forces to gather them together to form Malachite.

Remember that one of the main duties of these beings is to keep data records about the planets. These records include information about a planet's evolution and the life that lives on it—be it mineral, plant, animal, or human. These beings record how these life forms interact with each other and with the planet.

Some of these records are best kept on the planet; some are taken with the beings; and some are both kept on Earth and taken away. Malachite was formed to be the storehouse for information about the Earth. This includes information about the mechanical workings of the planet itself, as well as the planet's relationship to its solar system, moon, sun, and to a lesser extent, the galaxy to which it belongs.

Not just any rock can be planted on a planet and expected to keep information specific to that planet. In order for the information to be accurate, the material which contains it must be formed specifically from the elements of the planet. Therefore, Malachite is not found in any other place except the Earth. By the way, each planet has its own particular rock that contains information about that planet.

I differ from Quartz in the way I store information and in the kind of information I store. Anything you can imagine can be stored in Quartz, including dreams, ideas, formulas, and even illnesses. I have been programmed to gather information about the Earth. I can only accept and store information that I gather for the planet or that is given to me by the race of people who created Malachite.

The wave-like motions that you experienced just before meeting me are the key to the way I gather information. The black bands characteristic of my appearance initiate these waves. When worn by the human, the waves flow back and forth, and down and up the body. In the human body, my waves are limited by the confines of the skin. In the Earth, my wave motions do not penetrate the top layer of soil where the ground meets the air; they bounce off this layer and flow back into the Earth. When I am mined and taken out of the soil, I can no longer work for the Earth.

To explain the mechanics of how my wave motions collect information about the planet, I will speak simply and in illustrative terms.

Each wave motion, or frequency, that I send into the Earth is tagged with a certain date; as it travels throughout the Earth it gathers information. When it returns to Malachite, the information is deposited and cataloged.

My waves travel in a relatively straight line and perpendicular to the black Malachite bands that send them. They bounce back into the Earth whenever they reach the Earth's surface. For example, waves that originated from Malachite in the ground under Arizona might bounce off the underside of the Earth's surface in Florida and then flow back into the Earth. Then they might bounce off the surface somewhere in the middle of Antarctica, and then again off the surface in China before returning to a Malachite deposit somewhere else on the planet.

Eventually the waves will reach some Malachite somewhere, because there is an attraction between the Malachite and the wave frequencies it emanates. It does not matter whether the wave frequencies return to the Malachite from which they originated (in this example, to Arizona).

There might be as many as ten million pieces of Malachite scattered throughout the planet. Yet each of these pieces is part of the one body of Malachite, which in a way is me, the Guardian of Malachite. In this way Malachite is not like humans and plants. In order for humans and plants to maintain life, all of their cells must be attached to each other.

"If a wave motion originated in Arizona and reached Malachite in Canada, would the Arizona Malachite know the information deposited in the Canadian Malachite?" Michael asked.

When a wave frequency is received, its date and whatever information it has collected is logged in. This information is in the form of vibratory rate patterns. Then the Malachite in Arizona is told, "Your wave emanation has returned. You no longer need to attract that frequency. It came home in Canada, and we have received its information."

By the way, you have been using the words "vibratory rate," "frequency," and "energy" synonymously, when in fact they are different—at least as far as I am concerned.

Remember that the Malachite in Arizona is a part of the whole body of Malachite. On the physical level, it does not necessarily contain the information that was deposited in Canada. Yet, one can access from any single piece of Malachite all the information contained by Malachite everywhere. This can be compared to the way each cell of the human body contains genetic information about the entire body. This is just an analogy; it is only intended to help you understand how the whole of something can be reflected in just one part of it.

"Can humans tap into the information stored in Malachite?" Michael asked hopefully.

To help you understand the answer to your question, I will

first speak of Malachite's effects on the human.

If a human held an uncut rock of Malachite, it would do practically nothing for the human; it would only be an ornament. Now, if one placed that rock of Malachite in a potted plant, it would begin to send wave emanations through the soil contained within the pot. And, if one buried the Malachite rock outdoors in the Earth, it would work for the planet as though it had never been harvested.

When any form of Malachite is framed or mounted in metal, the Malachite's emanations will not be able to pass through the metal. It would be unfortunate if the individual wearing such Malachite wanted to experience Malachite's full healing effects, because it is through its wave emanations that one receives Malachite's healing qualities.

Those who wear Malachite that is in any way partially encased in metal might feel some healing energies. However, the wearer will only experience a fraction of what could be experienced if the Malachite were in spherical form and unencumbered by metal. The effects that people experience when Malachite is partially encased in metal come from the waves reflecting off the open face of the Malachite and into the aura. This is usually an indirect, haphazard kind of wave motion, and it is not necessarily soothing; the waves bounce around in erratic directions trying to find the Malachite from which they emanated.

When Malachite is worn in spherical form and not bound by metal, something magical happens between the Malachite and the human. Of course, something magical happens when any earthstone or gemstone is worn in spherical form.

I do not know whether you will ever understand all the mechanics of why the spherical form can touch a human so deeply and in a way that no other shape can. I am somewhat surprised that your people are ready for knowledge of the power of the sphere. Spirit which orchestrates all life, including the life of the gemstones, must have a reason for deeming your people ready and bringing them the knowledge of the spherical form.

Once the Malachite spheres are warmed by the wearer's aura, its waves move down the body and then up, down and up, in a soothing, rhythmic, wave-like flow. This is unlike the behavior of the Malachite in the Earth, whose wave frequencies often bounce from place to place to place before returning. On a human, when the waves move down and up, each time they pass the Malachite spheres being worn, information is deposited.

To understand how Malachite works with humans, you must understand more about harmony and disharmony. A good way to understand this will be to look at these concepts in terms of music.

The C-major chord is a simple, harmonious chord which consists of three notes: C, E, and G. When these three notes are played, the resulting chord is one that is pleasing to the ear, because it is in harmony.

Disharmony often occurs when notes that do not belong in the same chord are played at the same time. If, for example, instead of a C note, an F note was played with the E and G notes, disharmony would result.

Now, it is interesting to speculate about what would happen if the notes themselves could hear each other play. If the notes were aware of each other, and the F, E, and G notes were played, the notes might recognize that they were not in harmony with each other. Then, rather than the F note, perhaps the C note would be played, and the harmonious C-major chord would be produced.

Physical disharmony occurs when parts of the body do not know what other parts of the body are doing. It is as though parts of the body cannot hear which "notes" other parts are playing; therefore, the body has no awareness that a disharmony exists.

For example, if your ankles are playing a C note, your knees are playing an E note, and your hips are playing a G note, you will be able to run because your legs are working in harmony. (Remember, the notes C, E, and G are harmonious.) However, if your ankle starts to play a F note, instead of a C note, disharmony will result. Then, if you tried to run, you would feel discomfort or pain.

What I want to illustrate is that, if each part of your body does not work together, or if each part does not know what the other part is doing, it will be easy for disharmonies to develop. If a certain part of your body plays a note that is out of harmony with the rest of the body, there will be no awareness of the resulting disharmony and, therefore, no effort to prevent or correct it. If this disharmonious note continues to be played, the disharmony will evolve into a pain or disease.

When Malachite is worn, I hear the disharmonious notes being played in the body. I wonder why the body does not hear these disharmonies and therefore begin to play more harmonious music. Of course, the reason is that body is not communicating with itself. Its "ears" are shut, and the disharmonious music is therefore not heard. The first result of the Malachite wave frequencies moving up and down the body is that the "volume" is turned up. This allows the body to start hearing the disharmonious chords. Its reaction is then: "Whoa, that sounds awful! Ankle, stop playing the F note! You should be playing a C note instead."

When individuals have been wearing Malachite for a long enough time, they may begin to hear the harmonious music of the body. Although people often don't like to listen to the disharmonies they emanate, they may be able to hear the disharmonious music, too. Depending on how many disharmonies exist in the body, it may take several weeks or months before this point is reached. Even if they do not begin to hear music, they will have gained a greater knowledge and understanding of their physical conditions.

When worn in spherical form, I help every cell of the body to know every other cell, just as every little piece of Malachite on this planet knows every other piece. Human cells must be touching each other to work. I find it interesting that my "cells" are not all touching each other, and yet I know myself better than most humans know themselves. I can teach your cells how to know every other cell in your body, just as eons ago, when Malachite was first formed, Malachite was taught how each of its cells could communicate with all the others.

When one part of the body knows what is happening in another part, it is much easier for the body to call all its forces together to combat any disease it might find.

For example, you might have a tumor that your body has tucked away in your liver. It might even be malignant; yet still the rest of your body has no idea that it is there. I am not sure why physical bodies often tuck harmful things away. Perhaps—as the owner of your liver, your tumor, and the conditions that gave you the tumor—you might not want to know that certain actions of yours have resulted in a tumor. And since your mind is not aware of it, the majority of your physical body will not be aware of it either.

If you don't want to face the truth, your physical body is

not going to face it either. In this situation, I can let your physical body know that you have a tumor in your liver. I will tell your body to wake up and get its immune system into gear and its eliminative organs working. I will not be directing your body's functions like a drill sergeant. However, I will let every cell of the body know what is happening in every other cell. Then, if the cells find a tumor hidden in your liver, your body's natural survival mechanism will call on your eliminative organs, immune system, and whatever other systems the body needs to start to work on that tumor.

This whole process will be greatly facilitated if you are willing to let go of the circumstances that created the tumor. If you say, "Well, I didn't create the tumor. I was exposed to some chemical at work, so it wasn't my fault. It was my employer's fault," you may still have things to let go of. Have you let go of your anger toward your employer? Have you forgiven your employer? Are you willing to accept the lessons this experience is giving you, and are you now willing to take the steps to resolve it? Answering each of these questions positively and with honesty is another way of letting go.

Know that Malachite works to benefit its wearers, because when one cell knows what the others are doing, there is greater harmony. Individuals who do not want to know that there might be tumors lurking in their liver, and those who do not want to be in harmony with themselves, will not want to wear Malachite.

* * *

There are many beneficial side effects of Malachite's wave-like motions. When its wave-like motion flows up and down your body, you will probably feel soothed. Frazzled nerves will be soothed, and any feelings of impatience will be calmed. I have no effect on the emotions or mind, except in the way that they affect the physical body. Often when people are angry, the physical body becomes agitated; this agitation feels so uncomfortable, that the anger becomes further fueled. Those who become angry and are wearing Malachite may find that this physical irritation is soothed. As a result, the anger will become soothed.

Also, wearing Malachite will help to break up any

stagnations of fluid in the body, because my wave-like motion most resembles a wave of fluid.

These are some of my possible side effects. However, they will be different for different people.

"Now can you tell us how humans can learn about their planet from Malachite?"

So, you wish to know how to access the information that has been stored in Malachite. As masters of your planet—that is, if you assume mastery of your planet—you have the right to this information. At this time, you Earth people are still slaves to your planet and slaves to your limited concepts about your relationships with other planets in the solar system and galaxy.

For some reason, many people in power on your planet feel that the general public cannot handle certain truths that are already known. These truths concern your planet, your moon, Mars and the other planets in your solar system, as well as visitors from other planets. Knowledge is power; and, in this case, power is knowledge kept from the masses. As we hover between the moon and the Earth, with the sun behind us, I will tell you that the public is only being told a watered-down fraction of what is already known.

People pray for this information, and they are ready for it. Many are asking individuals from beyond the Earth for this information. Hence, much information about the planets, the moon, and the solar system is being given through individuals who "channel" beings from other places and other times. Unfortunately, much of the information being received this way is inaccurate. If the people in power would realize that the masses are ready for this information, and if they would share it, your people would not be running the risk of receiving incorrect information.

The individual from Planet X who is communicating through one of your people might have the best intentions and, in fact, might be giving you accurate information about Planet X. However, the laws of Planet X are not necessarily the laws that govern planet Earth. Therefore, if you utilize some of this technological information, you may waste a good deal of money, time, and perhaps even lives.

People on your planet seem to enjoy authority, especially when it comes from a distant source. For Earth humans, the farther away an individual comes from, the more authority that individual has. It doesn't matter whether this person comes from another country, planet, or far away in time.

The Earth is not what is was during the Age of Atlantis—not by any means. The world has changed considerably. Since Atlantis, crystals and minerals have been planted, vibratory rates have changed, people's consciousness has risen, elements in the atmosphere and weather patterns have changed, and the Earth's polarities, magnetic lines, and power points have shifted. The Earth is an entirely different planet from what it was during the Age of Atlantis.

If you want to know about the workings of your planet, do not communicate with an individual from Planet X who might have only visited the Earth once or twice. Do not communicate with someone from ancient Lemuria or Atlantis if you want to know about the planet today. If you want information about the Earth, you need not look beyond your planet to find a wealth of information beyond your wildest dreams. The information is here. It is within the planet. It is within Malachite.

"When you spoke of people in power who are withholding information, were you referring to people in charge of the government or to scientists with information that they aren't sharing?"

Your scientists, your military, and your government have collected more information about things such as the moon and extraterrestrials than you might like to think. However, since they are reluctant to share this information with the rest of the people on the planet, there are other ways to obtain it. It can be obtained from Malachite.

The longer that people wear Malachite, and the more that its waves move up and down the body, the more prepared people will be to accept the information contained within the Malachite.

After wearing Malachite for at least 24 hours, look into the sphere's bull's-eye. The bull's-eye is the center of the concentric circles formed by the black bands. Free your mind. Then imagine and feel the wave-like motions emanating from the center of the bull's-eye and entering your eyes and brain. Then imagine them flowing back into the Malachite, and back again to your brain. Back and forth, back and forth. Then close your physical eyes and allow this wave to move through your spiritual eye (or brow chakra) and into your brain, and then back again to the Malachite.

Malachite spheres work much better for this purpose than do polished Malachite rocks. However, as long as the rock has a bull's-eye, it can still be used for this purpose.

You will have to perform this exercise several times. Each time you do, your brain will unconsciously grow more in tune with Malachite. The wave motions which flow back and forth actually constitute a communication between your brain and the Malachite.

Your brain has a greater awareness than you might think. It can help you do an incredible amount of tasks, some of which you haven't even thought of yet. People are not using their brains to their maximum potential. Malachite communicates with a part of the brain that has only begun to be exercised by people today. This is the part of the brain that is exercised during meditation or contemplation, or whenever your attention is focused beyond the physical body during some sort of spiritual exercise.

Each time a Malachite wave reaches the brain, the brain is touched by certain frequencies. Malachite's information is contained in patterns of vibratory rate that are attached to these frequencies. Your brain reads these vibratory rates and copies them. Then the wave returns to the Malachite. Each time you practice this, and each time a wave reaches your brain, more patterns and frequencies will be copied by this special part of your brain. Eventually, your brain will have copied enough information that it will start to see and recognize patterns of information forming.

Your brain will also begin to use the language you have learned as a child to organize and sort out the patterns that the Malachite has allowed the brain to copy. Since your native language is English, these patterns will be translated into English. Then the part of your brain that understands English will consciously understand the information that has been translated from Malachite language.

The more that you allow these patterns to be copied from Malachite, the more coherent the messages will become. The picture will become greater and clearer, until you will simply begin to know the information. If you are a scientist who, for example, is working in the area of physics, you will start to have inspirations about how your field relates to the Earth. This will happen because a part of your brain will know what the Malachite knows.

If you do not have a scientific background, but just enjoy gazing at the stars at night and contemplating the Earth's position in the heavens, you will gain a greater understanding of these things.

Information will be available to you, because you will simply know it. Your brain will have copied it from the Malachite. If you are asked where you learned this information, you may feel like it came from a memory or a dream; or you may have the feeling one gets when one has read something in a book, but cannot remember which one. Of course, if you have been consciously working with Malachite, you will know where this information came from.

Prime numbers (those numbers divisible only by the number one and itself) are very significant. The information stored in Malachite is kept in sequences of these numbers, and my frequencies are all based on them. The more profound the information is, the larger the prime number will be.

When you look into the bull's-eye of Malachite and feel its wave emanations flowing to and from your brain, the information tied to the lower prime numbers will be copied first. The brain will also recognize the patterns of lower numbers first, because it is easier to see the whole of smaller numbers. The information in the larger prime numbers will take the brain longer to sort out, organize, define, and translate into your native language.

It will take many sessions with Malachite for the patterns of information contained in these larger numbers to be copied and then analyzed by the brain. Although it takes more time, this information is much more fundamental, and its ramifications can be much more profound.

This technique requires a commitment. You cannot put Malachite into a computer or an information-retrieval device and expect it to print out its information in black and white. It is only to the computer of the brain that I tell my secrets. Therefore, if a mental conversation begins as you perform this technique, realize that this conversation might not just be between you and yourself. You may be having a conversation with me, the Guardian of Malachite.

The spherical form of Malachite is by far the easiest form for a human to extract information from. Spheres with clear, crisp black bands will provide clear, crisp information; cloudy black lines may provide misleading and muddled information.

Also, the larger the sphere, the easier it will be to extract and understand the information associated with the larger prime numbers.

It is also easier to extract Malachite's information after its protective polish has been removed. Water will do this. However, removing its polish will limit the durability of the sphere and eliminate its shiny luster. Of course, the polish will wear off naturally as the spheres are worn, touched, and rubbed.

"Isn't information lost when spheres are cut from the Malachite rock?"

No, because the information is contained within the crystalline matrix of my molecules. Remember, you can extract all of Malachite's information from any of its pieces, just like you can find genetic information about the whole body in each of its cells.

"How else can the people of Earth master their planet?"

Are carpenters considered master carpenters if they have not yet learned how to use all of a carpenter's tools? No. They must first learn how to use all of the tools available to them.

At this point in time, people are ready to learn which tools are available to them. I think this is one of the reasons you are interviewing the Gemstone Guardians. The gemstones and earthstones are perhaps the most powerful tools you have on this planet. We are not just the hammers and the screwdrivers; we are sophisticated power tools. We are not simple tools; we are complex. Our users must possess intelligence, resourcefulness, ingenuity, and creativity in order to use us to our maximum potential. We also demand that our users have an understanding beyond the physical—an understanding of what you call spirituality.

When people have an understanding of Spirit and Soul, they have a greater respect and understanding for all things. They take greater responsibility for the tools they use and for the effects their tools create.

Malachite Therapy

Wherever you place the Malachite will become the epicenter of its wave emanations. Therefore, if you know that a certain area of the physical body is disharmonious, it would be most effective to place the Malachite over that area. Whenever it is not being placed over the area, it should be worn around the neck.

Malachite has been worn by people throughout history. Everyone claims that it does something different, but this is simply because the side effects of my wave-like motion are felt in so many different ways.

In some it will release congestion; in some it will increase circulation; and in others it will even open up chakras. Some say it will open up the spiritual eye, and these people give credit to the Malachite for the spiritual experiences that result. Malachite's wave-like motion will simply stir and break up anything that is in the way of establishing and increasing harmony throughout the body.

Malachite's goal is to have every cell in the body playing the note of a harmonious chord. The music emanating from one who has worn Malachite spheres for a long time is beautiful. An individual with inner hearing may be able to hear the music emanating from his or her body. This music is the result of the vibratory rate of harmony expressing itself in sound. When all the cells are in harmony, no note cancels out or dampens the sound of any other note.

Some parts of the body will harmonize faster than others. If you possessed some sort of a microphone which amplified the sounds of your body, after wearing Malachite for one month, you would hear some parts of the body playing harmonious chords and others playing disharmonious ones. There might also be some parts of the body from which you would hear no music. In these areas, the notes would be canceling each other out.

To hear discordant music is better than to hear no music at all. Once the body is aware of discordant music, it does everything it can to make that discordant music harmonious. The parts of the body where no music is heard are areas that you should worry about, because the body is still not aware that disharmony exists there.

This microphone I have spoken of is a fundamental diagnostic tool. It already exists, although perhaps not yet on this planet. With this microphone, individuals can actually hear the music emanating from various parts of the body. They can even hear the music of the stomach change after they eat a certain food that caused disharmony there.

Once people hear the disharmonious music that the body is singing, they may not want to eat the food or take the medicine that caused the disharmony. On the other hand, once they hear how beautiful the body can sound when it is working in harmony with itself, they will be inspired.

I mentioned the diagnostic microphone and a potential application of it just to hint at what is to come.

* * *

"I have heard that extraterrestrials have a special interest in Malachite. Is this true, and if so can you tell us why?"

Every living planet has a certain rock that stores information about itself, like Malachite does for the Earth. Malachite is special, because it is like an open book. There is no lock on its treasure chest; one must simply open the lid. I do not know why this is so. The technique I gave you for accessing my information is simple and remarkably easy, and you need no special technology to practice it. Those who meditate, contemplate, or perform spiritual exercises have already developed the part of the brain that accesses this information most accurately. Therefore, they will have the most success. Yet, anyone can develop this ability.

Although each planet in the physical universe has its idiosyncrasies, each also has much in common with other planets, especially those with similar mineral contents. Quartz-based planets have an affinity with the Earth like no others. It is only natural that the people from these Quartz-based planets would want an easy way to access information about another Quartz-based planet.

Extraterrestrials have a particular desire for freshly mined Malachite. This is because I can be contaminated after I am mined; the patterns of information I store can be disrupted by nuclear radiation in the atmosphere. However, the ability of the spherical form to absorb radiation from a wearer's aura may be beneficial to some individuals, even though the information contained within the Malachite will be altered.

* * *

Before we close, I would like to clarify why Malachite exists at all. Why does the Earth need a rock that contains so much information about itself, its history, how it works, and how it interacts with life and the solar system? It is a spiritual law that every living planet that supports a form of life must have a method for keeping records about itself. It is one of the rules of the game.

Libraries have always been treasured. I am like a library. Therefore, I am a treasure of your planet in a way that no other gemstone is a treasure. Now that you know more about me, you have the ability to open up the treasure chest and partake of what is inside. Those who do so are indeed honored and blessed, for they have will taken the steps to accept what is available and what, in fact, has already been given to them. I say they are blessed, because not everyone will have the strength and the stamina to accept the information that Malachite has to offer.

As the Guardian of Malachite, I do not take a physical form. That is why you did not see me when you placed your attention on me. It is an honor to be interviewed and to have the opportunity to share information about Malachite. Apparently, it is time that some truths about Malachite be known and that the directions for receiving greater truths be given.

That is all.

"May the blessings be," said Michael.

May the blessings be.

The wave-like emanations flowing within my body stopped, and I found myself looking down through my own eyes upon the planet Earth. The freedom of being in space without a spaceship and without even a spacesuit was exhilarating. I felt like flying around the moon to learn for myself the secrets that Malachite said are being kept from the people.

Alas, there is more to the moon than we have been told, but that adventure will have to wait for the telling of another story.

26
LAPIS LAZULI

I prepared to meet the Guardian of Lapis Lazuli and once again found myself hovering in space and looking down on the Earth. Michael, as usual, was at my side.

As we watched the Earth below, the light illuminating the planet began to bend. It was as though the Earth's image was printed on transparent paper, and some giant unseen hand was folding the paper over and over again. Paradoxically, no matter how many times it was folded, the Earth's image remained the same size. Then it came to me that I was watching the planet move backwards in time.

Suddenly I was back on the Earth. In front of me loomed a massive gold throne. On it sat a middle-aged man wearing a gold crown and blue and gold robes. His eyes were as royal blue as his garments.

I am the Guardian of Lapis Lazuli. I brought you to this time in history so that you could see that I was once a King. It was my power that gave all the kings of this era their power. I was a gemstone like no other.

We will remain in this time in history until I have answered your questions about the past. When we are done, we shall unfold time and return to the point from which we started. Then we will speak of the present and of the future.

The Early Years of Lapis Lazuli

I do not have a specific purpose or mission, either for the Earth or for its people. This is because I was not brought here to have a particular effect.

I was given to your planet in exchange for a large quantity of something that was taken from the Earth. I do not know what I was exchanged for. I do know that the people living on the Earth at that time had nothing to do with the exchange. Furthermore, those who made this exchange had no idea that what they were giving to the Earth would become so powerful. They did not know that when the Lapis Lazuli was planted in the Earth, the planet's vibratory rate would make the Lapis very potent.

The ones who left the Lapis have never returned to your planet. If they had, they might have been surprised at the way Lapis reacted to the Earth's atmosphere and at the powerful effects it had on the people who wore it.

Lapis Lazuli is not plentiful in the physical universe. However, I am abundant on a few planets, including the one from which I came. Interestingly enough, I react quite differently to each planet, whether I am brought there or grow there naturally.

You may wonder why so many crystals have been planted on the Earth. Yet it should not be surprising when you consider how many races of people are comfortable with and adept at interplanetary travel. Trade creates a diversity among planets, just as it does among the nations of the Earth. For example, because of such trade, the Japanese eat hamburgers and wear blue jeans, and Americans eat sushi and drive Japanese cars.

"Do you know when Lapis was brought here?"

It was during the Age of Atlantis. However, my greatest strength was realized during the Egyptian era. Although Earth people today associate Lapis with Egypt, my powers are universal, and I was used in many places on the planet.

"What effects did you have on the Earth and its people during the Egyptian era?"

I radiate the kind of energy found on my home planet. I am also the Guardian of the Lapis there, although there I am not called Lapis. My vibratory rate acts like a stimulant for the Earth. I send waves of stimulation through the channels of the Earth to the various power points, charging them as I do so.

On the physical body I do the same thing: I stimulate its channels and power points. You call the body's channels "energy meridians," and its power points "chakras."

During my prime, this stimulation of the meridians and

chakras was strong and its effects were profound. The fact that my energy flooded every chakra appeared to defy the laws of nature; and my energy gave those who wore me the awareness of how they could further bend those laws.

Particularly profound was the effect I had when my energy opened the higher chakras. The individuals of this time were not accustomed to having their higher chakras opened and stimulated. These people were more physically oriented. Their attention was rooted in the Earth, and they drew most of their energy from their lower chakras. The powers they experienced when their higher chakras were opened were very great. Indeed, they had tremendous power over the minds of those who did not possess Lapis Lazuli and over many natural forces, such as gravity.

"Did Lapis have anything to do with the building of the pyramids of Egypt?" Michael asked.

Although I was not directly involved, many of the architectural feats accomplished during the Egyptian era could not have been done without my presence. Remember, I gave those who wore Lapis Lazuli physical, emotional, mental, and spiritual powers. I was worn by the royalty. The powers I granted made the royalty seem like gods to the people who did not wear Lapis.

Lapis gave its wearers the awareness, understanding, and ability to accept the presence of interplanetary visitors. These visitors helped them to build the pyramids. Without Lapis, leaders of the time would not have been able to accept what the extraterrestrials wished to build on their land.

The pyramids were built for many reasons, and they had multiple functions. They possessed burial chambers and places for initiations and secret classes. There were also rooms where energies converged in such a way that great healings and transformations could occur. These particular rooms also served as terminals where people could be transported to other places, not only in consciousness but physically as well.

"Do you mean that people could be transported to other places on this planet or to other planets?"

Both. This transportation was mostly enjoyed by the royalty, who often made a game of transporting themselves from one pyramid to another. However, it was also practiced for the beneficial effects of the expanded state of awareness gained when they entered one pyramid and exited another.

"I can see how that could change one's concepts," commented Michael.

Exactly, and expand one's ceiling of limitations.

"Can this still be done in the Egyptian pyramids today?"

The pyramids have been destroyed. They are not what they once were.

"Can any pyramid be used for transportation?" Michael pursued.

Only if the transportation is done by leaving the physical body behind. It was not just the shape of the Egyptian pyramids and the way the energies flowed around them that allowed physical transportation to occur. Layers of special material were laid beneath the transportation chambers. This material played with the forces of gravity and magnetism. There were other forces involved too, but we are not here to talk about the pyramids.

During this era, Lapis Lazuli was used in many forms and fashioned into many kinds of objects, including ornaments, talismans, and intricate inlays. It was also cut into many shapes, including rounded ones. However, at that time, Lapis was so strong that it did not need to be formed into spheres in order to radiate its vibratory rate. Still, the larger the mass or the more surface area exposed, the greater was the effect.

People enjoy hearing about the past, because it is something they can dream about. However, the past cannot be accurately verified. My effects in the present can be verified, either scientifically or through direct personal experience.

"Shall we move back to the present?" suggested Michael.

Yes.

Instantly, we found ourselves hovering over the Earth again. This time the Earth's image began to open up and unfold. When it was finished, I noticed that some geographical changes had taken place during this unfoldment of time.

Lapis Lazuli Today

My energy has waned considerably. Today my effect on the chakras and meridians is only a fraction of what it used to be. Also, my focus is more on the heart, throat, and mind, and on the chakras in the head.

For the Earth, my stimulating effects have become mild. Instead of affecting the entire planet, I can only stimulate the areas within a certain radius of where I am found.

I can still help people feel the energy and power they possess within. This power is greatest when one's heart energy combines with one's mind energy, or when the emotional and the mental aspects are working in harmony and are not at odds with each other. This harmony occurs when the higher chakras are stimulated, and when the flows of energy through these chakras become balanced.

I can also help people to break free of past situations that may be causing them problems today. I do this, especially if they have had an association with me in the past, or if they were incarnated during the time when I was in my prime, regardless of where on the planet they lived. I can help these people most, because they have already made a connection with Lapis Lazuli. However, I can also benefit those who have not had a past connection with me.

Those who are attracted to me are attracted strongly. The energy I radiate can touch people very deeply. It touches them through the heart and the mind.

I work on creating a greater connection, communication, and understanding between one's emotional and mental aspects. When feelings are brought to the mind, mental processes become richer, more fruitful, and bountiful; and when mental processes touch the emotions, the emotions become understood.

When this happens, people tend to become easier on themselves. Often we are our own hardest masters. The feeling of relief I bring can be felt within moments of connecting with Lapis. It may be one of the reasons people are drawn to me.

The establishment of a good connection between the emotions and the mind opens possibilities. It expands horizons and increases one's potential. I give my wearers courage and the fearless, adventurous spirit needed to realize their dreams. I show them their dreams and give them the feeling that they can attain them. Once you have a feeling that you can attain your dreams, resources will be drawn to you like iron filings are drawn to a magnet.

Since my energy is waning today, I must be worn in spherical form in order for my energy to flow freely into the aura. The more gold pyrite flecks I possess, and the more royal blue is my color, the stronger I will be. Also, the more I am worn by an individual, the stronger I become—although I will never again be as strong as I was in my youth.

The vibratory rate of my color can affect an individual deeply, because it touches the optic nerve in an unusual way. Lower quality Lapis is usually dyed to enhance its color. Unfortunately, any dye applied to such Lapis will further inhibit its energy, which is already weak because of its low quality. Dye will also prevent the vibratory rate of my true color from having its effects. The color of dyed Lapis will still leave an impression on the optic nerve. However, its effect will represent only a fraction of the effects of the undyed variety.

Not only will dye inhibit effects, but because quality will be poor in the first place, what effects there are will be further inhibited.

Your optic nerve picks up impressions of what you see with your physical eyes, as well as impressions of what you see in your dreams and inner visions. All of these impressions stimulate this nerve, which is connected to the part of the brain that serves as the storehouse for memories.

The vibratory rate of my color will impress the optic nerve in such a way that the brain is reminded of a primordial memory. This memory is basic, fundamental, and from the individual's core. It is a memory of that which links the individual to his or her source.

"What do you mean by source?" Michael asked.

God. And it is not only my color that reminds people of the energy, or Spirit which connects them with God. My vibratory rate also plays a large part in stimulating the optic nerve, and hence the brain, to recall this memory. This is another reason that natural Lapis is much more powerful than dyed Lapis.

Although they might not know why, people are comforted by my royal blue color. When people feel comfortable, they feel freer; and freedom gives people confidence. When people feel more confident, they begin to feel that they can attain their goals, aspirations, and dreams. The vibratory rate of Lapis gives them the courage and understanding to attain these things.

* * *

I do not directly initiate physical healing. Any healing effects credited to me are only the result of how I integrate the mind and the emotions.

Placing Lapis Lazuli over the brow chakra or around the head in a tisrati can result in a profoundly heightened spiritual awareness. This awareness will only be on the mental level, but the mental world is Heaven for many religions on your planet. Any state of consciousness beyond the physical has something to teach. It can give the individual feelings of expansion, as well as greater wisdom, knowledge, and awareness.

I have little effect when placed anywhere on the body other than the brow, with the exception of around the neck. When worn around the neck, I have my greatest effect if I am worn directly over the heart or as close to the heart as possible.

In the past, Lapis was treasured by one owner, and one owner only. It was not passed from one person to the next, unless it was given to another family member at the time of death. Otherwise, it was buried with the individual. The more that one individual wears Lapis, the more deeply and effectively I can work. The longer I am worn, the more an individual can become attuned to and accept my powers.

Lapis need only be wiped with a cloth to enhance the shine of its polish. This is all the cleansing that is necessary.

"You have the reputation for being very wise, and I sense your wisdom. I have wondered what the overall purpose of gemstones is. Do you know why Spirit has created them?" Michael asked.

From one point of view, Soul was thrown out of the glory of Heaven, had bodies dumped on it, and was given a destiny to fulfill. This destiny was to be full of trials, tribulations, lessons, and experiences until Soul realized who it was and returned to its true home in Heaven with God.

Yet God did not abandon Soul in the worlds of matter with all its burdensome bodies and with nothing to help it. Signposts, guiding lights, and religions are provided all along the way. There are also spiritual masters, guides, healers, and others who can help. Tools, such as books and gemstones, are also there for Soul. All of these are available to help individual Souls to fulfill their destinies and return to their true home with God. Each of these helpers of Soul are distinct and different. Each is powerful and not to be underestimated.

"So, gemstones are another set of tools available to assist Soul," concluded Michael.

Yes. Gemstones are among the many tools provided to assist Soul, whether or not Soul uses them. Those who are wise utilize the tools that lie at their feet, rather than struggle constantly with their bare hands. Yes, God created your hands; but God also created tools when God created tasks.

"What is the overall purpose of the Gemstone Guardians?"

To direct life force toward the gemstones of which they are in charge, and to keep this connection flowing. Sometimes we are not supposed to do this—as in my case with the Lapis of Earth. I am not supposed to feed the Earth's Lapis with energy. I have been told not to.

Although it exists there, the Lapis of Earth does not exactly belong on the planet. On my home planet, I continue to feed this royal blue gemstone and to awaken people's awareness of it. On planets where Lapis is located, I sometimes work in the dreams of those who wear me. I open their awareness to what this tool is doing for them and how they can use it to greater advantage.

"Is it common for wearers of gemstones to have dream experiences about the gemstones they are wearing?"

This is truer today than it has ever been. Today awareness is being expanded, and invisible clouds and congestions are being removed from people's consciousness. The gemstones themselves are waking up and becoming more energized and enlivened. As Gemstone Guardians, we are being given a greater awareness of our own capabilities.

In other words, we have been given the awareness that we can work directly with people. We can teach people and work with them in their dreams, meditations, contemplations, or even in the waking state. Although we always could work with people, and some of us might have done so, today we are being asked to work more directly with people. We have been asked to work with each other, as well.

"Why do you think this is happening at this time?"

Destiny. It was predicted eons ago that there would be a time—and the time is now—when, in the semi-darkness, a greater light would start to shine. Since the end of the last century, an opening and awakening has been occurring. This is happening everywhere—on every planet in every galaxy, in every world and in every universe.

Everywhere there is a rejoicing, and yet with it comes a profound responsibility. With the rejoicing also come many lessons, and perhaps even hardships, for this is also an opportunity to grow. Growth means change; and change means letting go of things that are no longer necessary, even though we may dearly want to hold on to them. However, we cannot remain attached to who we once were—and grow—at the same time.

This opening began with a crack in the door, and slowly, slowly, the door is opening. By now it has only opened a few inches, but it will continue to open over the next several decades.

It is indeed an interesting time that you have been born in.

Lapis Lazuli Tomorrow

Today my power is waning, and I will probably become increasingly rare on the Earth. I was not deposited in many places. Although I grow on the Earth, I do not grow fast, because I am not indigenous to this planet. Lapis does not proliferate. It grows, simply because it is alive.

Those who are fortunate enough to own high quality Lapis specimens are indeed blessed with a powerful tool. Feel the power that I radiate today, and then imagine what I must have been like in my prime, when my abilities on this planet were a hundred or five hundred times what they are today. It is awesome, humbling, and perhaps even frightening to realize the power and potential of those who wore me in the ancient days.

"Have the effects of Lapis Lazuli also waned on its home planet?" Michael asked.

They have not waned nearly as much as they have on Earth. I may look like an old man; but remember that when we turned back time, I only appeared to be about ten Earth years younger than I am now. My life span is not dictated by the life span of Lapis Lazuli on Earth. It is dictated by the life span of Lapis on my home planet.

"Then why would the Earth's Lapis have lost so much of its strength?"

It is because the Earth's atmosphere does not have the energy to sustain and enliven Lapis Lazuli. If you remove a tree from the forest and plant it in a flower pot in your home, it will not live as long as it would have if it had remained in the forest.

"Is there anything else you would like to share?"

The beginning pianist can only play a few notes at one time and make them sound beautiful. A master pianist can play a seemingly infinite number of notes and make them sound still more beautiful.

Michael, you are working toward mastery of Spirit and Self. Since Spirit is life, there is no reason that mastery of Spirit and Self cannot not be reflected in the mastery of everything you do in life. This might include business or any other activity you enjoy.

You have experienced time and again the plight of the beginning pianist struggling to make a composition sound beautiful. You will have to work on mastering greater and greater pieces of music. Set your sights in that direction, and you will attain it.

It takes practice to become a master, but the potential to do so is available to everyone. Lapis Lazuli can help you to attain mastery, perhaps more so than any other gemstone. This may be mastery of bread baking, piano playing, or of Spirit and Self. To become a master, you must first see your goal. I help people to see and then to attain their goals and dreams.

To become a master, you must own the experience. You must feel that you have already attained it. I can help you have these feelings; but you must know that you have the ability to take the steps necessary to attain mastery. I can give you the courage to take those steps.

You have experienced Lapis Lazuli before. Let it place music in your heart. Let it strike the chords, for they have been played before. And don't accept your own limitations.

"That is good advice."

Now I shall leave you. May the blessings be.

"Thank you, and may the blessings be."

The Guardian of Lapis departed, and I began to speed through a tunnel of light so quickly that the atmosphere around me shook. Several moments later, I found myself back on the Earth, sitting comfortably on the living room sofa.

During my "re-entry," a technique for using Lapis Lazuli was planted in my heart.

This technique is to be practiced after you have been wearing Lapis Lazuli spheres for a while or at least until they have become warmed by your body's energy. Remove the strand. Hold about four or six of the spheres on the skin over your brow chakra, placing light pressure on the area. Close your eyes, and clear your mind. Then feel the Lapis energy flood through the brow chakra and into your head.

Feel your head filling with this energy. When it reaches the back of your skull, allow a question to enter your thoughts. Then place your attention, not at the brow chakra, but inside the Lapis spheres resting on your forehead. In your mind's eye, watch the scene that unfolds. It will give you or help to explain the answer to your question.

27
ONYX

I expected to meet the Guardian of Onyx in a dark place, perhaps in a dimly-lit cave deep within the Earth. So I was surprised when Spirit led us to a grassy area near a mountain brook. There the Guardian of Onyx sat waiting on a large rock. When he saw Michael and me, he stood, stretched out his hand to shake ours, and greeted us warmly.

The Guardian of Onyx looked as ordinary as any Earth human. He had jet black hair and dark brown eyes, and he spoke in a quiet, gentle voice. This Guardian seemed to be a rather likable fellow. Judging from the location he chose for his discourse, he dearly loved nature. I felt this love—a kinship with all living things—as I entered his aura.

Although it is considered an earthstone, the material you call Black Onyx has not been made entirely by the planet. It is comprised of the Earth's elements, but has been enhanced by humans. Yet it is not manmade, like plastic, either. Plastic beads do not have Guardians.

Onyx is surely alive. It has a special vibratory rate, even though its color has been enhanced to make it appear blacker. In fact, this enhancement only contributes to its mission; indeed, it gives me my effect. The effects of some other gemstones are dampened by treatment. Without treatment, Black Onyx would not be.

As its Guardian, I have been assigned to watch over Onyx, to guide its vibratory rate, and to care for and work with the people who wear it.

"Does your mission include only the Black Onyx on Earth?"

Michael asked.

Yes. My guardianship is for the Earth's Black Onyx only.

"Are you also the Guardian of the material from which Onyx is made?"

There is another who acts as Guardian for the material you call Gray Onyx. When Gray Onyx is made black, its effects change considerably. This is because of the way light reacts with the color.

"What is your mission?"

My mission is for humans exclusively. The mission of my vibratory rate is to stabilize, strengthen, and support the base chakra. My vibratory rate, combined with my color, works on stimulating all the chakras, except the crown chakra. At the deepest level, I give the chakras the strength to function properly. My energy first enters the base chakra. Then it rises up through the body, giving the chakras the message that it is all right for them to open up and accept vibratory rates or colors as the body needs them.

Although, from a certain point of view, it may seem paradoxical—when all light converges, there is darkness. When this phenomenon occurs on a spiritual level, the negative pole of the universe is formed. Perhaps this is why black is a symbol of the negative, and white is a symbol of the positive. Yet, please do not consider Black Onyx a negative stone.

The nature, purpose, and importance of the negative force is that it tempers Soul. Ultimately, it strengthens the individual—the hard way. When Onyx is worn during a negative situation, its vibratory rate allows light to shine on the situation and reveal its positive side.

Sometimes people have negative attitudes about the base chakra or consider it much less important than the other chakras. If the base chakra were not needed, it would not have been included in the human body. When the base chakra is balanced and functioning properly, the individual has the strength to develop the higher chakras. The strength of the base chakra is also needed to help withstand the changes that the development of the higher chakras will bring into one's life.

It is the nature of my vibratory rate and my color to absorb the seven color rays and bring them into the body through the base chakra. After entering the body, some of my vibratory rate leaves through the sex chakra, but most of it rises up the body. As my energy passes each chakra, it deposits the vibratory rate of the colors each chakra is programmed to accept. My energy reinforces the chakras' ability to accept these color rays. It also enlivens their receptivity to all colors.

When my energy reaches the stomach chakra, I let go of the green and yellow vibratory rates, because that energy center has a magnetic attraction for these two rays. The heart chakra has a magnetic attraction for the red and orange rays; this attraction calls the red and orange vibratory rates from my make-up. At the throat chakra I release the blue ray vibratory rate; and at the brow chakra I let go of the indigo and violet vibratory rates. In some individuals, I deposit the indigo ray with the blue at the throat chakra. My energy does not reach the crown chakra.

I can help the body become strong enough to accept the proper amount of these colors on its own. When the body does this, the individual's vibratory rate rises. When one's vibratory rate rises, one often recognizes patterns and habits in one's life. This is because a habit is a form of disharmony; and where all colors of the rainbow exist in balance, there can be no disharmony.

With the rise in vibratory rate, the individual might also see that a certain habit is not all bad, because through that habit certain lessons are being learned. Nevertheless, the individual might also come to realize that the habit is no longer needed. Then, it will just be a matter of further raising one's vibratory rate in order to totally dissolve one's ties with the habit.

Actually, in most cases, habit resolution involves dissolving karmic ties with the entity associated with the habit—for example, tobacco, in the case of a smoking habit.

My effect on patterns and habits is a side effect of my primary mission. However, it is a very noticeable one and common to everyone who wears Onyx. The side effects of most gemstones are not experienced by everyone who wears them; in this way, Onyx is different from most gemstones. Still, the details of each person's experience with Onyx will be unique.

People who are attracted to Onyx are often looking for a way to break out of certain patterns or habits. These habits may be physical, emotional, or mental.

A change of habit must be preceded by recognition of the habit; otherwise the change cannot occur. When people see the reason for certain habits, and understand why patterns keep recurring, they will have taken the first step required to change those habits, or at least to change their underlying causes.

"Would you explain the mechanics of how you help people let go of habits?"

First, I allow the individual to become aware of the habit. I do this by intensifying the individual's attachment to the habit. Yet I intensify it only to the point where the individual recognizes that the attachment exists. In this way, I help the person see that what is destructive is not so much the habitual behavior itself, but the individual's attachment to it.

How many people do you know who smoke or drink, but don't think that they have a smoking or a drinking problem? When Onyx is worn, an individual who has, for example, a habit of smoking will find that the attachment to this habit is intensified. This does not mean that the person will smoke more cigarettes or that the habit will get worse. Instead, the attachment to smoking will intensify. This, in turn, will encourage the person to recognize that the attachment exists. With this recognition will come the realization that "I am out of control! My habit is controlling my life!"

As the attachment to the habit intensifies, I also give strength. I do this by making sure that each chakra is receptive to the color rays and that the color rays entering the body are being distributed equally.

This is important, because it will prevent the individual from losing balance when the realization dawns that he or she is out of control. Then the individual will have the strength to let go of the attachment and say, "This habit once controlled me, but no more. I accept self-mastery, and I have mastered this habit. It is no longer a part of me." Perhaps the person will even continue to smoke, but the attachment to the habit will have been released. The individual will have mastered the habit.

In other words, if people continue to wear Onyx, they will have the strength to break the karmic ties with the habit that is controlling them. Onyx will also protect their aura whenever the habit tries to return.

One can use one's knowledge of how Onyx works to focus my effects. If my wearers understand my effects, they can decide to put attention on the habit that concerns them most. On the other hand, when people who are unaware of my effects wear Onyx, they will simply realize that certain habits are controlling their lives.

"If someone wearing Onyx has, for example, twenty habits, would the habits be addressed one at a time; or would the attachment to all of them be intensified at once?"

The attachment to the habit that is most destructive will be dealt with first, unless the individual chooses a different habit to focus on. However, if one chooses a habit that is really just a manifestation of a deeper habit, I will work on the underlying habit first. For example, if the individual chooses to release an attachment to food—when the underlying attachment really concerns the person's concept of giving and receiving love—my attention will focus on the person's underlying attachment.

Letting go of habits can be uncomfortable, but it is not my intention to give individuals more than they can handle or to cause an imbalance.

My work can be gentle, because my goal is to allow changes to occur in balance. This is supported by my effect on the chakras; when they are better able to accept the proper balance of color rays, overall balance is enhanced. Breaking habits causes a change in overall balance. Therefore, if the body's balance is being supported by Onyx, the individual will not be overburdened by the changes that come with the breaking of habits. The individual will have the strength to make those changes.

Larger spheres or longer strands of Onyx will not necessarily make my effects stronger, because people can only accept whatever changes they can accept. If you enjoy a particular size and length of Onyx, it is because you are most in harmony with that size and length. Therefore, that particular strand will be most effective for you.

It does not matter where I am placed on the body. You could wrap me around your ankle, and I would still affect the chakras in the same way. However, when worn around the neck, I can affect the higher chakras more easily.

One can place Onyx over the base chakra to give strength and support to individuals who feel particularly insecure and unstable. This insecurity may be emotional or mental, or it may be felt in terms of the person's energy. This treatment will also be beneficial for those who have been imbalanced by influences that forcibly open the chakras, such as hallucinogenic drugs, narcotics, and marijuana. These individuals may even be naturally drawn to Onyx. It will be good if they are, because I will help to strengthen their chakras and counteract the damage they have done to their inner bodies.

"Do you have any other effects on the inner bodies?"

Some individuals would have a better perspective on their inner worlds if they were to become more secure and grounded in the physical body. Onyx will give them that secure and grounded feeling. It will allow them to view the mind and emotions from a grounded, physical point of view, and thereby gain a greater understanding of themselves.

People who tend to feel "spaced out," disoriented, or detached from themselves will benefit from Onyx. So will those who have difficulty concentrating on important tasks or who tend to live almost exclusively on the emotional level. Often such people struggle to maintain adequate awareness of what is occurring around them on the physical level. Onyx can be a helpful tool for these individuals, especially when they must drive, use potentially dangerous power equipment, or perform a task that requires intense concentration for safety reasons.

At such times, these individuals should place Onyx in whatever part of the aura that is most comfortable for them. The Onyx could be worn around the neck, placed in a pocket, or laid in the lap.

Onyx Therapy

"Are there any specific therapies that involve Onyx?" Michael inquired.

When you ask for therapies, I believe you must be asking for the peculiar ways in which the vibratory rate of my gemstone affects the human body.

There is a technique for using Onyx that gives people a greater awareness of the physical body and allows them to experience the chakras. Specifically, it helps them to recognize, understand, and become acquainted with their chakras. The results of this knowledge can be profound, but I take no responsibility for this increased awareness. This technique is more accurately called an "experiment," for it is an experiment you perform with yourself. You are the scientist using the tool called Onyx to discover yourself.

Begin by holding a strand of Onyx spheres over the base chakra. Then hold it over the sex chakra, and then over the stomach chakra, and so on up the body. The amount of time you hold the Onyx over each chakra is not important.

During this application your mind should be quiet; it should be open to experiences and willing to accept knowledge and a greater understanding of the chakra over which the Onyx is placed. As you proceed, focus your attention on each chakra, and feel its energy.

When you are finished, place the Onyx over your forearm, shoulder, or thigh, and then back over a chakra. Feel the difference. This technique should give you the understanding that the seven chakras are important and profound centers, different from all other parts of your body.

Onyx Tomorrow

"Do you anticipate that your effects on humans will change in the future?" Michael asked.

Although humans might think that they change slowly, you really change quite quickly compared to the rate at which gemstones evolve and change. As long as humans continue to make Gray Onyx black in the same way they do now, my effects will remain the same.

All beings react to light; and all beings have energy centers, including animals. Perhaps plants do, too; and if one knew how to look for them, their energy centers might be found. Therefore, I believe that all living beings will react to Onyx in a similar way.

* * *

"Since you are the last of the Earthstone Guardians to be interviewed for this book, is there anything you would like to say to summarize the work of the earthstones?"

Now that you have an understanding of how I work and what I do, feel free to experiment with other therapeutic uses. Be creative! I believe this would be the message from all the Earthstone Guardians.

When you learn the true nature, purpose, and mission of

a stone—whether you call it an earthstone, oceanstone, or gemstone—you will have gained the freedom to combine this basic knowledge with your creativity and your own knowledge of the human body. In other words, you can experiment.

There is not just one way to use a tool. With creativity, you can use most tools in a hundred different ways. For every gemstone, there are at least a hundred and one applications of it, especially when one has a more complete picture of the world of gems.

Do not underestimate your intuition when working with gemstones therapeutically. Some say intuition is God, Spirit, your higher Self, or your Guardian Angel speaking to you. If you feel insecure about using your intuition, substitute the phrase "inner knowingness" for "intuition." Always use your inner knowingness to guide you when using any gemstone.

There are some who will always need to prove their intuitive insights with mental equations. These people either have not adequately developed their intuitions or do not trust them enough. Of course, there are instances when mathematical equations are essential, especially in the case of complex situations.

The earthstones are not greater than the gemstones, and vice versa. They are just different. Earthstones are crucial for the planet, just as crystals are.

People have already accepted medicinal plants as gifts from the planet. We Guardians believe and know that people are now ready to accept medicinal gemstones as gifts from the planet. Both plants and gemstones can be medicinal and therapeutic. Nevertheless, they are very, very different from each other. Both plants and gemstones are alive. However, the amount of life and healing force contained in the molecular structure of plants is miniscule compared to the amount contained in the crystalline structure of a gemstone.

The life force of a plant starts to diminish once it is plucked from its roots. The life force of gemstones does not change when it is plucked from the planet. In fact, the harvesting of gemstones is the first step taken in preparing gemstones to directly assist humans. If one tears off a piece of leaf, that piece will immediately start to die. If one breaks off a piece of a gemstone, it will stay as alive as the stone from which it was broken.

Plants lose their vibratory rate once they are ingested by

the body. The body soon forgets the plant's gift and needs another dose. If you wear a gemstone for one minute and take it off, your body will soon forget the gemstone's vibratory rate. However, it is much easier to wear a gemstone continuously than it is to eat a plant continuously.

My comparison between plants and gemstones could continue. I respect plants. I love them, just as I love all the gifts the Earth has given us, and I am deeply grateful for them. Plants and gemstones can work well together. You can receive as much gemstone therapy as you wish and as much herbal therapy as you wish at the same time. As long as the therapies are beneficial, they will not conflict with each other.

The more you know about gemstones, the more freedom you will have to choose from a wider variety of the planet's gifts. These gifts will help you through your changes and support you in your growth.

* * *

"We will be interviewing some of the Oceanstone Guardians next. Would you like to introduce the first Guardian?" asked Michael.

The oceanstones are out of my realm. Although we exist on the same planet, we are of different worlds.

"Thank you for sharing your wisdom with us."

That you have recognized wisdom in my words tells me that there is wisdom in you, as well. Otherwise, how else could you have recognized it?

I expect that we will meet again, perhaps even on the physical level.

"I will be looking forward to it," Michael replied.

I looked at the Guardian of Onyx, who smiled. He had a twinkle in his dark brown eyes. I reached out my hand to shake his, and we said our good-byes.

He spoke privately with Michael for several minutes while I waited, enjoying the scenery. They seemed to be enjoying each other's company and forming a true friendship.

When their conversation ended, the Guardian stretched his arms, and inhaled the refreshing, clear blue mountain air. Then he turned to watch the water as it tumbled over rocks in the stream next to us.

It was indeed a glorious day.

28
MOTHER OF PEARL

I closed my eyes and was greeted by the sound of waves and the cries of sea gulls. Soon the waves I heard began to move through my body, sending a stirring, rhythmic motion through every cell. It was as though my cells were particles of sand on a beach, and waves of life force were surging through them, then receding, and surging again.

Then I let my attention go deeper, and I heard the sound of the water molecules themselves. They sang.

When I opened my eyes, I was not surprised to find myself and Michael by the sea. A small white cloud was moving toward us over the waves. When it arrived on the beach, I saw that it was actually the transparent form of a woman. Her image was that of a ghost, shimmering and iridescent. Her wrinkled face made her look old; yet her perfect posture and the love radiating from her aura gave her an ageless beauty.

She sat between Michael and me on the sand. She seemed to know Michael well, and they greeted each other warmly.

Turning to me she said, There is no need for you to enter into my aura. Just close your eyes, relax your mind, and connect with me on a deeper level.

Mother of Pearl is part of a sea shell. The shell is the house of a sea animal. Every species has its own Guardian Angel, including humans. I am not the Guardian Angel of the sea creatures in whose shells Mother of Pearl grows. I am the Guardian for the Mother of Pearl that has been harvested and fashioned in some way to be worn by humans.

If you wish to know the history of Mother of Pearl, study

the evolution of the sea creatures that bear shells: the mollusks.

My purpose is not for the planet. It is for the humans who wear me. I also have a responsibility to assist the Guardian of Pearl. She needs assistance because of the ways in which Pearl is being used and worn by people today. The Guardian of Pearl has withdrawn. She has been battered and beaten by the vibratory rate of cultured Pearls; their vibratory rate dilutes and breaks down the power of the true Pearl. It also places strain and stress on the Guardian of Pearl.

My mission is to stir. I stir physically, emotionally, and mentally. I stir the life force in the cells of the physical body. I stir the emotions in the emotional body, and I stir thoughts and memories in the mind. This stirring helps to remind my wearers of their true origin.

Every cell in your body and every aspect of your emotional and mental bodies has a subconscious, a primordial memory. My stirring awakens this memory. It reminds you of the time when you were part of the sea.

Now, if you have a scientific background, you will say, "Ah yes, humans evolved from the sea. Humans, as did all creatures, originated as single-celled organisms which lived in the ocean." If you have a spiritual orientation, you will say, "Yes, humans originated in the ocean, the ocean of God and love—that spiritual ocean where all Souls dwell." Some might call this place Heaven.

There are many side effects, or results, of my stirring. On a mental level, I stir memories, especially recent ones. When memories are stirred, they are remembered. Specifically, I stir the memories of dreams, including daydreams. I make their symbols clearer, so that they can be understood. I also stir the thoughts to look within and beyond the mind; from this stirring comes the realization that, indeed, there is something beyond.

When I stir the emotions, they become more balanced and harmonious. Positive and negative emotions are two completely different entities, and the stirring effect is different with each. The sharpness of negative emotions, such as sharp tempers and the sharp pangs of fear, is smoothed and calmed. This alone makes the individual appear to be more emotionally balanced.

On the other hand, those who have difficulty expressing their positive feelings, such as love, will find these feelings becoming stronger and more defined. Then it will not be long before these emotions are expressed. I also give the strength and support needed for this expression to take place.

When I stir the life energy of the physical body's cells, there is an overall calming effect. My stirring is relaxing, rhythmical, and steady, like the rhythm of waves lapping the shore. Yet I may not be strong enough to help one sleep. Insomnia is often related to strong mental activity. When I stir the thoughts, they tend to turn inward; they are not suppressed. I am calming, sedating, and relaxing, but I am not a sleeping aid.

Physical imbalances are often caused by mechanisms in the body that have become either overactive or underactive. I help to calm any mechanism that is overactive.

My stirring action is like the motion of breathing. It increases the flexibility of the cells. The more flexible the cells are, the more life force and oxygen they can accept.

I also give the feeling that one is resting in the arms of a loving mother. Therefore, I will help those who need some motherly love, whether or not they are aware of it.

I have another effect that is a specific result of my vibratory rate: I scatter or absorb any negative wavelengths thrown at the individuals who wear me. These include the wavelengths of thoughts, emotions, and electromagnetic forces, as well as the emissions of televisions, radios, and microwave transmitters. These can all produce disharmonious effects on humans.

These wavelengths are not homogeneous; they contain different parts. Some parts I absorb, and some I can only scatter. I am able to do this because of the way my vibratory rate charges the aura.

This action can be considered a side effect of my mission. Nevertheless, it is a profound effect of my vibratory rate. It occurs when the wearer's aura is saturated with my vibratory rate. In an adult's aura, saturation will occur after wearing a strand of six-millimeter spheres for about five or ten minutes. Four-millimeter spheres may take ten to fifteen minutes to saturate the aura. In a child's aura, saturation will occur within five minutes if a strand of four- or six-millimeter spheres is worn.

When the Mother of Pearl vibratory rate has saturated an aura, it affects the wavelengths that enter it, as I have just described. It also affects certain other wavelengths that are already contained in the aura. These wavelengths are the individual's unfulfilled needs and desires.

Inside of each of you are needs, desires, feelings, and hurts. All of these are reflected in your aura. When Mother of Pearl has saturated your aura, it recognizes the needs and desires that are unfulfilled. It sees them for what they are: holes in the fabric of your being.

I shall explain. Humans have a natural, innate need to be nurtured, cared for, and loved. These needs are first felt in the womb, and are most apparent in infants and young children. Mothers and fathers are surely aware of all the love, attention, and nurturing that a baby needs.

Yet people do not stop having these needs as they get older. In fact, they have these needs for life. I am not talking about the need to own the latest invention on the market. The needs I speak of are part of your fabric. As an infant, you needed to be loved and nurtured in order to survive. Now that you are an adult, these needs are not as critical for your physical survival. However, they are absolutely critical for your emotional survival.

No mother is perfect. I have been a mother myself for thousands and thousands of years. Not only have I had children of my own, but, as the Mother of Pearl, I have performed a motherly role for Pearl for a long, long time.

Even with all this experience, I am still not perfect. Although we do our best, no mother can fulfill all the needs of her children. As children grow into adulthood, they find that Mother is no longer there to fulfill their needs for love and nurturing, and that often life does not fulfill them either.

The unfulfilled needs of the individual become holes in the fabric of the individual's being. I am speaking of every unfulfilled need—every one. These holes may include the lack of attention you received as a child; the inability to receive the education you wanted; the lack of food, shelter and clothing; or the lack of a relationship that would fulfill your need for love. You may have had a relationship that went awry or experienced a situation in which you loved someone, but that person did not return the love in the way you needed it to be returned. No doubt this created a vacuum, an unfulfilled need; it created a hole in the fabric of your being.

Mother of Pearl detects these holes. Then my vibratory rate

sings the song of love, of motherly love; the more that you wear Mother of Pearl, the more I will be able to fill or repair these holes.

Often it is not just my vibratory rate that repairs the holes. I may also have to help you help yourself, since often these holes must be acknowledged before they can be repaired. Sometimes the individual must cry many tears before a hole can be mended.

Yet know that these holes can be mended, for my vibratory rate sings of the source of infinite love, and it stirs within every part of you the memory of this source. I am speaking of that primordial ocean out of which we all grew. It is an ocean of love. As your memory opens to this ocean of love, the love will flow into you and help repair the holes created by unfulfilled needs.

* * *

Mother of Pearl is an ideal gift for young children. I will protect the child's inner nature from harmful wavelengths—namely, negative thoughts, emotions, or other influences, such as the radiation from television sets. However, if I am exposed to too much television radiation, I can become saturated in about two years; then my other effects will also be weakened.

My protection will deflect the brutal thoughts and emotions that accompany abuse. On the other hand, I do not protect a child from emotions that are important for the child to experience. For example, a parent's anger may be needed to teach a lesson or prove a point. However, if a parent or anyone oversteps the boundaries of teaching anger into destructive anger, I will take it upon myself to deflect this anger away from the child. Although the child may cry and appear shaken, the inner core of the child's being will be protected. It is important that children's inner natures are protected and allowed to grow unharmed and undamaged, because this is the foundation upon which they will be building the rest of their lives.

"Does Mother of Pearl have specific effects when placed on different parts of the body?" Michael asked.

I may have a more concentrated effect on the cells of a certain area if I am placed over that area. However, I easily affect the whole aura when I am worn around the neck. I do not know everything there is to know about the human physical body. If you wish to experiment, and you are moved by your intuition to place Mother of Pearl over a certain part of your body, go ahead and do so.

"How does bleach or dye effect Mother of Pearl?"

Bleaching has a negligible effect, since it does not change my vibratory rate. However, a dye will change my vibratory rate and therefore prevent me from working in the same way.

"What is the effect of your opalescence?"

The shimmering, reflective quality of Mother of Pearl helps my vibratory rate to enter the aura. It is one of the reasons I saturate the aura so quickly. The more opalescence I possess, the more deeply I can work—be it physically, emotionally, or mentally—and the more clearly the individual will receive my effects.

The larger that the Mother of Pearl spheres are, the greater effect I will have for protecting individuals from electromagnetic radiation and other wavelengths. This is probably obvious. On the other hand, the size of the spheres worn will have no influence on my calming and stirring effects. These happen as a result of the aura being saturated with Mother of Pearl vibratory rate. As long as the aura is saturated, these effects will occur, regardless of the size of the spheres.

"Do you see your involvement with humans changing in the future?"

I hope I do not disappoint you when I say that I do not see into the future very well. I cannot answer your question.

* * *

You will have one opportunity—and only one—to speak with the Guardian of Pearl. It is vital that her attention be kept on maintaining her strength. After her discourse, I will answer any additional questions you may have about Pearl.

The energy shifted, and the Guardian turned her attention away from Michael and me. She seemed to be calling to a force that lay hidden deep within the sea.

29
PEARL

The air grew humid and became gently charged with an energy that felt like electricity. I was sure we were surrounded by the presence of the Guardian of Pearl.

The Guardian of Mother of Pearl reminded us to listen to Pearl's words with our hearts. Then the Guardian of Pearl spoke.

You wish to know Pearl. Pearl is as ancient and timeless as the ocean from which I come.

During the Age of Lemuria I was young, strong, and vibrant. I was a gift from the seas of the Earth to humans: I reminded humans of the source of life. I was also like a mirror in which they could see the reflection of their true inner selves, as well as visions of the future.

I was more powerful than the crystal balls used by mystics today. I was a living gift from the Earth, naturally formed into a perfectly round shape with luster beyond your wildest dreams. Pearls were much larger than than they are today; their average diameter was approximately one inch. The largest Pearls, which were approximately three inches in diameter, were rare and treasured by royalty.

During the Age of Atlantis, my size was halved, as was my ability to reflect wisdom and to offer visions. However, I was still used, worn, and loved. Often I was given as a gift to a loved one as a symbol of love and life. Even today, the Pearls given in this manner and worn around the neck shine with the love in which they were given. I absorb the feelings of the giver and reflect them upon the wearer.

Today I am still treasured as a gift from the sea, but only a faint memory of my youth and strength lingers. I am very, very tired. Yet I am willing to share with you what information I can. You see, I am old, and my power has been diluted by the vibratory rate of cultured Pearls.

Once I was able to reflect both the positive and negative aspects of people's natures. By gazing into me, people could see their faults and shortcomings, and then work to correct them. Now, with the little strength I have left, I choose to reflect only the pure and positive qualities in an individual. This is less stressful for me, and it is uplifting for the wearer.

This effect is the result of the vibratory rate of my luster. When worn around the neck, on a finger, or as earrings, I reflect the beauty contained within the aura. The life span of each Pearl is short. Pearls age as their wearers age and, in the process, their luster diminishes.

To some, my life cycle symbolizes reincarnation or rebirth. First, I have a life beneath the sea. The opening of the shell is like the transition from the watery womb into the world of humans. Then I begin life anew.

Pearls that are allowed to live beneath the sea to a ripe old age are the most powerful of all.

My natural and most powerful shape, the sphere, is the shape of the Earth and the sun. It represents the source of life for humans. The naturally formed sphere can reflect the inner bodies. The rounder my form is, the more encompassing is my work. Those which you call cultured Pearls, whose seed has been planted by man, only reflect the physical body of humans.

My color is a reflection of the purest light that shines within the aura. Those who are attracted to rose-colored Pearl are drawn to it because they have beautiful shades of red and pink in their auras. The white-colored Pearl reflects the greatest overall beauty. The gold variety reflects the highest connotation of the color gold: the pure light of Soul. Not everyone can wear such golden pearls, simply because not everyone can handle the reflection of this high vibratory rate.

Those who would most enjoy wearing Pearl are those who would benefit from being reminded of their positive qualities. They are also those who would benefit from being reminded of life, since my spherical shape represents the source of life. I have little or no therapeutic value, but as a gift of love I am most dear. When given by a lover, my wearers benefit from being reminded of the love that surrounds them.

My nature is patient, understanding, calm, and tranquil. Those who want these qualities in their lives may also be attracted to me. So will the individuals who wish to express beauty and purity.

Now it is time for me to go. In a way, I am sad to leave you, for my mission is a lonely one. Old age is a lonely place to be.

I wish that one day you might be taken in your dreams to a time when I was in my prime. Then you might experience for yourself the youthful beauty, power, and energy I once expressed.

The electric charge in the atmosphere intensified for a brief moment. It seemed to be Pearl's way of thanking us and of saying good-bye. Then the Guardian of Pearl was gone.

* * *

The Guardian of Mother of Pearl spoke up. I would like to clarify a few things that Pearl said and offer my point of view at the same time.

Pearl was once extremely powerful. Thousands of years ago, this gift of the sea gave people of the land the power to understand themselves. The Pearl reflected the individual accurately and clearly.

When people see themselves in a mirror, they have an opportunity to closely inspect their physical bodies. Pearl gave people the chance to closely inspect their inner selves. She let people examine the way their inner selves were reflected outwardly. Pearl's mission was to allow people to see themselves as they truly were.

Pearl has let go of the burden of showing people the entire truth about themselves. Truth is often a burden to show and to accept. Today Pearl only reflects the highest beauty within each of us.

Every one of us contains beauty beyond description. In order for Pearl to reflect this beauty, she must draw upon the life force within the individual. The stronger the individual is, the more effective the Pearl will be. Therefore, it is not advisable to wear an entire strand of true Pearls unless you naturally have plenty of strength and energy. Pearl will help to balance overabundant energy. At the same time, she will continually remind you of the beauty within yourself. It is also not wise for those who are very weakened to wear Pearl, because they need all the life force available to them to sustain or heal themselves.

The beauty I speak of is beyond vanity. It is that part of you which is pure Spirit, pure light and sound, Soul itself. This part of you contains no negativity and no aberrations. That is why it appears so beautiful.

"Why do cultured Pearls drain and weaken the Guardian of Pearl?" asked Michael.

As the Guardian of Pearl, she is responsible for all Pearls, including cultured Pearls.

Although we Gemstone Guardians do not take responsibility for the occasional misuses of our gems, we must do so if too many people misuse them. Such widespread misuse usually occurs if the Guardian has not been careful or responsible enough to share only the positive or correct applications of the gem. It might also happen if the Guardian has shared too much information. Therefore, if the misuse of our gems is widespread and great enough to cause an imbalance, we Guardians must take responsibility.

When worn, cultured Pearls do not behave in the same way that natural Pearls behave. Cultured Pearls begin as seeds that are planted in seashells by humans; the Pearl is then allowed to grow around the seed. Therefore, the very core of a cultured Pearl is devoid of life, thereby making it incapable of affecting the inner core of a human.

For a long time, the Guardian of Pearl used her own energy and love to compensate for the deficiency in cultured Pearls. This allowed cultured Pearls to behave like real Pearls. However, it was a tremendous drain on the Guardian of Pearl and consequently diluted her energy. Today there are so many cultured Pearls, that the Guardian of Pearl does not have enough love and energy in her heart to go around.

Imitation Pearls—those made from plastic and designed to fool people into believing that they are true Pearls—are simply an insult to the Guardian of Pearl. They drain her in the same way you would feel drained if you were bombarded with insults all day. The mental aberrations that cause people to create imitation Pearls is certainly not her responsibility. Still, it hurts her feelings that such things are made.

Imitation Pearls are completely empty of life. Cultured Pearls, on the other hand, are only half-alive and will drain energy from anyone who wears them. Therefore, cultured Pearls should not be worn by those who are already in a weakened state.

The true Pearl benefits its wearers by reflecting the beauty within them. You will also find that when Pearl is combined with other gemstones, it will draw energy and life force from those gemstones instead of from its wearer.

If I had only so much money to spend and wanted to buy a Pearl, I would invest in one very special Pearl. If I decided to wear it, I would mount it in a ring, because then it would be easy to gaze at its beauty. It would also be easier to see my reflection and therefore to provide some level of self-awareness.

I am not referring to spiritual self-awareness. I mean self-awareness in a practical, day-to-day sense. In other words, I would start to take notice and ask myself, "How are my thoughts and emotions being expressed? How am I presenting myself? Is this the way I want to present myself?"

Often we are not aware of the silly things we do that we may regret later. Pearl will help one to be more aware and refined, more like the person one would like to be. It helps one to move closer to the ideal image of oneself.

If I wore the Pearl around my neck, other people would tend to see the Pearl more than I would. Therefore, others would see more clearly the kind of person I am. As a result of their feedback, I would become more aware—consciously or unconsciously—of the image I was projecting. I could use this feedback to start smoothing the rough edges of my personality.

I wish to make it clear that I am not the Guardian of Pearl. I have only given you my point of view, and I do not know all there is to know about Pearl.

"Thank you for sharing your wisdom," said Michael.

You are welcome.

Her form became more and more transparent until it was only a faint shimmer of sparkling light. These sparkles rested in the air between Michael and me until the next gentle breeze scattered them. Then the Guardian of Mother of Pearl was gone.

30
CORAL

I readied myself to seek out the Guardian of Coral. But before I could begin my search, three beings entered our living room. Faceless and formless vortexes of swirling color, they hovered in the air above us. One was red, another was pink, and the third was white.

We have decided to meet you in the atmosphere of your living room, said a voice emanating from the red vortex. For the sake of simplicity, call us Red, Pink, and White Coral.

Over the millennia, Coral's shape and color have changed along with the chemical nature of the oceans. Coral is also found in different places than it once was. Those who live by the sea have always enjoyed Coral. Yet only those who wear Coral in spherical form can fully experience its therapeutic qualities and benefits.

We, the Guardians of Coral, care for the Coral that lies under the sea, as well as the Coral that is worn.

Once Coral is removed from the ocean, it goes to sleep until it is enlivened in a human's aura. It takes several hours for this enlivenment to occur, because the Coral must make an adjustment. It must learn to respond to the human aura, rather than to water.

Our purpose and mission is to provide the human wearer with the opportunity to build strength. We do not have a specific purpose for the planet. We live to house other ocean life; when we are in the sea, we are just another one of its inhabitants.

We only affect humans when we are shaped into spheres.

In general, people are not drawn to Coral as they are drawn to other gemstones. The decision to wear Coral will probably be based on knowledge of what Coral can do. Therefore, we are much like a tool, chosen for a specific purpose.

We do not saturate the aura as other gemstones do. We work on a layer of energy that lies closer to the physical body. This layer is comprised of the vibrations, or life essence, emitted by your body's cells.

Electrical currents run up and down your body. These currents give an accurate picture of what is going on in your physical body. Coral senses and reads them. When Coral is worn around the neck, its vibratory rate touches virtually every one of these currents. That is why it is best to wear Coral spheres around the neck.

These currents flow both inside and outside of the body. Coral accesses the currents that run inside the body through those that run on the outside. Incidentally, these currents are not physical manifestations.

There is another aspect of the body which is essential to Coral's work. Like the electrical currents, this aspect would not be found if one were to dissect the body. It is a vortex of energy which swirls within your torso. It is somewhat, but not entirely, associated with the chakras. It is known as your "powerhouse."

The powerhouse is one of your most important sources of energy—energy you use for life, growth, and evolution. It is made up of electrical currents and the life force itself. In a sense, these electrical currents form a structure which contains and stores the vortex of life force within you. Therefore, when we refer to the powerhouse, we mean both this life force and the structure of energy which contains it.

The Coral in the ocean builds a structure for the animals that live inside it. When worn by a human, Coral can strengthen, rebuild, and cleanse the structure that houses the vortex of life force contained within the wearer.

Red, Pink, and White Coral each affect this powerhouse in a different way. Before we get into specifics, do you understand what the powerhouse is?

"Perhaps if you elaborate, it would help us to understand it better," replied Michael.

The powerhouse is located inside the body in front of the spine and behind the chakras. Think of it as a building, and imagine a roofless, cylindrical structure.

At its top in your crown chakra, it is quite narrow. It remains narrow behind your brow chakra and then begins to widen just below your throat chakra. From there it continues to widen until it reaches its greatest circumference in the area between your stomach and sex chakras. Then it quickly tapers off and ends at the base chakra.

You eat food for energy, and you breathe air for life. Your chakras give and take yet a different kind of life-sustaining energy. The powerhouse acts as a storehouse for this energy.

People who are overweight do not have bigger powerhouses than people who are skinny. It is not the kind of energy reserve that fat is; it is a life-energy reserve. People who are ill or weak have depleted powerhouses. Healthy people have full powerhouses.

Yet, no matter how healthy or vital you are, you can always become stronger. It is the nature of the world in which you live that your powerhouse is constantly being battered by harmful influences, both internal and external. Internal influences include thoughts and emotions. External influences include such things as the food and drink you consume and the air you breathe. Any of these influences that are negative whittle away your powerhouse.

Coral can do more to cleanse, strengthen, repair, and rebuild the structure of this powerhouse than practically anything else on this planet.

Whenever you are very, very tired and need a little boost, you call upon the reserves in your powerhouse. Whenever you want to eat something that you know you are allergic to—and you eat it anyway—you call on the reserves in your powerhouse. Whenever you go somewhere that is polluted, you call on the reserves in your powerhouse to protect you from the pollution.

The life force contained within your powerhouse feeds your enthusiasm for life and your joy for living. It nourishes your desire to grow, evolve, and learn. These activities take a great deal of energy. Therefore, people who are depleted and weak are usually not interested in learning new things or in growing or changing.

The powerhouse feeds cells through electrical charges, which act as little packages or jolts of energy. Without the use of Coral, you can strengthen, rebuild, and cleanse your powerhouse with anything that is constructive, strengthening, or "good for you"—clean air, good food, harmonious thoughts, positive attitudes, or any form of spiritual nourishment.

Now, I, the Guardian of Red Coral, will speak to you about Red Coral and about its effects on the powerhouse.

Red Coral

The blueprints of your powerhouse were given to you as you were forming in your mother's womb. There the foundation of your powerhouse was also formed.

Therefore, one of the best things a pregnant woman can do is to wear Red Coral. Red Coral will do the same thing for the growing fetus that it will do for the mother: it will evaluate the entire individual and determine what improvements need to be made in the blueprint, and hence the foundation, of the powerhouse.

I, as Red Coral, compare the vibratory rate of the powerhouse with that of the individual. I evaluate and analyze the difference. Then I pinpoint the specific ingredients that should be added to the vibratory rate of the powerhouse to make it more harmonious with the vibratory rate of the individual.

By the time this cycle of work is completed, the individual's entire vibratory rate will have been raised. Then I perform another even greater cycle; because when the individual's vibratory rate has been raised, there will again be a discrepancy between it and the vibratory rate of the powerhouse. So I work again to harmonize the two by uplifting the powerhouse and making it stronger. This process continues for as long as I am worn. Therefore, the longer I am worn, the stronger the powerhouse and its owner become.

I know how to make the strongest possible powerhouse foundation. The deeper and darker is the natural red color of the Coral, the better I can work, and the stronger my effects will be.

Red Coral will always find ways to improve the blueprint of your powerhouse, no matter how healthy you are. Your blueprint is alive. It will change as you change. For example, if you deny yourself certain minerals, the lack of these minerals will soon be reflected in the blueprint of your powerhouse.

I rely on what the body knows about itself. The body knows

what it lacks and what it needs. The individual, on the other hand, often has no conscious awareness of what these needs are. I do not work on a conscious level. I have found that the individual's awareness of my specific effects only gets in my way. I do better work on an unconscious level.

The body, on the other hand, knows what ingredients are needed to make its powerhouse stronger. I simply give the body the strength and ability to draw these things to itself. I do this by magnetically charging key areas of the body.

Let's say, for example, that the foundation of your powerhouse lacks a mineral, such as calcium. Your body will recognize this need. I will then "magnetize" the body in such a way that it attracts more calcium to itself. The way that each body does this will vary. Sometimes the body will become more efficient at extracting calcium from food; other times it will begin to crave foods that contain calcium.

I do not work just with minerals. All sorts of things may be missing from your powerhouse foundation. No matter what these things are, I will work in the same way to draw them to the body. These things might include a color ray or some kind of emotional nourishment. Most often, however, the powerhouse foundation lacks oxygen or a nutrient that can be obtained from food.

When Red Coral is worn alone, the strand should be choker-length: sixteen, eighteen, or twenty inches long, depending on the size of the individual's neck. Now, I must caution you, that the effects of a solid Red Coral necklace can only be handled by those who are brave and truly aware of what will happen when they wear it. Changes in one's foundation are often upsetting. Afterward, things will not be done the way they used to be done. Energy will not be stored the way it used to be stored. Because the body's ability to absorb nutrients may be altered, even one's diet may change.

A plain Red Coral necklace is more appropriate for men than for women, because men tend to have stronger physical constitutions than women do. Therefore, a woman may not be able to handle the changes as well as a man would. Besides, when women build physical strength, they must simultaneously build emotional strength for balance. Combining some Pink Coral with the Red Coral will support the emotional aspect, strengthening its foundation at the same time the physical foundation is being strengthened.

Red Coral attracts the red ray. It does not carry the red ray, nor can it open the body to accept it. It simply attracts the red ray to the wearer.

Do you have any questions about Red Coral?

"How do the impurities and irregularities commonly found in Red Coral spheres influence your effects?"

It is important that the Coral be in spherical form; and the closer it is to a sphere, the better. Small nicks, holes, and irregularities; slight color imperfections; or little flat or white spots have little effect. This is because Red Coral is so strong. However, this may not be true of Pink or White Coral.

"Are there any specific therapies for which Red Coral can be used?"

Yes. I work most effectively with bones that are close to the skin. Red Coral can be used to strengthen these bones after a disharmony, toxicity, or disease has been removed from them. The bones are likely to be in a weakened state after the disharmony has been resolved.

For example, in the case of spinal deterioration, Red Coral can do wonders. It will build a strong foundation by stimulating the necessary minerals to gather at the spine. This process will also lay the ground for the work of Pink Coral. Pink Coral can later be used to stimulate the body's cells to build on this new foundation and thereby form a stronger spine.

The procedure I am about to describe should be performed with love and respect, and only after asking the Red Coral for permission.

First, grind the Red Coral into a powder. Then mix it with a neutral salve to form a paste. Rub the mixture into the spine, working it in well. Place a thin cotton cloth (such as cheesecloth) over the area and tape it to the skin. Then apply a hot cloth over the area, and replace the cloth whenever it loses its heat. This treatment should be performed for about an hour.

The individual should lie quietly during this entire procedure. After the heat treatment is completed, the individual should continue to wear the salve.

Balance is the key when mixing Red Coral powder and salve. The mixture should be strong, yet not wasteful. The salve used could have a slightly penetrating quality. Also, only the finest Red Coral spheres should be used. Undrilled spheres are preferable for this purpose, because they are whole. It is also best to use small spheres, because if they are red on the outside, they are more likely to be red on the inside, too. Red Coral powder will lie dormant until awakened by an aura; it should be stored in a ceramic or enamel container, and not in glass.

Any area of the body that has been completely covered for some time will become white and wrinkled—signs of a lack of oxygen. The salve should be periodically removed so that the skin can absorb the oxygen it needs.

Your physician may want to change the salve once a week or—if the condition is severe—every three, four, or five days. Each time the salve is replaced, the hot-cloth procedure should be followed.

While the individual is undergoing salve treatment, he or she should also wear a necklace containing a harmonious combination of the three Corals. This necklace should be made of mostly Pink, some White, and some Red Coral. By the way, wearing a Red Coral necklace alone—that is, without undergoing salve treatments at the same time—will not be an effective therapy for spinal degeneration. It would work eventually, but it would take much longer.

Soon after the salve treatments begin, the patient will probably feel some changes occurring in the area. The strengthening effects may not be felt immediately, since strength takes time to build. However, it probably won't be long before the patient feels more movement and less pain in the area.

"So, this therapy is for specific areas of the body, and not for general powerhouse foundation building," concluded Michael.

This therapy is appropriate for any bone that lies close to the surface of the body. It will not work as well for organs. Spinal degeneration is only one example. This therapy can also be used for broken or bruised bones—especially when a broken bone is not placed in a cast, as with a hairline fracture.

If a cast has been used, apply the salve after the cast is removed. The salve will strengthen and rebuild the bone. Although an x-ray may indicate that the bone has healed and the cells have mended themselves together, it will not truly be healed. One must ask why the bone broke in the first place. Of course, accidents can cause broken bones. However, if you were just running or walking, and you fell and broke your leg, it probably means that the bone was not strong enough to withstand the fall. Chances are good that every other bone in your body is in the same weakened condition. In this case, you should also wear Red Coral around your neck to strengthen the rest of the bones in your body. The Red Coral necklace should be worn both during and after the salve treatments.

"Would this therapy work for individuals paralyzed from a spinal injury?"

That condition is a function of the spinal cord, not the bone.

"What about cases in which spinal weakness is due to lack of use, and there is no disease?"

In these cases, it would be best to wear a necklace containing a balanced combination of Red, Pink, and White Coral.

Now let's talk about Pink Coral.

Pink Coral

The red vortex of energy receded into the background, and the pink vortex moved forward and began to speak.

Your powerhouse is not just a blueprint or a foundation. It has substance to it. In this way it is also similar to a building. A building is not just its foundation; it is made of building blocks or bricks. Ever since you were born, more and more "bricks" have been laid—one on top of the other—on the foundation of your powerhouse. This process continued until your physical body stopped growing at adulthood.

Now, no one lives in such a perfect environment that they are provided with the nutrients they need exactly when they need them. By nutrients, I mean both food and emotional nutrients. When needs are not met at the moment they are needed, holes form in the powerhouse. These holes are also created when great stresses are placed on the body. Such stresses tax the powerhouse and result in improperly laid bricks or the placement of insufficient "mortar" between them.

By the time people reach adulthood, all the bricks of the powerhouse have been laid. At that point, if one does not have the energy one would expect to have, it is probably because either there is some mortar missing or some bricks have been put in the wrong place or are absent altogether.

We can also compare your powerhouse to a well. Instead of water, the powerhouse stores life force that can be called upon whenever it is needed. If there is a hole in your well, water will drain out of it. The lower down in your well the hole is, the more water will drain out. I work to fill the holes in your powerhouse by rearranging its "bricks." In other words, I rebuild the powerhouse.

This is why Pink Coral is such a wonderful gift for children. The younger the child, the deeper within the powerhouse I can work. It is easier to rearrange bricks in a well that is only two feet high than in one that has grown to five feet. Pink Coral will rearrange the bricks so that they fit in the optimal places in the child's powerhouse. It will do this no matter what stresses the child may experience or what nutrients life may not provide as the child needs them.

The bricks are just "sections" of vibratory rate, and therefore are easily moved under my influence. Of course, I will also readjust and shuffle the vibratory rate of an adult's powerhouse in order to make its bricks fit properly.

If your powerhouse has many holes, energy will seep out of it in all directions. Since your powerhouse is located in the vicinity of your organs, the energy seeping out of it will often cause hyperactivity in these organs, especially in the intestinal tract. The abnormally high intestinal activity will cause food to pass through too quickly. This can result in a decrease in the intestines' ability to absorb nutrients.

There will also be situations in which the powerhouse has been incompletely built. This occurs for many reasons. In these cases, because the powerhouse has only gotten halfway off the ground, it will not be able to store much energy. People who wake up in the morning feeling just as tired as they did when they went to bed often have incomplete powerhouses. During the night, the powerhouse is most effective at gathering and storing its energy for the following day's activities. If the powerhouse is only half-built, little or no energy will be stored.

Pink Coral will attract whatever is needed to build on the foundation of the powerhouse. To do this, I recreate the natural process which directs the flow and expression of energy in the body. In this way, I increase the individual's overall strength and vitality.

"Are there any specific therapies involving Pink Coral?"

The best way to wear Pink Coral is around the neck in a strand that covers the heart. Your powerhouse affects your entire being; the only way I can affect your entire being is when I am worn around your neck. Being worn over the heart gives me better access to your powerhouse.

"Pink Coral is found in many shades. Does your color affect your strength?"

The deeper and richer is my natural pink color, the stronger I can work. When Pink Coral has patches of White in it, the wearer will benefit from the effects of both Pink and White Coral. In fact, it may be silly to wear pure Pink Coral by itself, just because the presence of White Coral with the Pink greatly benefits the wearer and enhances my effects.

Pink Coral strengthens and builds on the foundation that the body has already accepted for itself, whether that foundation is good or bad. Therefore, if someone starts to wear Pink Coral and then begins to feel even more tired and weak, it may mean that the Pink Coral is building on a foundation which has been laid improperly. This situation can be prevented by wearing Red Coral before or along with the Pink Coral. The Red Coral would correct any deficiencies in the powerhouse foundation before the Pink Coral starts to build on it.

I will build on the foundation chosen by the Red Coral; this new foundation will be beneficial to the wearer. However, it is often difficult to alter one's basic nature—that is, to replace the weak with the strong and the old with the new. It is a strong, determined, and brave individual who can wear Red Coral by itself, for it will change the whole structure on which the individual is built.

There is another situation in which I work particularly well with Red Coral. This is when the individual's building blocks have been weakened by certain disorders or dysfunctions, especially those of the bones and, to a lesser extent, of the blood and lymph systems. After healing rays have been introduced, and the affected area is cleansed and ready for rebuilding, Red Coral can prepare the foundation. I will then build on the new foundation created by the Red Coral.

Now let's speak of White Coral.

White Coral

This time the Pink vortex of energy receded, and the vortex of pure White energy intensified and moved toward us.

I protect the powerhouse and keep it pure. That is one of

the reasons I am so important and wonderful for children. Children often yearn to explore and experience the world around them, but their explorations don't always lead them to positive experiences.

Like Pink Coral, I am much more effective on children than adults, because children's powerhouses have not yet solidified. Nothing about them has solidified, since they are still growing and changing. Therefore, it is easier to protect them and keep their powerhouses free from impurities.

I have a particular love for people, perhaps more than Pink and Red Coral do. My feelings for humans may have much to do with how I affect them. I am like the mother who wishes to protect her children from all that is unpleasant. Of course, you would need to wear a large amount of White Coral to do this completely.

I work well with Pink Coral. When Pink Coral rearranges the powerhouse structure, making it strong and resilient, changes occur in the wearers' lives. During these changes, individuals are often somewhat more susceptible than usual to outside influences, particularly negative ones. These negative influences can include anything that is not completely nourishing, whether it be thoughts, emotions, or foods.

I have a reflecting or repelling action. I am like a mirror. But this mirror does not surround you; it is more or less inside of you. Therefore, everything I reflect passes your consciousness. This prevents you from being blind to what is not good for you. You will see everything that I reflect.

"I'm not sure that I understand," said Michael.

If, in order to deflect outside influences, you place a mirror around you, the mirror will be outside of you. Then, if a negative thought comes your way and is reflected in the mirror, you may never even know that it came.

On the other hand, if the mirror is placed so that it is somewhat inside of you, the negative thought will come in, but it will be reflected back to the sender before it can affect you. I will not let the thought affect you. More accurately, I will not let it affect your powerhouse; I will not let it affect the core of your being. However, you will still experience it. Hopefully, you will also learn from it, so that in the future you will avoid similar, potentially harmful experiences.

Is that clear?

"Yes."

Although the other Corals may not be completely aware of it, you also have a powerhouse in each of your inner bodies. Red Coral's work focuses on the physical. Pink Coral focuses on the physical and the emotional. I work physically, but I also protect your emotions and your mind. That is why I can protect the core of your being, not only from your own negative thoughts and emotions, but from those of others too. I also protect your core from any disharmonious influence that enters your physical body.

Any kind of negative influence can act like a battering ram on the building blocks of your powerhouse. If the influence continues, blocks can loosen and fall out, creating a hole in your powerhouse. I will protect the body from anything harmful, including harmful chemicals or any other physical irritants. However, if damaging elements are continually introduced to the body, I will not have the strength to maintain my protective influence.

It is best to wear White Coral around the neck in a strand long enough to reach the heart area. White Coral can be worn alone. However, the Pink Coral works best when I am included with it. In fact, all of us—Red, Pink, and White Coral—will work most holistically if we are all worn together.

"Are there any ways to use White Coral therapeutically?"

I affect the whole being. When worn around the neck, I can touch every part of you.

All Corals work best and do great work with those individuals who understand our purpose. We are most effective with those who are willing to let go of the things that inhibit their vitality, energy, and basic strength. Those who have self-defeating or destructive attitudes, who are confirmed pessimists, or who have little hope that they can change or grow will not benefit from Coral as much as those who have at least a glimmer of trust, acceptance, or hope.

Even if the individual is unaware of Coral's effects, Coral will work—as long as the individual has an optimistic nature or is at least willing to accept change or acknowledge that it can occur. Most people are willing to be healed; they just may not know what they are in for when they ask to be healed.

"How do you see Coral being used in the future?"

As long as we exist, we can be used as a tool. We will work for the benefit and strength of any individual of any age. You will see changes occur more swiftly in children. Children are easier to change, because they are already in a state of change.

Children should wear a combination of Pink and White Coral. It should be worn continually for several days until the Coral becomes attuned to the child. Then the child should wear the Coral every day for at least several hours. It can also be worn only at night. The ideal duration is twelve hours a day.

If you follow this protocol, you will find that the child's resistance to infection will be strengthened. The child will not get sick as easily and will be less susceptible to negative influences. Children who wear Pink and White Coral will experience an increase in self-confidence, because they will recognize what is good for them and what is bad for them. This heightened discrimination will be the result of the White Coral. Few children will need Red Coral, since it is usually too strong for them.

You may also notice that children who wear Coral will want to move beyond their previous limitations. Because they will feel stronger, they may try physical activities that they would have never tried before. For example, they might do things on the "monkey bars" they have never attempted before. They will have a greater sense and awareness of their bodies, and their growth will be more stable.

Children who have growing pains often do so because their bodies are experiencing many rapid changes. Children going through adolescence, and experiencing the great changes it brings, will benefit from wearing Pink and White Coral. They will benefit even more if their parents have the foresight to encourage them to wear it before they go through this adolescent stage. Pink and White Coral will help to prepare them, to ease the transitions, and to increase their self-awareness on a fundamental level.

Although it will take longer, these same effects will be experienced by adults. An adult will probably have to wear the Coral continually for many days at first. Then it should be worn for at least half a day every day. An adult will begin to feel stronger after wearing the Coral for one or two months, but it will probably take several months before he or she notices radical changes.

In contrast, differences may be noticed in children after only a few weeks. It is sometimes difficult to get verbal feedback from children; so watch their actions and be aware of their immunity level. Be aware that cold weather, or any other kind of stress, may not affect them as deeply.

Older people, or anyone whose life force reserves are seriously deficient, will also feel the effects of Coral more quickly than will the average healthy adult.

An older person will need more Red and White Coral and less Pink Coral. Why? Because they will need the Red Coral to draw to themselves the ingredients that will strengthen their foundations. They will need White Coral to repel anything that might deteriorate their foundations. They will need a minimal amount of Pink Coral, because Pink Coral will re-shuffle the bricks of the powerhouse; and when people's bricks are first being rearranged, they sometimes feel even weaker than usual. Pink Coral's effect is ultimately strengthening. However, there may be some discomfort when bricks that have been stuck in the same space for decades—and don't want to move—get re-shuffled. The influence of Pink Coral should be minimal, so that the movement and rearrangement of bricks will happen gently.

People who are taking drugs or chemicals to help a certain condition can benefit greatly from wearing Coral. The three of us must be worn together for this. By working together, we will keep the negative influence of the drug out of the powerhouse, and the core of the being free from the disharmonious vibratory rate of the chemicals. Chemicals may lodge themselves somewhere in the body, or they may be eliminated; it is not our purpose to know how chemicals behave or to direct their behavior in the body. We will, however, protect the individual's core, or powerhouse, from the chemicals' destructive effects.

If you foresee that you will be taking drugs or chemotherapy, prepare yourself by wearing Coral. Do this for at least two weeks—or as long as you can—before you begin the therapy. We cannot protect an individual from the focused radiation administered for therapeutic purposes.

White Coral can repel normal amounts of radiation. By normal, I mean the levels of radiation commonly found in the atmosphere these days. You may need to wear more than one strand of White Coral if you are in an environment where there is an unusual amount of radiation or other disharmonious influence.

My purpose is to protect the core of your being. Remember that, when I am worn, whatever influences come toward you will touch you. I only reflect them away from your powerhouse. Is that understood? I am not like Rubellite, which will shield your aura. I only shield your powerhouse. Do you see the difference?

"Yes, thank you. Now, would you summarize the functions of the three Corals and the differences between them?" Michael requested.

Certainly. Red Coral rebuilds the powerhouse foundation; Pink Coral rebuilds the powerhouse itself; and White Coral protects it and keeps it balanced.

Red Coral builds the strength of the powerhouse foundation by drawing to the body the basic nutrients it needs. It entrusts the actual building and maintenance of the powerhouse to the Pink and White Coral.

Pink Coral builds—or rebuilds—the powerhouse itself. It rearranges its building blocks, or sections of vibratory rate, so that they are all in their optimal places. It builds the powerhouse on the existing foundation, be it good or bad. This is why it is often important to wear the Red with the Pink. Of course, the effects of the Pink are also enhanced by White Coral. There are also cases in which all three work best when worn together.

White Coral keeps the powerhouse strong by keeping it clean and pure. It maintains the vitality of the powerhouse by deflecting all negative and harmful influences.

* * *

We Guardians each have our own missions, and we work in our own individual ways. Yet, on another level, we are united. I do not mean just among ourselves. I mean we are united with all life.

We are united with the life of the Earth, with all animals and plants, and with all humans who wish to be united with us. The difference between humans, plants, and animals is that humans can consciously choose whether or not they wish to work with gemstones.

We are united for the singular purpose of spiritual unfoldment. No matter what our effects are, no matter how we can benefit, and no matter how we can assist, it is all in the name of greater unfoldment.

Gemstones do not just help humans. Humans help gemstones, too. Within you flows a force that emanates from the highest place—the source of life itself. By wearing gemstones, you enliven them with your aura. In this way, gemstones are touched by the flow of this life force, and their evolution is fueled by it.

We Gemstone Guardians have done our best to give you an overview of who we are, what we do, and what our potential is. We have done this, because if humans and gemstones band together and share with each other, we can help each other move towards greater spiritual unfoldment.

Never forget that all gemstones contain intense concentrations of the light and sound of the life force. As long as you have a physical body, the gemstones, earthstones, and oceanstones will continue to be some of the greatest tools available to help you grow beyond your current limitations.

Those who are blessed with wisdom will consciously take the steps to use the tools that are available to them.

"Ginny and I thank you and all the Gemstone Guardians for sharing this wealth of information with us," said Michael.

On behalf of all the Gemstone Guardians, may I say that you are welcome. May the blessings be. . .

The swirling vortexes of Coral energies faded until they seemed to disappear. Yet their effects remained. I felt as though their presence had strengthened the foundation of our house and solidified the walls of our living room. Even the air seemed purified.

The interviews we had agreed to do were now over. Returning to physical consciousness, I became fully aware of my physical body sitting comfortably on the sofa. I smiled into Michael's happy eyes. We felt truly blessed and honored for having had these inner world experiences—and for being given the opportunity to accept the gifts of the Gemstone Guardians.

Afterword

Soon after their interviews were completed, the authors met several times with the Overseer of the Gemstone Guardians. During these meetings, the Overseer stressed the importance of using only the finest quality gemstones for therapeutic applications. She explained that the average or "commercial" quality gemstones commonly available today should not be expected to have the powerful effects described by the Guardians.

She also gave the authors invaluable information about combining gemstones within the same strand. Although many gemstones are compatible, some gemstones may nullify another's effects or produce disharmonious energy when combined. When gemstones that are in harmony with each other are placed together in a necklace, each gemstone enhances and focuses the power of the others. This creates effects that could not occur if the gemstones were worn alone.

During their conversations with her, the Overseer described specific gemstone combinations that provide the greatest benefits and are the most in harmony with the consciousness of people today. Naturally these combinations are designed to be worn around the neck. In these necklaces, the numbers, patterns, and placement of gemstones are highly significant; in fact, they are nearly as important as the choice and quality of gemstones used.

So that anyone who wishes to enjoy the benefits of these necklaces may obtain them, many of the Overseer's designs have been compiled into a catalog. Also included are single-gemstone strands of many of the gemstones described in this book. An order form for this catalog appears on the next page.